"Over the past 50 years and c[...] helped hundreds of thousands, [...] themselves from emotional mis[...], [...] teaching them how to accept reality for what it sometimes is: a bumpy road."
—MICHAEL E. BERNARD, PH.D.
California State University, Long Beach

"Dr. Albert Ellis, with co-author Dr. Emmett Velten, has created a useful and witty self-help manual. The authors give us 20 Rules for Optimal Living and Aging, and provide the tools for charting a path toward optimal aging. I highly recommend reading and using Optimal Aging, both for those who, like Albert Ellis, are in their 80s, and for those of us who are not so old, but hopefully will be so some day! Unfortunately our society often irrationally looks at old as bad or else glorifies old as antique-best. Optimal Aging gives us the ammunition to take on some of our own and society's ageist beliefs and challenges us to reshape our culture's view of aging and our own growing old."
—SUE C. JACOBS, PH.D.
Associate Professor and Director, Counseling Psychology Training Program, University of North Dakota

"A wise and practical guide to maintaining—even increasing!—enjoyment of life as one ages. Despite the physical changes and despite the negative attitudes of society and sometimes even ourselves, Drs. Ellis and Velten show how we can create joy and peace of mind in our mature years. Millions of people could be helped by reading this book.
—BERNIE ZILBERGELD, PH.D.
Author of The New Male Sexuality

"A wise, warm, and funny book about getting older! There are tough things about growing old, but if we approach aging with the clear thinking and canny problem solving Drs. Ellis and Velten demonstrate in Optimal Aging, the future begins to look fascinating and worthwhile. The authors balance three important elements in this book: accurate information about the good and the difficult aspects of aging; teaching the use of REBT principles through fascinating human examples; and application of these principles to problems we can expect to face as we grow older. Living a full, rich, long life is a goal worth embracing, and this book shows how to do it."
   —ANTONETTE M. ZEISS, PH.D.
      Past President of the Association for Advancement of Behavior Therapy

"One does not really 'get over' getting older—one does get older. And older can be better; it is not necessarily 'badder'. No book can erase the process of aging, but Optimal Aging presents a realistic, optimistic, affirmative, and even adventurous approach to these welcome new years of our lives."
   —BETTY FRIEDAN
      Author of The Fountain of Age

"Regardless of age, no reader can afford to ignore this unique prescription for better living. As I read on, even my cynical self became convinced! Optimal Aging finally lays to rest many myths about aging and offers a down-to-earth set of rules for aging with grace."
   —CYRIL M. FRANKS, PH.D.
      Professor Emeritus of Psychology, Rutgers University

Optimal Aging

Get Over Getting Older

Albert Ellis (signature)

Albert Ellis, Ph.D.,
and
Emmett Velten, Ph.D.

Open Court
Chicago and La Salle, Illinois

To order books from Open Court, call 1-800-815-2280.

Open Court Publishing Company is a division of Carus Publishing Company.

First printing 1998

Printed and bound in the United States of America

Library of Congress Cataloging-in-Publication Data
Ellis, Albert.
    Optimal aging: get over getting older / Albert Ellis and Emmett Velten.
        p. cm.
    Includes index.
    ISBN 0-8126-9383-3 (paperback : alk. paper)
1. Aged—Psychology. 2. Self-realization in old age. 3. Happiness in old age. I. Velten, Emmett Charlton. II. Title. HQ1061.E378 1998
158.1'084'6—dc21   98-4017
                                                                          CIP

Dedicated to Janet L. Wolfe
Albert's lover and Emmett's fine friend

Contents

Preface

Change What You Can and Do the Best with What You Can't Change

This book is for people who want to learn ways to maintain—even increase—their enjoyment of life as they grow older. It speaks to people who aren't yet older—but who know they will be someday—and to people who are already older than they'd like to be. Instead of just looking at present trends, this book does something quite different. It shows how you can *take control of the trends of aging. You can take the lead to create change and make for yourself the kind of life you desire.* Harmful attitudes can hold you back. This book shows you ways to recognize and combat them, and ways to develop more helpful attitudes. These methods and tools come from well-researched, practical forms of self-help and psychotherapy, particularly from Rational Emotive Behavior Therapy (REBT). These methods are easy to grasp and can help you at any time of life to take control of your emotional growth and happiness. They can help you improve how you cope with hassles and practical problems, including those that relate to age.

This guide to optimal aging can meet some vital needs for our rapidly maturing population. In it we will outline many ways in which those of you who want to live—and expect to live—long lives, can apply Optimal Aging methods to troublesome, and even obnoxious, aspects of aging. You can learn to:

- break free of harmful myths, negative expectations, stereotypes, and prejudices about age, and then create new roles and experiences;
- apply your knowledge and brain power to cope with the practical hassles and inconveniences of older age;
- discover and invent ways of lessening these hassles and inconveniences;
- make the most of age's opportunities—empty nest, retirement, longer life;
- see that creating your life must never stop and it has little to do with age;
- accept, even though you don't cheer about, the pains of growing older;
- refuse to disturb yourself about things you can't change—such as incessant aging itself;
- develop flexible views about the opportunities afforded by longer life;
- grow positively happier, more committed, involved, and vital as you grow older;
- get more of what you want and less of what you don't want in your longer life.

Are we assuming that aging is mostly bad? Not at all! It has many charms, bonuses, distinct advantages, and benefits, which people often overlook. We'll look at some of the unsung pluses of aging before we help you learn ways to prevent self-disturbance, dread, and complaining about the minuses.

This book includes personal anecdotes and other examples that illustrate the methods we want to convey, as well as how people can gain by using them. These illustrations include ours, those of well-known personalities and friends, and of therapy clients or self-helpers. When we refer to clients, we changed all identifying information—often including gender—to safeguard their privacy and confidentiality.

The graying of America is one of the most important facts about our future. Roughly 80 million Americans—about a third of the population—were born in the years 1946-1965: the baby boomers. Their generation has dominated American culture for four decades. The boomers' preferences and desires, and now their pocketbooks, are the dominant concerns of American business and pop culture. As it has aged and matured, this huge generation has changed the ways of our culture.

- The boomers were the flower-power, drugs, sex, and rock'n'roll generation of the 1960s and early 1970s, who opposed the war in Vietnam.
- They are the first generation to embrace pronounced women's liberation values, with men's liberation rising rapidly, with racial equality, and with gay rights.
- They are the first generation with large numbers of people who did not marry at all and did not have children. An estimated 20 percent of the baby boomers will have no children; another 25 percent will have only one child.
- They are the first generation where living together without matrimony is common.
- They are the first generation where divorce reached 50 percent, where significant numbers of people practice "serial monogamy," and where families with layers of in-laws, stepchildren, and visitation rights are commonplace.
- They are the first generation heavily "into" technical innovations, like faxes, cell phones, computers, email, and the Web.

It's possible that you, baby boomer or not, will carry the baby boomers' values and experimental frame of mind into your "golden years" and really shake up America's concepts about aging. We hope this book encourages you to do so and provides you with many helpful how-to's.

The main message of this book is Seize The Day—Carpe Diem! Instead of drifting into older age with no map, no compass, no sail, and no oars, decide where you want to go and what you want to see, do, and experience along the way. Remain open to new destinations and experiences, and then set your sails. We believe people can shape their destinies, individually and together, and this book gives you some tools to do so and thus achieve optimal aging.

Until recently, there weren't enough older people (and people who would soon join those ranks) to accept the challenge of this book—to reshape our culture's attitudes and values about aging and about you, a person who is aging. Don't forget that it is unusual for a large percentage of the population to reach its fifties or sixties. Among humans, it still only reliably happens in the more developed countries. Among most other animals, it is rare for an individual to reach old age outside a zoo or the safe confines of a human home. Human beings have changed the natural order—short life—that held sway throughout almost all of human history. We have vastly improved the prenatal care most women get, eliminated many diseases of infancy and youth, and developed medicines and procedures to combat diseases largely affecting older people.

By 2020, one fifth of the American people will be over 60. Until fairly late in this century, there was hardly any such thing as a voting bloc of older people. We older people were rare birds. The phenomenon of large numbers of older people is still in its youth, even its infancy. We are at square one.

Older people are not the only johnny-come-latelies. Childhood, too, as we know it in the developed nations, is fairly new. Not too long ago, most children who lived much past infancy went to work in fields and factories—"little adults." Science, education, democracy, and relative affluence have provided a foundation for other subcultures to develop, too. The women's movement has created new opportunities for women to try on new roles, and women are breaking out of many traditions. Their mental and physical health and their longevity have improved. Men's liberation is now building up steam as a movement. With it, men can forge new lives, expand their horizons, and improve their happiness and health, too.

Unquestionably, more people are freer to create and live the lives they want these days than even just a few years ago. While homosexuality has been around as long as people have, the developed countries in the last two decades have seen an immense growth of gay and lesbian involvements. Similarly, the present-day tendency for people to seek their ethnic roots is another form of self-creation. The same is true of the rising trend in America for people of mixed racial heritage to create new identities for themselves.

While there is an undercurrent of respect for elders in our culture, it is hardly predominant. Perhaps it was stronger in the past. Many social and economic forces have shaped the current culture of older people. These forces include fewer jobs; forced retirement; frequent stories in the media about how the greedy old geezers will break the financial backs of poor but honest young people paying into Social Security; lower income; a pervasive message that the young are more valuable than the old; expectations that your children automatically deserve what you have; and debility and ailments.

With the right attitudes, tools, and hard work, our increasing numbers, especially with the baby boomers hitting fifty, will make possible new strength. We have the chance to invent our own lives and to write part of our own stories. No longer need we just live out the scripts provided by an ageist society. We have the chance to reshape our society's warped and restrictive ideas about aging. Instead of agreeing with a vision of decline, you can create new meaning. If you do it now, while you are still younger, you will increase your enjoyment of the one life you have to live. That one life will likely be much longer than you ever expected—yes, you did somehow survive to 30, 40, and beyond! That one life can be independent, vigorous, full, and fun—*if* we end prejudice against aging, *if* we refuse to take its dictates seriously.

Ageism is a crucial fact of life in our culture, and talking openly about it is taboo. Older people—and *you*—had better break the taboo, not just with talk but with action. We had better do something about it. Our culture is prejudiced against older people. It is, or will be, prejudiced against *you*—if you expect to remain alive and kicking for an average amount of time and live a happy life. *You* will be the target of prejudice. It will limit your options the way prejudice has done for other groups and kinds of people. Don't like that prospect? Then do something about it. Starting now.

If you are young and not yet the target of ageism, just wait. Your turn will come. At the heart of ageism is the assumption that human worth depends on age—the older the worse, the younger the better. It also assumes that self-worth depends on not *showing* the natural biological changes associated with increasing age. A ridiculous standard! Another contributor to prejudice is the common belief that the inconveniences and hassles of older age are too awful to endure. Every age has its inconveniences and hassles, but we can rid ourselves of those caused by our culture's rampant ageism.

We will not pass lightly over the unpleasant facts of ageism. In its many guises, it harms people of all ages. It contributes to immense suffering and can rob us of our futures. If we do not conquer it, if younger people do not vigorously join this battle, part of our futures— your futures—can be kissed good-bye. If you are young, chances are that you knowingly or unknowingly share some aspects of ageist attitudes. It would be hard not to, given the incessant bombardment of youth, youth, youth in the media and advertising. If you are older, it's possible that you have internalized some ageist beliefs and apply them to *yourself*. Suppose that you would rather feel younger, be more physically agile, and not join a frowned-upon minority group. These preferences would be sensible if they motivated you to keep fit mentally and physically and fight for your rights. However, you may also feel prejudice against yourself and other older people. The preference not to suffer prejudice is sensible. It can motivate you to battle ageism, rather than cling to vanishing youth, hate your older body, write yourself off as vital, and segregate yourself from the rest of society. It takes a lot of energy to cling to the illusion of youth—energy that you could devote to creative pursuits.

Why do we use the term "older" and not just say "old"? Because there is no category called "old." There is no point at which you have to "act your age" or act differently because you "are" old or have fallen into the last category or stage of life. Age continually varies, from the moment you are born until the moment you die. Every day you live, you get older. Every day you live, you can continue to create yourself and your life.

Prejudice against older people and against aging itself is, we contend, a dominant reason many people dread older age. To the degree that you share this prejudice, then you collude in ageism. Such prejudice is a major way you might prevent yourself from enjoying and making as much of your future as you can. Think of it this way: The longer you live, the more you join a disadvantaged minority group— older people. Tough! There is only one alternative to aging. Need we name it?

Therefore, we who are older or who expect to be older someday had better buckle down and get to work. With work, we can change ourselves and our culture so that we all can enjoy and develop our lives more as we age. To advance that cause, this book will show how to cultivate attitudes designed to make the most—individually—of being alive. It will show how to develop and recreate yourself and your culture as long as you live.

Acknowledgments

Many people reviewed early versions of the manuscript for this book or otherwise provided feedback, suggestions, and inspiration. The following individuals were particularly generous with their time and expert advice: Michael Edelstein, Hank Robb, Ricks Warren, Sophia Wolfe, Ava Wolfe, Bea Tracy, Alma Knubel, Bobbi Beelman, M. Joan Hansman, Sharon Peppler, Kitty Fouty, Dell Velten McCall, and Billy Bob Branch. Special credit is due to our editor at Open Court, David Ramsay Steele, for his many thoughtful contributions to this book as well as for his superb editing of the manuscript.

1

Aging: the Good, the Bad, and the Attitude

There is no such thing as instant experience.

Oppenheimer's Law

If you view a problem closely enough, you will recognize yourself as part of the problem. Why is this saying true? Because you *choose* how you act and how you feel. The choices you make can add to your problems. They can lead to suboptimal existence. Or they can help you live optimally.

Practical problems, such as aging, don't hold power over you. *You* have the power, though you may give it away. An ancient idea, but easily forgotten. You *can* change how your think. You *can* change your beliefs and attitudes. You cling to them. You can drop them if they don't work for you.

This book will show you how to do that. It will show you how to work on your attitudes and change them so that they help you deal effectively with problems rather than hinder you. Realistic attitudes—Rational Beliefs, as we call them in this book—are the key to optimal living. And to optimal aging.

We have put some of these realistic ideas into a set of 20 Rules for Optimal Living and Aging. This is the first of the lot:

Rule #1: FACE REALITY

Aging has its good and indifferent aspects, as well as bad ones. When reality has a bad side, accept the reality of that fact. Then change it if you can. If you cannot do much about it, live with it and make the best of it. Then look for and focus on the good side. What you make of your future—what you make of your *now*—depends on you. It depends on your attitudes *toward* practical problems that happen to you, such as those problems brought by aging.

The Good . . .

Aging has its good aspects that you may often ignore or forget. Let's first look at the good, and then at the bad. As we list some of aging's benefits, think about what you could add to our list. Later, you can review and build on your list. Ponder each possible benefit to aging. How does it apply to you? If you really *think*, you can teach yourself to develop a healthful perspective about aging.

Here are some of the advantages of growing older:

- You have had more experience in life, and you could be the wiser for it. You may have had several families and careers, many jobs, and different homes. You may have accumulated skills in getting along with other people.

- You can see more clearly how the parts of your life fit together. You can know more about and better understand life's many contradictions and paradoxes.

- You can show younger people the essential value of experience. You can share with others the information you've had the time to learn.

- The longer you live, the greater chance you have to learn good skills for coping with life. Trial and error is the way human beings learn. Older people often know a thing or two younger people don't know.

- People may treat you with more respect and take you more seriously. They may assume that older means wiser, even when it doesn't!

- You have had time to learn how to accept frustrations that you can do nothing about.

- You may learn to live with fewer gender stereotypes as you mature and to accept yourself with fewer strings attached. Men may discover and express more often their tender, sensitive sides. Women may do the same with their assertive, take-charge side.

- You may also stereotype others less often and accept them more often as they are.
  The longer you live, the more chance you have to find or develop a special niche—or several niches—for yourself.

- With longer life, you can have more time and experience to come to grips with larger questions of existence.

- You have more opportunity to experiment. Having lived longer and having lived through your many mistakes and false starts, you can have less fear of taking risks and trying new things.

- You have the chance to create yourself many times, to try many of life's options.

- You have more opportunity to realize some of your deeply-held, long-term life goals. You have the natural goal and challenge of living as healthfully and joyfully as possible, as long as possible.

- You have a rich store of fond memories to contemplate whenever you wish. You have the opportunity to see your grandchildren and great grandchildren grow and mature. You know how to savor experiences.

- You have the excitement of contrasting the world before and after—space travel, computers, fax machines, McDonald's, and so forth.

- You can benefit from the latest scientific discoveries and medical advances that improve health and longevity.

- You often get discounts and other benefits for movies, theater, travel, food, and many other amenities.

The Bad . . .

Bette Davis advised, "Gettin' old ain't for sissies." She knew what she was talking about. Most of us know deep down that we'd *better* face life realistically and develop courage and optimism. It's difficult at times to cultivate such attitudes and to hold onto them when the going gets tough. But life becomes *much more* difficult when you don't! You usually do better and feel better when you actively face reality and change its lousy aspects if you can. If you can't? Then do what you can to cope with life gracefully, and remain resolved to have as much fun as possible. This is the Second Rule for Optimal Living:

Rule #2: TAKE ACTION

Build your life actively and you will usually get more of what you want and less of what you don't want. Passivity will not work. If you don't row, row, row your boat, you will drift down the stream. And sometimes not gently.

While growing older can have its joys, adventures, and other benefits and advantages, it does have its negatives. Very definitely! Would that the "rotten" aspects of aging were only myths or were entirely brought on by our own stupid lifestyles, which we *could* change! But no, some aspects of aging *seem* rotten because they *are*. The same is true for some aspects of all the other stages of life.

Some of the unfortunate aspects of aging stem largely from society's attitudes and from ageism. You can work to change those attitudes in society. You can break free of them in your own life. But other disadvantages of aging stem from your own attitudes. You may have gotten those attitudes from the culture. From TV. From your parents. From your teachers. From your peers. You may have invented some of them yourself. No matter. They are yours now. You hold them. You can change them.

Still other unpleasant features of aging arise from years of not taking care of yourself. Again, you can do something to change that—*if* you change the beliefs that interfere with your taking care of yourself. Another large portion of the downside to aging comes from physical changes that happen in your body. Some of these you can prevent; some you can hold off or minimize; and some you can do very little about. But you *can* govern your own attitudes *toward* those realities.

You can change some adversities, and some you cannot. The methods of this book apply in either case. The optimal living methods of Rational Emotive Behavior Therapy (REBT) can help you develop your courage and fighting spirit. They can show you how to minimize some of the badness of aging, while also reducing your disturbance about it. Now let's look at some of the bad aspects of aging. Let's face them to see what we're up against.

- ageism: some people's prejudiced attitudes and practices and

biased views that older people are less valuable and worthy as humans than younger people;
- retirement, fixed income;
- the empty nest;
- losing friends and relatives through disability or death;
- physical decline and ailments;
- larger medical bills;
- limitations such as losing your driver's license;
- less mobility;
- the possibility of getting stuck in a nursing home.

Quite a list! Before we tackle them, we'd better show you more about the methods of Rational Emotive Behavior Therapy that apply to *any* age group. We will show you how to buckle down and *use* those methods, especially the famous ABC model. It's a powerful tool for optimal living and self-change. It has proven itself effective in the lives of thousands of people who have learned and explicitly used it. As you will see, the ABC model is empowering. It states what *really* causes our emotions and our actions. It shows what we can do to change ourselves.

Your Attitude Is *All in Your Head*

There are many disadvantages and costs of older age. In Rational Emotive Behavior Therapy, we call them Adversities. They are "A" in the ABC model. These Adversities clearly do exist, but they do not determine your reaction to them. Your Beliefs (B) largely produce the emotional and behavioral Consequences (C). The basic formula for optimal living, then, is this:

$$A \times B = C$$

Activating Events	**Beliefs**	**Consequences**
Adversities	Attitudes,	Actions/inactions
Experiences—past,	Thoughts,	Emotions/feelings
present, and predicted	Assumptions,	
Aggravations	Images	

Suppose, for example, that you are getting on in years, you have barely enough money to get by, and you feel quite depressed about this.

A (your Activating Event/Adversity) is lack of money.

C (your Consequence) is depression.

What, do you think, is the cause of your depression? Is it lack of money? Why not?

To take another example, imagine that you are now in your 40s. Whenever you think about "getting old," you feel anxiety and dread.

A (your Activating Event) is the prospect of "getting old."

C (your Consequence) is dread and panic.

So what's the cause of your dread and panic? Why is it wrong to say that the cause of your dread and panic is the fact that you're getting old? (Consider this: Don't some people get old without feeling that dread and panic? What makes the difference? Could you feel differently?)

You're a middle-aged woman. Another woman you are getting to know at the health club asks you your age. You feel anxious and instead of telling the truth, you say your age is less than it is.

A (your Activating Event) is your true age and being asked your age by someone.

C (your Consequence) is anxiety and lying.

What makes you anxious? What makes you lie?

You are a man in your early 50s and your erections are less firm than when you were younger. You avoid having sex with a new partner.

A (your Activating Event/Adversity) is less firm erections.

C (your Consequence) is avoidance of sex.

What makes you avoid pursuing sex?

Does A cause C? No. *By itself*, A can never cause C. If Activating Events "gave" us our reactions, then we'd all react the same way to the same things. We don't. If Activating Events made us do what we do, then we could never change ourselves unless our circumstances changed. But experience and observation show that we can change our responses, even if the environment remains the same.

In each of the examples above, we omitted the essential cause of C. Namely, B, your Beliefs or attitudes. Your Beliefs (B) *about* A cause you to act and feel the way you do. Your Adversities in the examples above—lack of money, thoughts about "getting old," being asked your age, having less firm erections—can *help* you choose your actions and feelings. Yet, they do not make you choose what you choose. That's your responsibility. But how *do* Adversities "help" you choose poorly?

If you did not lack money, and in fact had tons of it, you would probably not depress yourself about lack of money. Lack of money— Adversity at A—helps you depress yourself because *you already hold* Irrational Beliefs *about* what lack of money means. Remember, there are street people who are not depressed, and even cheerful. And there are miserable millionaires. So, lack of money *itself* does not give you your emotions. You do that.

Similarly, if you never had the thought about "getting old," you would not have the opportunity—at least not at that moment—to make yourself feel dread about it. When you were a fifteen-year-old, you most likely did not feel dread at the thought of getting old enough at sixteen to get your driver's license. Dread stems from your Beliefs at B—about aging.

And, yes, if the other woman at the health club had not asked your age, you would not have felt anxious and then told her a lie. So, the Activating Event of being asked your age played a part in your reactions. Your response to the woman's question, however, comes from you. It does not come from her question. It does not come from your age. Your response came from your Beliefs about your age.

When you avoid having sex with a suitable partner, that choice is made by your brain, not by any other part of your anatomy. You make your choice based on what you think at B, your Beliefs. But, yes, again, if you did not have the opportunity to have sex with a suitable partner, then you could scarcely choose to avoid it.

Activating Events, therefore, are important, but you, not they, directly produce the ways you act and the ways you feel. You have the power. Don't give it away. That is why we sometimes use a different graphic of the A x B = C formula, like this:

Activating Events × Beliefs = Consequences

This version of the ABC model illustrates that your Beliefs are much more important than your Activating Events in producing your reactions and emotions as Consequences at C. Your Beliefs can be helpful or harmful to you; they can be rational or irrational. The choice is yours.

What Do You Tell Yourself?

If you lacked money at A, what would you have to *tell yourself* at B to make yourself feel truly *depressed* about it at C? Not displeased about it, not frustrated with it, not concerned over it, not determined to do something constructive about it—but despondent, despairing, depressed? What would you have to tell yourself at B to make you feel dread about "getting older"? Or to feel anxious and lie when someone asks your age? Or to avoid sex play with someone you like when the opportunity arises?

Beliefs that hinder your pursuit of happiness and your solving or adapting to practical problems we call Irrational Beliefs (IBs). When you combine Irrational Beliefs with your Activating Events, especially if they are adverse ones, you get self-defeat as a Consequence at C.

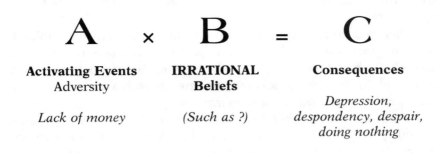

A ×	**B** =	**C**
Activating Events	**IRRATIONAL**	**Consequences**
Adversity	**Beliefs**	
		Depression,
Lack of money	*(Such as ?)*	*despondency, despair,*
		doing nothing

You have the power at B to choose self-helpful Rational Beliefs rather than self-defeating Irrational Beliefs. The optimal choice is yours. If you choose Rational Beliefs and if you dispute and defeat the

Irrational Beliefs, you get helpful results as a Consequence at C. Then you have much more chance to do something constructive about your practical problems at A—such as lack of money. Or lack of erections. Or "being older." If you find you cannot change your adverse Activating Event soon, or perhaps ever, what then? Rational Beliefs at B allow you to accept frustrating reality and adapt to it as gracefully as you can, rather than continue to spin your wheels and complain about unkind fate.

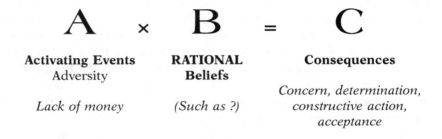

A ×	**B** =	**C**
Activating Events	**RATIONAL**	**Consequences**
Adversity	**Beliefs**	
		Concern, determination,
Lack of money	*(Such as ?)*	*constructive action,*
		acceptance

I Command the World and You to Obey My Wishes!

How do "depressing" (irrational) Beliefs about lack of money differ from realistic Beliefs that could motivate you to take constructive action or to adapt to your situation as best you can? They differ in the same way "I command" differs from "I prefer."

You take your desire or preference for having more money—"I'd like to have more money"—and *make it into* an unrealistic demand: "I absolutely NEED and MUST have more money. My life is *devastatingly horrible* unless I have it." With that command (which reality ignores), you make yourself depressed instead of realistically disappointed that you lack money.

If you want to feel *un*depressed about not having enough money as you grow older, you dispute (D) your Irrational Belief (IB), "I absolutely NEED and MUST have more money. My life is *devastatingly horrible* unless I have it!" You ask, *"Why* MUST I have more money? Where is the evidence that I NEED more money or else my life is *devastatingly horrible?"*

If you keep strongly disputing your Irrational Beliefs (IBs), you will very likely create an effective new philosophy (E). For example: "It is highly inconvenient and a pain in the rear if I do not have more money, but I do not absolutely NEED it. My life will be frustrating without it but not horribly devastated." Then you will most likely feel the healthful negative emotion of disappointment rather than the unhealthful negative feeling—that *you* produced—of depression.

To get or not to get what you want—namely, more money, better erections, or youth. That is the practical question. But do you NEED to have what you want? MUST you absolutely have what you want? That's the psychological question.

People often ask whether there are exceptions to this idea that you do not NEED things, you merely *want* them. Yes, in the sense that we need—in order to stay alive—oxygen, water, food, shelter from extreme weather, and perhaps certain medications. Those are true needs. Money is desirable, and your life can be more comfortable with it than without it. But NEED it to have *any* degree of happiness? NEED more of it or else not be happy *at all?* Unlikely. The same thing is true of our "needs" for success, approval, and comfort. They are not absolute, or true, needs—they are desires, wants, preferences, wishes.

We will show you how to use the ABC's of Optimal Living to your advantage in chapter 2. Meanwhile, here's the Third Rule for Optimal Living:

Rule #3: CREATE YOURSELF

You create yourself—your Beliefs (B's), your actions, and your feelings (C's). You cannot always change the circumstances of your life (A's), and one of them is your age. Therefore, if you desire optimal living (and optimal aging), it's advisable to focus your energy to create change where you can. You *can* change your Beliefs *about* life's circumstances. Your Beliefs *about* aging itself.

2

The ABC's for Optimal Living
You Mainly Feel the Way You Think

Believing is seeing.

Disimoni's Rule of Cognition

Helen, now 70, contracted polio just before the release of the Salk vaccine. She almost died and was confined to an iron lung for months. Paralyzed from the chest down since then, she remains a model of good cheer and lives a full life. She has been employed full-time—in a variety of jobs—for decades. Once she moved across country to a new location, with no job to go to and not even knowing anyone there. Yet she soon re-established herself and flourished.

How did Helen do it? How could anyone do it? What kinds of attitudes might Helen hold that help her get good results despite an exceptionally poor physical situation? Her secret? "I concentrate on how to solve problems," she said, "and I force myself to have an upbeat attitude even when I don't feel like it. After all, there are many people worse off than I am."

Helen's cousin, Joanna, was in good health until the age of 50, then had a car accident that left one arm almost useless but did little other damage. She complains bitterly—sometimes to Helen—"Why did this have to happen to me?" She hasn't worked since that time although she could easily return to her teaching job. She feels certain no one will

11

hire her. She also feels very embarrassed over her handicap and won't consider dating ("They'd just feel sorry for me"). She calls her life "miserable." She forces herself to have a downbeat attitude. Consequently, she feels wretched.

Helen now faces impending blindness due to macular degeneration. At first she felt shock, numbness, grief, and for a time cursed the universe for giving her this latest extremely inconvenient malady. However, she soon began to prepare with her usual practical attitude. "This is the hand of cards I've been dealt," she said. "I'll play the game as well as I can."

How do you teach yourself the philosophy that Helen chose to live by? And avoid Joanna's?

It's Your Philosophy That Makes the Most Difference

A Roman philosopher of Greek origin, Epictetus (Eh-pic-TEE-tus), said "People are disturbed not by things, but by the views they take of them." Shakespeare had Hamlet express a similar thought in remarking, "There is nothing either good or bad, but thinking makes it so." Milton said, "The mind is its own place, and in itself can make a Heav'n of Hell, a Hell of Heav'n." These ideas can empower you—*if* you dispute the *disempowering* notion that almost rules in our society. Namely, that Adversities such as aging—A in the ABC model—*make* you feel your disabling feelings as Consequences at C. REBT shows you *how* to work energetically on what you *can* change—your Irrational Beliefs at B, *about* growing older. Your Beliefs lead to your emotional and behavioral Consequences much more than your Adversities do.

Adversities *help* us disturb ourselves, of course. If your job, let's say, is wonderful and you thoroughly enjoy it, you probably will not depress yourself about it. This is true even though you hold the Belief, "I MUST have a great job, or else I'm *a nothing*." But what happens when your great job gets worse? Or goes down the tubes? Back to wormhood you will go! So, in that case, your Adversity—having lost your great job— *does* help you depress yourself. You would not depress yourself had you *not* lost your job. But your job loss can help you depress yourself only because you already hold the Irrational Belief, "I MUST have a great job, or else."

Emotions are useful, because they motivate us. They help us

communicate. Without emotion, life would be far less worth living. So we are not suggesting that it's a good idea to try to have no emotions. It's a question of whether the emotions are healthful or unhealthful. In chapter 3, we will discuss the important distinctions between healthful *negative* emotions and unhealthful *negative* emotions. The point we make here is that our emotions, no matter what their kind or degree, do come from ourselves, from our attitudes and mindset. We ourselves supply the B that's the link between A (Activating Events) and C (our emotional and action Consequences).

There are some Adversities of huge proportions, such as earthquakes, floods, war, terrorist attacks, genocide, rape, torture, murder of your loved ones. Most people experience powerful negative emotions as Consequences after such extreme Adversities. Your emotions in such extreme situations seem automatic. They seem to directly come from the Adversity itself. Nevertheless, your reactions, your emotions, still come from *you*. Consider that not everyone's reactions are the same in similar, "horrendous" circumstances. A friend of ours lost her home and almost everything else in the gigantic flood in 1997 of the Red River of the North. What was the story about it that *she* came away with? How people helped each other, pulled together, cooperated, coped as best they could with the immense hardships. Another friend lost her home in the Oakland Hills fire of 1991 that destroyed some 5,000 homes. She had thought their house was in a safe area, but firefighters woke her and her family early Sunday morning ordering them to flee. Within 15 minutes their house was destroyed. She was at work the next day, taking care of her business, thankful that she and her family had survived. Exceptional people? Well, yes. Exceptional people *because of* their exceptional use of a simple philosophy. In a nutshell, that philosophy is this: How you think is how you feel and act—even in the face of real catastrophes.

Why can the simple idea voiced by Epictetus, Shakespeare, and Milton, empower you?

- First, because B in the ABC model is under your control! You can do something about your thoughts and your attitudes.
- Second, because you cannot change many disagreeable situations. This includes all of them in the past and many in the future—death, for example. In these cases, your only chance for feeling better is to change *how you think*.

- Third, because if you *can* change a disagreeable situation, your efforts will often be much more effective if you do not terribly disturb yourself.

Aging Does Not Cause Emotional Problems

It is not the *sheer fact* of growing older that causes emotional problems, but your attitudes *toward* growing older. Yet our society views aging as a cause of emotional problems. Decades ago, women with "involutional melancholia" occupied many beds in mental hospitals. Oh, never heard of it? What happened? Was a vaccine invented that prevents it? Not at all. Back then, women were almost entirely limited to the roles of housewife and mother. When they could no longer have children, or the nest was empty, they often believed nothing was left for them. They got depressed. Involutional melancholia was not the result of a biological change of life, though it was thought to be. It resulted from women's having few alternative roles and their buying into society's views about their worth as people. Involutional melancholia is now an almost unknown "disease." The idea once prevailed that women are nothing without husbands and children, but now that idea is weak and getting weaker. Our culture, however, has many other widely held Irrational Beliefs that hurt large numbers of people. Including many pertaining to aging.

What can we learn from Helen and Joanna? First, we can learn that it's *good* that we largely create our feelings and actions with our thoughts. Why is it good? Because what we think, believe, and do, we can think, believe, and do differently. We have control. This is the heart of the justly famous ABC model for optimal living.

The ABC's for Optimal Living

Let's break out Helen's and Joanna's situations, their Beliefs, and their reactions into the ABC's for optimal living. As you recall, the "A" of the ABC's stands for Activating Events or Adversities. Activating Events can be good, indifferent, or bad (adverse). It is the Adversities that most people usually want help with. These can be *actual* (my spouse was late) or *inferred* (my spouse was deliberately late). Activating Events can be *accurate* (my spouse is late) or *inaccurate* (my spouse is late [but your watch is wrong]). They can be *past* (my spouse was late yesterday), *present* (is now late), or *predicted* (will be late tomorrow).

In the example of Helen and Joanna, the Activating Events at A are clearly Adversities. Helen is paralyzed from the chest down, and Joanna's left arm is useless. These Adversities are similar in kind, but different in degree. The reactions of Helen and Joanna to their Adversities differ radically. In the ABC model, we use the word Consequences for people's actions and emotions at C. Joanna's Consequences at C are that she "can't" work and will not job hunt or date. She feels bitter, depressed, and embarrassed. On the other hand, Helen's Consequences at C are that she works full-time and has a wide range of friends and interests. She is noted for her upbeat mood.

The ABC model is a tool for optimal living. It can especially help you because you may *disempower* yourself by mistakenly accepting the highly popular A→C theory. According to this theory, Adversities at A automatically "make" you act poorly and feel emotionally disturbed at C. This A→C theory says something bad happens outside you—such as your having a neglectful child—and consequently pushes your buttons and "makes" you upset. It says that you have no choice about how you *feel and act* at C when A occurs. If it were true that A directly causes C, then Helen's reactions would be bitter, complaining, miserable, depressed, withdrawn, and self-pitying—as Joanna's reactions were. And Joanna's reactions would be more like Helen's—cheerful, optimistic, involved, interested in others. Helen's Adversity is objectively much greater than Joanna's. But Joanna's suffering (at C) is much greater. Fortunately for Helen—and potentially so for Joanna—Adversities do not directly lead to your responses and emotions at C. What does?

What's missing in the A→C formula? B, of course. Consider any Adversity at A. For example, part of your body may be paralyzed, as was true of both Joanna and Helen. Or you could have a very neglectful adult child. Or you may have lots of wrinkles on your face when you would rather not have them. According to the ABC model, these Adversities can *help* you disturb yourself as a Consequence at C. But A alone doesn't make you horrified, hurt, and depressed. It doesn't make you refuse to job hunt or to go out socially. It doesn't send you repeatedly running to the plastic surgeon. Instead, the missing and most important link is B, your Belief System—your B's (Beliefs)—*how you evaluate and think about A's (Adversities)*—that produces C's, your emotional and action Consequences. Your Beliefs are *yours*. This brings us to the Fourth Rule for Optimal Living:

Rule #4: ACCEPT RESPONSIBILITY

Life deals you a hand of cards, but YOU play that hand. That is your responsibility and you'd best accept it. You choose your actions and you choose the Beliefs that ultimately create your emotions and your actions. You choose how you react to the hand that life deals you. Accepting responsibility puts you in the most powerful position. If you do accept responsibility for your thoughts, feelings, and actions, including your emotional disturbances, you will save much time and energy by not defensively blaming others and blaming social conditions. Directing your own life sensibly also usually means cooperation with others, while not NEEDING considerable support, "strokes," and coaxing from them.

Most of us can learn to help ourselves—emotionally and practically—rather than persistently plaguing ourselves about Adversities. That's the main "what for" of this book: to learn how to help yourself so you'll feel less disturbed, happier, and better able to solve and live with practical problems like aging. What about "when to"? *When* do you help yourself? Right now! When you upset yourself, you can quickly, promptly *un*upset yourself—if you really acknowledge that your Beliefs are *yours*, and that therefore you can examine them and change them. Yes, *now*.

Is It Your Parents' Fault?

A popular, but mostly mistaken, idea common in our culture is that your past makes you what you are. This idea implies that older people cannot change because they have longer pasts. We will address that erroneous idea more fully in later chapters. Right now, however, let's examine one version of it: *Your* behavior is your parents' fault, and your children's behavior is *your* fault.

Mike and Jean sought counseling because they felt guilty and depressed over their inability to help their daughter, Lori, who had turned out badly. She addicted herself to drugs and worked as a prostitute. It *was* a fact that their daughter had (so far) turned out badly. Mike and Jean blamed themselves severely for the path Lori had taken. She nicely took advantage of their self-blame. She told them they had been too tough on her. She told them they had been too easy on her. She told them they had tried too hard. She even told them they had been too good as parents—she would have turned out better if they had been more average! None of this stopped Lori from calling Mike and Jean collect, desperately asking them to send her money to pay for drug detox programs and telling them it would be their fault if she ended up dead. They sent the money. This happened a number of times, with continued collect calls from Lori for ever larger sums of money.

In terms of the ABC's, Lori was telling her parents that her actions (Consequences) at C were caused by them (Activating Events, such as sending money, not sending money, and how they raised her) at A. What happened to B?

Jean's hairdresser, himself in recovery, recommended that Mike and Jean ask Lori to sign a release giving the drug program permission to tell them how she was doing. Perhaps they could find out about her progress. Lori signed and mailed back the form without protest. Mike and Jean sent the release to the drug program and then called to see if they could get some insight into how their daughter was doing in treatment. The drug program had never heard of her. Lori then told her parents they had called the wrong place, that she actually was registered at a different location of that program. Mike and Jean found she was unknown there, too.

By the time I (Emmett Velten) met Mike and Jean, Lori's story had passed through additional stages, punctuated with pleas for more money, to which Mike and Jean acquiesced. The additional stories Lori offered? 1. She was in the drug program but somehow was not in the program computer. 2. The drug program must have her under the wrong name, one of her aliases, perhaps. (None of those checked out.) 3. The program intake worker didn't like Lori, or was on drugs herself, and had (sadly contrary to program rules) borrowed money from Lori and "therefore" would not admit there was a Lori. This led to Mike and Jean's calling the program's director, who indicated his program would be very happy to treat Lori, if she registered. If they chose to pay for her treatment, the director told Mike and Jean, there were several payment methods for making sure the money went for treatment, not drugs. It was 99.99 percent likely, he went on to tell them, that all their money had gone for drugs. Then he referred Mike and Jean to me.

I first showed Mike and Jean how their profound self-downing and guilt about Lori's addiction and prostitution led to their unintentionally helping her feed her drug habit—as if she needed any help! Mike and Jean agreed with me on that one. They said they would follow the program director's suggestions about paying for Lori's treatment. If anything, however, this left them feeling even more miserable. Why?

While they agreed that it was bad to help Lori buy drugs, and good to refuse to do so, wasn't it true that her problems were basically their fault? Weren't they supposed to feel miserable about her having problems?

I showed Mike and Jean that their self-downing was detrimental to *them* because it produced miserably guilty feelings and depression. It also led to their falling for Lori's many cock-and-bull stories. Their putting themselves down *helped* her keep her drug habit. If, I told them, they only felt sad and regretful about their daughter's behavior rather than guilt-ridden and self-damning, their emotions might help them think more clearly about an admittedly bad situation. They might then see more clearly where the responsibility lay for Lori's behavior. What were they supposed to feel about their only child being a heroin addict and a prostitute? Uncaring? Righteously, cruelly angry? Of course not. But keen sadness and regret about their daughter's irrational actions could be quite healthful and rational.

At first Mike and Jean stuck to their idea that their upbringing of Lori—too strict, too easy, too average, too perfect—really *had* caused her problems. Fortunately, they did see that *their* current emotional reactions stemmed from their Beliefs about themselves rather than from the *fact* of having a child who turned out badly. If they were responsible for their current reactions, then who was responsible for Lori's?

By the end of their second session, Mike and Jean had realized and *accepted*, after years of self-blaming, that Lori was responsible for her own behavior. They realized and accepted that their paralyzing guilt and depression did not stem directly from the sad fact that Lori was in trouble. Instead, it stemmed from their Beliefs *about* her predicament. From their Beliefs that they were responsible for her self-defeating actions and therefore were *bad people*. Beliefs that they could, and later did, change.

So far, so good. At the beginning of their third session, Mike and Jean said that they no longer felt guilt-ridden since it was true that Lori was responsible for her own conduct. They felt sad and regretful about her and hoped that somehow she would change herself. "And what about your depression?" I asked. Mike and Jean felt less depressed, but still depressed. Why? Well, they *had* made mistakes as parents. Not all the mistakes Lori claimed, but some mistakes. After a little discussion I learned, without surprise, that Mike and Jean's child-rearing practices seemed about average—not even especially lenient. The worst example of their "childrearing" behavior this middle-aged, educated, profession-ally successful couple could think of took place in the late 1960s—well before Lori was born in the early 1970s! They had driven across the country in a VW bus, and they had smoked, even inhaled, pot.

I immediately agreed with Mike and Jean that they had made mistakes all over the place—like sending Lori all that money. They probably would make some mistakes later in the day, if not the session, as likely would be true of me, too. But how did mistakes make them bad people? This was the remaining essence of their lingering depression, their Irrational Belief that their mistakes made them *bad people*.

"Your Beliefs," I said to them, *"define* you as bad (or good) people. Once you believe you have the essence of badness, there's little chance for change. Your actions, like Lori's, can be good or bad, judged according to your goals, the standards of society, and social reality. Lori's actions, for instance, in conning you out of money and trading on your guilt, were bad, but they do not give Lori an essence of badness. She is not *a bad person*, even though she is *responsible* for behaving badly." In time, these ideas helped Mike and Jean accept themselves as fallible human beings, who had made mistakes, who loved their daughter, and who would no longer let her con them.

Blame Is Different From Responsibility

What can we learn from Mike and Jean's example and from Lori's? One important lesson is that it works better for most of us to accept responsibility for our actions and emotions. Responsibility and blame are quite different. In blame, you damn yourself or others as total human beings for their poor behavior. In responsibility, you accept yourself and other people as fallible human beings. Then, you *may* damn, disagree with, or try to change your and their poor *actions*. If your actions and feelings really were someone else's responsibility, you would be powerless to change. If you recognize that your actions and your feelings are your responsibility, you make yourself powerful. You have the chance to take control of your life.

Another lesson we can learn from Mike, Jean, and Lori is to see how easy it is to believe widespread, but incorrect, ideas "given" to us by our culture. We learn and believe some ideas, and we assume they are simply facts. Instead, they are just ideas. They are theories about facts. In Mike and Jean's case, they automatically assumed that if their child was behaving badly it had to be their fault. They learned that idea and assumed it was a fact. The ABC model taught them a different way to look at things. It taught them how to get better results in their own emotional lives—by accepting responsibility for their actions and feelings. And letting Lori remain responsible for hers.

Rock'n'Wrinkle

You could have a good many wrinkles (at point A) and create severe anxiety and embarrassment about the wrinkles (at point C) because you are telling yourself (at point B), "I MUST NOT have numerous wrinkles. I *can't stand* them! How *terrible* if I get more! I look so old!" Then you can dispute (D) your Irrational Beliefs (IB's) and make them over into reasonable, optimal Beliefs that *promote* optimal living and that *demote* unhappiness. This is what Karen, a client of mine (Emmett Velten's), did.

At A, Karen was quite wrinkled, far more so than most women her age. Maybe her smoking played a part in it, maybe she got too much sun, maybe it was genes. No matter. Several of the best dermatologists had done what they could, and it wasn't enough. Twenty-five years ago, Karen had been an entertainer, whose real name most baby boomers would recognize. But she had changed careers. After a couple of decades as an executive in a record company, what became her true desire? Yes, to go back into entertainment. So why couldn't she just come out of retirement as a wrinkled rock star and tour like the rest of the wrinkled rock stars who never retired? What was the problem? As indicated above, Karen devoutly believed she *couldn't stand* it if her old fans, to say nothing of "kids," saw her wrinkles. "It would be *awful!* They'd think I'm *an old lady!*" she lamented.

We worked not on Karen's wrinkles at A, but on her Suboptimal Beliefs at B, which had produced as a Consequence at C, her feelings of humiliation and avoidance of doing what she wanted. Karen worked hard in her therapy and sang rational humorous songs, several of which appear in chapter 10. She concluded, "OK, I'm clear on the idea that it's what things, such as wrinkles, *mean* to me that leads to any emotional difficulties I might have about them. The wrinkles themselves don't make me wish I were dead."

"Right. Wrinkles aren't popular in our culture, but there's no proof they cause depression, horror, and avoidance of public appearances! As Epictetus might have put it, 'People are disturbed not by wrinkles, but by the meaning that they give to wrinkles.'"

"So, in a way," Karen butted in, "regarding my feelings about myself at least, I really am only as old as I think?"

"That's right. Most people, as they get a bit older, feel a lot younger than they are. If you buy into the stereotypes about getting older, you'll *feel* older, maybe even much older than you are."

"Maybe people aren't supposed to act their age!"

"Exactly! I don't know who thought up that quaint idea, but it's stupid for us to hide our faces and limit our lives because of our age."

Nevertheless, you may wonder, as Karen did, whether *any* of the possible disadvantages to aging can truly disturb us. Maybe not the wrinkles, but what if you are weaker or get tired much more easily than was true just a few years ago? Disappointing, yes. Disturbing, no, not by themselves. Many other people have the same disabilities and do not feel terribly upset about them. How come? And what about people who disturb themselves about even more minor handicaps? Or those who disturb themselves about not being perfect *enough*?

Undisturbed people have a different outlook—different Beliefs— about their afflictions. They *dislike* them, but do not *demand* that they not exist. Is this true of you? Or do you, like most people, contend that damaging Adversities SHOULD NOT, MUST NOT exist? Oh? So, you often do. So your aging problem—if you have one—*plus* your Belief that it SHOULD NOT exist, is the issue. Disappointment you may have, but get free of your demand, and will you really have your disturbed Consequences? Most likely not!

We Have Met the Enemy . . .

It's fortunate that we largely disturb ourselves. Why? Because it shows we have the ability *not* to do so. Oliver Hazard Perry, the famous naval commander in the War of 1812, sent a message back to General William Henry Harrison after Perry's forces had won the Battle of Lake Erie: "We have met the enemy, and they are ours." This victorious message became a well-known quotation. Then Pogo, Walt Kelly's comic strip character, applied it to human nature and gave it a humorous twist, by saying, "We have met the enemy, and he is *us*." All too true! Most of us don't need enemies. We do that job very well ourselves. In the battle for happiness, we defeat ourselves. Often we don't realize that the most important enemy lies within. Until we do realize it—and do something about it—we may lose battle after battle. The ABC method can help you win.

3

There's No Time BUT the Present

There's no time like the present for postponing what you don't want to do.

Hecht's Fourth Law

Insight is over-rated. According to psychotherapy as it's usually practiced, insight is the key that will unlock your prison. Most therapists hold the following notions to be self-evident. We think they are harmful nonsense:

1. The past is responsible for your feelings and actions.
2. You MUST get insight into this gruesome past and who's responsible for your unhappiness and poor choices—your parents, your culture, your peers—before you can get better.
3. Insight itself will change you or make you easily able to change yourself.

This standard psychotherapy Belief System—otherwise known as B.S.—says that your past screwed you up and is still wrecking your life. It has made many psychoanalysts rich and stopped hordes of their clients from admitting their own complicity in making themselves disturbed. It blocks people's own creative potential for *un*disturbing themselves.

22

   This cop-out credo is appealing (for it blames your parents and other villains), but it is misleading and futile to believe it. The more persistently and strongly you whine about your gruesome past—yes, even if it *was* gruesome—the less time and energy you will have to get on with your present and future life! The B.S. that your past is all-powerful and that you are all-powerless is *especially* futile the older you get. Why? Because you have less time to waste in poring over your lengthier past for magical insights and answers and for people to blame.

   Blaming others—especially your parents or "society"—for your poor behavior will hardly help you improve your life. It prevents your taking responsibility for your actions and feelings. It fosters the notion that no one is responsible for anything, which can have a corrosive effect on the whole moral fabric of society. It leads to an absurd infinite regress in the effort to show "why" you now have your problems. A good example of this is offered by John Bradshaw in his 1990 book, *Homecoming.* He says that the neglected, wounded inner child of the past (courtesy of your parents) is responsible for "much of the violence and cruelty in the world." He attributes World War II and the Holocaust to the wounded inner child. On page 10 he claims that Hitler's inner child was neglected and wounded, and that Hitler was the victim of "toxic shame". It seems that Hitler's father gave the wounded inner child and the toxic shame to him. Hitler's father—"the bastard son of a Jewish landlord"—in turn got *his* mishegoss from *his* father. Oh. With Hitler's Jewish landlord grandfather, the chain of cause and effect identified by Bradshaw—the sins of the parents being passed on to the children— ends. He says nothing about the Jewish landlord having had a wounded inner child or even parents.

   Thinking of yourself as a victim will make things worse for you. Whatever led to your bollixing yourself up at this point in your life is past. The past *influences* us, yes, but it is we ourselves who carry on— right now—the slop from the past. Endlessly exploring it and "understanding" it is a delaying tactic. It will not change the fact that the one and only time any of us can change is *now.* This is the Fifth Rule for Optimal Living:

Rule #5: DO IT NOW

If you're going to change, there's no time BUT the present. To get better, you can take responsibility for changing yourself—starting now.

Dear Inner Child: Grow Up!

Mary, at 49, had only one session with a therapist who wanted to explore her "past lives." The therapist had "sensed" that all those past lives involved Grecian royalty, rather than the Albanian peasants Mary knew her distant forebears had been! She easily saw that this kind of therapy was silly and harmful, and didn't go back to that therapist after the first visit. But Mary then spent two years and thousands of dollars on "inner child therapy." She intensely got in touch with how her parents—those offspring of peasants!—hadn't loved her enough to support her going to medical school, as she had wanted. Instead, they had encouraged her to enter nursing, which she'd done but never liked as much as she thought she'd have liked being a doctor. Mary resented her parents, but she wanted to make peace with them as they were getting up in years.

What did inner-child therapy do for Mary? It fanned her hatred for her parents and made her feel like a helpless victim. It encouraged her to blow her savings on interminable therapy that did nothing to help her. It focused her on the awfulness of nursing. It focused her on how her life was wrecked because she had been forced into the Florence Nightingale role, instead of what she'd wanted to be, by parents who didn't care enough about her. Besides, Mary added doubtfully in her first REBT session, they hadn't supported her in other ways. Such as? Mary admitted she had never been able to think of anything worse than that once she had wanted to have a big birthday party and her parents had put a cap on the number of children invited. This hadn't seemed *horrible* to Mary, though the inner-child therapist had wept over the incident, had hugged Mary as well as her own teddy bear, and had wanted to "probe" the incident, Mary suspected, for more years and more dollars than Mary cared to spend. At this point, Mary fired the therapist and turned to Rational Emotive Behavior Therapy.

Within a few sessions, Mary found that yes, her parents probably had treated her shabbily, but not because they didn't love her. Instead, they thought she lacked the stamina to get through medical school and that is why they wanted her to try nursing. So they undersold her. However, her parents' failure to support her goal to become a physician (A) did not cause her intense hatred of them (C). It was mainly her Irrational Beliefs (IB's) *about* A that caused C. Namely, "They SHOULD have backed up my desires to be a doctor, which they did not, and therefore they are *rotten people!*"

When Mary disputed her IB's, she effectively changed them to, "It would have been nice had they supported me in doing what I wanted, but they surely didn't have to. No law of the universe says that they MUST." In time, she gave up her rage at her parents and went on with the rest of her life. She decided to obtain additional training as a nurse practitioner, which, in her home state, has a wide scope of independent practice and would involve fewer years of training than going back to medical school.

The Past Is Gone Forever

Tad also got sidetracked by the idea that your past Activating Events cause your present reactions and emotions (C). He spent three years in traditional psychotherapy "understanding" that his eldest sister, Amy, had been cruel to him as a child. Therefore, according to this "insight," he resented older women (including his two divorced wives) and hated getting older himself. After his analysis was "successfully" completed, he married a third wife, and soon he began to hate her. His fear of getting older remained as strong as ever, if not stronger.

Within three months of starting Rational Emotive Behavior Therapy, Tad realized that he was the victim of his own low frustration tolerance (LFT). He *couldn't stand* his "cruel" sister and his various wives because he demanded that they do everything—yes, practically everything—his way. He had no forbearance whenever they even slightly thwarted him. During courtship, Tad kept his demandingness under wraps, but not after marriage. Then he switched to believing that his spouse SHOULD be faultless. The same demand for an impossible, no-fault guarantee that he never be thwarted by his aging body also underlay his fear of growing older. Tad applied the ABC method, and gave up his insistence that his spouse, and his body, always do things his way. He accepted his third wife with her faults and began his first successful relationship in 25 years. At last report, they were aging happily together.

The most important point of our stories is that Mary and Tad could not do anything to change their past—what's done is done—but they could and did change their *present* Irrational Beliefs. Mary changed hers about her parents and their treachery and thereby saved herself more years of heartache and therapy. Tad changed his demands that he not be thwarted in any way, whether by his wives or by the inevitable hassles of growing older.

What can *you* change? List the influences—past, present, and predicted—that you think "make" you feel how you now feel about any topic, such as aging. They may include gender, upbringing, nationality, culture, social status, income, genes, schooling, the amount of dietary fiber consumed, and your attitudes. But what can you change *now?* The past is not one of the factors you can change. You *can* change your current and future attitudes. You *choose* to hold on to them or get rid of them, today. Yes, it's your choice.

Your childhood is irrelevant to handling your present problems. The past is gone forever. It's not in existence. It can't "make" you feel bad and behave self-defeatingly now. Fussing and cussing about your childhood and other *unchangeable* factors gets you nowhere fast— except worse off. Your present Beliefs about the past, however, *can* really affect you. But fortunately, if they make you unduly upset, you can always change them. For if you *now* have Beliefs, they are yours, and you can *now* replace them. This brings us to the Sixth Rule for Optimal Living:

Rule #6: You Can't Change the Past

Feeling Bad Can Be Good

"What about *really* bad things in my life—like disability or dying or maybe going to a nursing home someday?" we are sometimes asked. "Am I supposed not to care about those things at all?" Our answer is, "By all means, care. In fact, it's often helpful to feel very bad about things."

There is a great difference between healthful and unhealthful negative emotions. Many psychotherapists give the impression that feeling good is always the goal. Not so! Success at self-help may be for you to feel bad—yes, *bad*—about something. Not serene, not neutral, not cheerful. If a situation *is* bad for you, then you can constructively feel bad about it—it would be nutty if you didn't!

The theory of REBT says that you can legitimately feel healthful negative emotions when things go wrong in your life and even feel them very strongly. If a close relative or friend dies, you can experience intense sadness, sorrow, or grief. Because you *did* really feel attached to that person, you suffer a loss, a profound deprivation, by his or her death. If you were only mildly attached to a person who died, you would probably suffer only mild or moderate sadness.

Similarly, when you are unsuccessful or frustrated in important ways you may feel the healthful negative emotions of disappointment, annoyance, regret, frustration, sorrow, or displeasure. These feelings may be mild, moderate, or strong, depending on how much Adversity— a frustrating situation—you experience and depending on how strong your desires are. If your negative feelings are healthful, you are telling yourself something like, "I *don't like* this frustration. It really is annoying, and I *wish* it didn't exist." You are also thinking or implying, "*But* it's not the end of the world. *But* I can find other things to enjoy. *But* even with this frustration, I can still lead a fairly happy life."

In other words, when you *desire* or *prefer* something and do not get it—or if you have it and you lose it—you are deprived. You can create healthful negative emotions of sadness, annoyance, or displeasure. Otherwise you would hardly have a meaningful life. You might not even survive! For if you felt happy or indifferent about your frustrations and losses, you would not try to replace losses or cope with them. You would not try to change or avoid bad things (such as dangers and illness) and you might well die. So when you don't get what you *do* want or do get what you *don't* want, some negative feelings are healthful or self-helping. They help you live optimally.

Most important, however, you have a choice of *healthful* or *unhealthful* negative feelings. For when you want, say, success and approval, and you get, instead, failure and rejection, you can appropriately feel healthfully sorry and frustrated. And you usually do. You also can choose to create the *un*healthful negative feelings of depression, horror, rage, or hopelessness. Why are these unhealthful? Because they usually give you bad or self-sabotaging results. Thus, if you feel disappointed about failing a driving test, your disappointment motivates you to study and practice more to pass it next time. But, if you feel depressed or humiliated about failing the test, you tend to cop out, put off taking it again, refuse to study for it, drive without a license, or perhaps give up on driving.

When something is undesirable in your life, healthful negative feelings will probably help you cope with it and change it. Unhealthful negative feelings often make you too upset to cope with or change undesirable happenings and may even "help" you make them worse. If your bad feelings are generated by Rational Beliefs you will:

1. Accept that life has a right to give you bad things.
2. Go ahead and have strong, healthful negative feelings about those things.
3. Use those healthful negative feelings to motivate yourself to change what you can change.
4. What do you do with what you *can't* change? *Accept* those Adversities with serenity. Not resignation—because when we feel resigned to something we often continue low-level whining about it—but complete acceptance. As theologian Reinhold Niebuhr, and Alcoholics Anonymous after him, recommended: Do whatever you can to learn the difference between the things you really cannot change and those you can change. Accept only the former.

Niebuhr's advice and A.A.'s Serenity Prayer really go back to the time of the ancient Stoic philosophers. The A.A. version is: "God grant me serenity to accept the things I cannot change, courage to change the things I can, and wisdom to know the difference."

Rational Emotive Behavior Therapy says that you'd better feel—and often strongly feel—annoyed and disappointed. Not panicked, depressed, or enraged. These emotions, healthful or unhealthful, arise from your Beliefs, which you control. You have a choice, and your choice is mainly at B, your Beliefs about Adversities. If B is a *preference* for success, approval, and pleasure, you will tend to feel healthfully frustrated and disappointed when your preference is not fulfilled. But if B is a *demand*, a Belief that you absolutely MUST succeed, you will tend to feel at C (your emotional Consequence) panicked and depressed. If you keep telling yourself, "I absolutely MUST win everyone's approval or else I *can't stand* it!", see how you feel when anyone disapproves of you. Our bet is you will feel quite disturbed.

The concept of having *healthful* negative feelings about bad situations helps you build on the ABC model of self-disturbance. Life situations, or Activating Events—such as certain features of aging—can be fortunate (favoring your interests), neutral, or unfortunate (adverse to your interests). The latter, of course—the Adversities—are what self-helpers want to help themselves with. It is *healthful* to feel negatively about such situations if—but make that a big IF—those negative feelings motivate you to try to remedy the situation or to sensibly adapt to it. It is rational to have healthful negative emotions—such as concern, regret, and determination, for example, when you think about your friend requiring live-in assistance as an alternative to a nursing home. Or for when you realize how easy it is to get physically out of shape and how hard it is to get back in shape. Those negative emotions could help you motivate yourself to do as much as you can to promote your goals and purposes.

When they are healthful, negative emotions can motivate you to work for what you want, work *against* what you do not want, and learn to cultivate philosophical acceptance—*when you can't do anything else about it*. When, however, your negative feelings are *unhealthful*, they can block your efforts to solve problems effectively, make you frantic, and create misery.

Older people create their emotions the same way younger people do. Depression is not a rational adaptation to getting older. Nor is it an inevitable consequence of getting older. Depression is a negative, *un*healthful emotion based on Irrational Beliefs. Such as, *"Either* my whole body works as well as it used to *or* life is miserable and I can't be happy *at all."*

"So," one of our clients, Diane, said, "your point is that feeling bad, but not disturbed, about unfortunate happenings is good. It can motivate me to change what I don't want, right?"

"Yes. And to *accept,* but not cheer about, and learn to cope with the bad things that you *cannot* change."

"That makes sense. I probably could use some specific tips about how to keep from disturbing myself and how to calm myself down if I do disturb myself."

Before we get to those specific tips, let's explore more fully the difference between healthful and unhealthful *negative* emotions.

Your Feelings Are Important

What optimal emotional outcomes does Rational Emotive Behavior Therapy strive for when people feel depressed, anxious, or enraged? A common misconception about REBT stems from its use of the word "rational." As REBT uses the word, it means "in your long-term interests." Some people, however, think of "rational", like Mr. Spock's "logical", as cold and calculating. They infer that REBT aims to make people feel neutral or serene about bad events, such as losses. Definitely not! Another misconception stems from REBT's approach to unhealthful emotions like depression. Some people, at first, think that the only alternative to feeling depressed about a loss is not to care. Untrue!

REBT makes an important distinction between healthful and un-healthful *negative* emotions and considers them different in kind, not just in degree. Depression, for example, is not simply *very* great sadness or grief. You may feel depressed about a loss and also feel sad or grief-stricken. An important loss, therefore, could be the relevant Adversity at A that happens before your feelings of depression or sadness or grief. Depression, sadness, and grief do overlap, yet they are distinct emotions.

Why do we define depression as different from sadness and grief? Because, first, different Beliefs underlie depression, on the one hand, and sadness or grief, on the other hand. You don't even "have to" feel sad and regretful. Theoretically, you could train yourself into thinking you don't care about various losses you may incur. The downside there is that you would also miss out on the far greater *emotional benefits* of caring.

Second, depression differs from sadness and grief in how it helps or hinders you in adapting or coping with unkind fate. Sadness and grief stem from Rational Beliefs. Rational Beliefs acknowledge the seriousness of a loss and rate the loss as very bad. Rational Beliefs then lead you to feel very sad or grief-stricken. In time, they motivate you to move on and cope with and adapt to the loss. Depression, on the other hand, acknowledges the loss but includes exaggerated and maladaptive ideas like "I can't *ever* be happy now," "*Everything* is lost," or "Now life is *not worth living*." REBT targets the maladaptive Beliefs and *respects* the adaptive Rational Beliefs about the seriousness of your losses.

When It's Worthwhile To Feel Bad

Some self-help methods and therapy systems imply that feeling good is always the goal. On the other hand, some philosophies and religions advocate desirelessness as the highest goal. The REBT approach is different. Successful self-help and optimal thinking can be quite consistent with feeling bad about something. Not serene, not neutral, not desireless, not cheerful. If a situation *is* bad from your perspective, then you can constructively feel bad about it— there would be a conflict with your values if you did not. Serenity or desirelessness in the face of something bad could defeat your purposes. Negative feelings—such as concern, sadness, grief, disappointment, annoyance, and frustration— may inspire you to do something constructive. Alternatively, feeling bad about a situation may inspire you to accept it gracefully, adapt to it, and then to move on with life and focus your energy where possible on other, more rewarding matters.

Once you really have achieved thorough acceptance of something bad that you cannot change, then you will have more chance to let go of it. To forgive it. In time, you may reach the point that you hardly think about whatever the bad event was—*nor* do you then feel much sadness, regret, displeasure, annoyance, or concern about it. As was true of 70-year-old Helen, whom we mentioned in chapter 2. She has been paralyzed from the chest down for over 40 years. She has built many adaptive habits for dealing with the inconveniences of her condition, as she goes about her busy life. Though still afflicted with a mammoth Adversity, it would hardly pay for Helen to hold negative feelings about her condition except now and then—when she comes across a novel situation. Helen has accepted and adapted to an ongoing Adversity that she can never change. Negative feelings are partly there to help you. In Helen's case, *ongoing* negative feelings—even healthful negative feelings—would be superfluous.

Six Healthful Negative Emotions and Their Unhealthful Counterparts

Let's now compare some healthful negative emotions with their unhealthful counterparts.

1. *Concern vs. anxiety and panic.* Concern is a healthful emotion that stems from such Rational Beliefs as, "I hope that this threat or loss does not happen. If it does, it would be unfortunate. But there's no reason that I NEED a guarantee that I won't lose what I love!" The unhealthful negative emotions of anxiety and panic, on the other hand, stem from the Irrational Belief "This threat MUST NOT happen and it would be *awful* if it did."

2. *Sadness vs. depression.* Sadness is a healthful emotion that stems from Rational Beliefs along these lines: "It's very unfortunate that I have experienced this loss but there is no reason that it

should not have happened." Depression, on the other hand, stems from "This loss SHOULD NOT have occurred and it is *terrible* that it did." When depressed, you may feel responsible for the loss and damn yourself for the loss. "It's all my fault. I am *no good.*" If, however, the loss is outside your control, you may tend to damn the world and life conditions: *"Life sucks* and isn't worth living."

3. *Regret vs. guilt.* Healthful feelings of regret or remorse stem from admitting responsibility for a bad act you have done, but accepting *yourself* as a fallible human being. When regretful, you feel bad about the act or deed but accept yourself. You hold Rational Beliefs along the lines of these: "I *prefer* not to act badly, but it's not carved on stone tablets that I MUST NOT do so. If I do, I do. Too bad! I'll try to learn from my mistakes." Guilt stems from damning yourself as bad, wicked, or rotten for acting badly. You feel bad about the act *and* you damn yourself because of the Irrational Belief, "I must not act badly and if I do it's *awful* and *intolerable* and it makes me a *rotten person!*"

4. *Disappointment vs. shame and embarrassment.* Your rational feelings of disappointment stem from acting "stupidly" in public, acknowledging the stupid act, but accepting yourself in the process. You feel disappointed about your actions but not with yourself because you prefer, but do not demand, that you always act well. Shame and embarrassment stem from recognizing that you have acted "stupidly" in public, followed by self-condemnation for acting in a way that you absolutely SHOULD NOT have done. Shame and embarrassment also stem from expecting the watching audience to think poorly of you, and then agreeing with those perceived judgments. We like to quote former First Lady Eleanor Roosevelt's observation, "No one can make you feel inferior without your consent."

5. *Annoyance vs. rage, anger, hatred.* Healthful annoyance, irritation, or determination occur when another person disregards your rules of living. When annoyed, you do not like what the other has done but do not damn him or her for doing it. "I *wish* the other person had not done that and I *don't like* what he or she did. It does not follow, however, that he or she MUST NOT break my rule." In unhealthful anger, however, you *do* believe the other person absolutely must not break your rule, and thus

you damn, despise, vilify, hate, or deeply resent the other for doing so.

6. *Frustration vs. horror.* When you don't get your way, your frustrated feelings are unpleasant, but such feelings can help you. They can motivate you to try harder or to try another way. Feelings of frustration stem from Rational Beliefs and thinking, "I don't like this! It's annoying! What can I do to get past this obstacle and get what I want?" Frustration motivates you to keep working for what you want. It also, ironically, increases enjoyment because you contrast the frustrated feelings with the pleasurable feelings. Feelings of horror, on the other hand, stem from your Belief, "This obstacle is *horrible!* It *can't* (MUST NOT) be this way! How can life give me such an *awful* obstacle!? I *can't stand* it!"

4

Three Key Questions to Beat Self-Defeat

Life is too serious to be taken very seriously.

Jilly and Rob's Conclusion

When increasing age brings you Adversities, how can you promote your optimal, rational thinking? How can you reduce your irrational, suboptimal thinking? You can learn to ask yourself, and to answer correctly, Three Key Questions. If you do this, you will probably get more of what you want in life and less of what you don't want, and the Adversities can go fly a kite.

1. Does my particular thought help me or hinder me over the long run? If it hinders me, what thought would help me reach my goals better? What thought would help me feel better over the longer term?
2. Is my thinking consistent with the facts? If it isn't, what thought *is?*
3. Is my thinking logical? If not, what would make more sense logically?

What About Positive Thinking?

People often mistake rational thinking for "positive thinking," but there is a big difference. Emile Coué popularized positive thinking some 75 years ago with what probably was the world's best-known saying: "Day by day, in every way, I am getting better and better." Coué and the many other purely positive thinkers, such as Mary Baker Eddy, Henry Wood, Dale Carnegie, Napoleon Hill, Norman Vincent Peale, and Louise Hay, saw that how you think is immensely important. It *is* immensely important! They saw that fact, but they saw only its "think positive" aspect. Some of them thought that positive thinking could overcome *all* Adversities, such as diseases. Some of them thought that positive thinking would bring you untold riches. And not just in the Hereafter, either. In *this* life! Have positive dreams, they said, and they'll come true.

Some of today's purely positive thinkers with a New Age flair believe that your thinking *literally* gives you diseases like cancer, MS, TB, and AIDS. Oh? What happened to bacteria? What happened to viruses? What happened to smoking? What happened to unsafe sex? What happened to heredity and genes? (What happened to the brains of some of these New Age folks?) No, real life has real Adversities. Lots of them, including many you can do little or nothing about. You'd better think quite realistically in coping with, and accepting, those Adversities.

The positive thinkers also fail to see that no matter how much you practice so-called positive thinking, you do *not* thereby eliminate your negative thinking. Yes, *while* we think positively, we may temporarily sidetrack our deadly negative thoughts. But what happens when we take a break from telling ourselves "Day by day, in every way, I'm getting better and better"? Back to negative thinking we instantly go. We especially do so when adverse reality intrudes and we notice what almost certainly will be true, namely that we are *not* getting better day by day in every way! Day by day, and in every way, we remain humans. We remain riddled with fallibilities. We keep our tendency to think irrationally (as well as rationally). Almost every day, and in far too many ways, we remain beset with Adversities. What do we do about these realities? Positive thinking, anyone?

So, don't for one minute suppose that we advocate mere positive thinking. Nor will we tell you to dwell fondly on positive mental images. Such "positive" sentiments as "Everything will probably turn out for the best" and "Things aren't as bad as they look" are often not only unrealistic, and even silly, but negative! Why? Positive thinking can be impractical if it inspires you to sit around waiting for Godot rather than to do something to help yourself. It can also be unrealistic and does not logically follow from your *wish* that everything turn out for the best. Most fundamentally, the practice of positive thinking in itself does nothing to uproot the Irrational Beliefs that generate emotional disturbance.

Reality Testing

Let's look at some examples of both rational and irrational, optimal and suboptimal, thinking and ask you to judge for yourself which is which, and why. You will thereby improve your thinking about your thinking. You will build your crucial skills at detecting irrational, suboptimal thinking and at disputing it. Disputing suboptimal thinking means attacking it vigorously in its own territory. Irrational thinking almost always masquerades as obviously true, as logical, even helpful. When you dispute an Irrational Belief, you call its bluff. You make it put up or shut up. You analyze its helpfulness. You study its logic. You compare its claims with the facts. You ask it the Three Key Questions (which we'll explain next). If it fails these tests, you revise your Belief so that it's more helpful, more realistic, and more logical.

Suppose you are thinking about taking an early retirement, as one of our clients, Jim, was, and your thought, like Jim's, is: "I can't retire early, even though I would like to do so, because people wouldn't respect me. They'd think I was lazy. I *couldn't stand* their disapproval. I NEED their respect and would be pretty *worthless* without it. Damn! I'll have to keep working at least five more years. Otherwise, if people didn't respect me, I'd be *worthless*." Are those thoughts rational or irrational? Well, we admit we stacked the irrational cards in this example, but let's look at *why* it's irrational. Ask the Three Key Questions of these Beliefs about retirement, and see.

Key Question #1: *Does it help me over the long run to believe this?* When Jim worked out his answer to this question, he came up with this: "No, that thought is useless, because I *want* to retire now and enjoy myself. Who knows if I will be around five years from now—or in any condition to enjoy my retirement? Also, when I tell myself I absolutely NEED something, it depresses me and makes me grumpy and nervous—which I definitely don't need!"

Key Question #2: *Is my Belief consistent with the facts?* Jim concluded, "No. Some people might not respect me for retiring early, some wouldn't care one way or the other, and some would respect me more for doing what I wanted to do. If a good many people did not respect me and thought I was crazy, I *could* definitely stand it. I would hardly die of it. Despite their disapproval I could lead a happy life. In fact, if I retired early from this job I might well be happier than if I let fear of disapproval influence me to keep working."

Key Question #3: *Is my Belief logical?* Jim said, "Three for three! No, even if I were lazy and retired early, and even if a good many people didn't respect me for doing so, it doesn't logically follow that my worth as a person would be zero. At worst, I would be a person with *defective behavior*. But I wouldn't be a *defective person*."

If you ask yourself these practical, realistic, and logical key questions, you can see whether your Beliefs are rational (that is, promote optimal living) or irrational (promote suboptimal existing). If your Beliefs are self-defeating, knowing this can further motivate you to give them up and replace them with Rational Beliefs (RB's). This brings us to the Seventh Rule for Optimal Living:

Rule #7: ACT LIKE A SCIENTIST

When nondisturbed, you will tend to think more objectively and scientifically than you do when you feel disturbed. You can feel deeply and act concertedly, but you can learn to regulate your emotions and actions by reflecting on them and evaluating their consequences in terms of how they help or hinder you in reaching your short-term and long-term goals.

Can you always figure out whether one of your Beliefs about success, approval, or pleasure is rational or irrational, self-helping or self-defeating? Or whether it promotes optimal living or suboptimal existance? Maybe you cannot *always* figure this out, but practically always you can. For if a Belief will probably help you fulfill your desires for long-range gain, is realistically attainable, and is logical and not self-contradictory, it certainly looks good.

Thus, if you are 30 pounds overweight and you want to lose some weight, your Belief that it is *preferable* to eat less and exercise more will help you lose some pounds. Your Belief is realistic (for you *can* diet and exercise more), and it is factual (for fewer calories consumed and more burned will usually help weight loss). On the other hand, your Belief that you absolutely MUST at all times eat less might lead you to fast for three months, which is likely to be harmful. Your "must" is unrealistic, because you will probably fail to always do as you MUST, will seriously blame yourself, and out of anxiety may end up by vastly overeating. Besides, if you did not eat anything for three months, you'd possibly be dead before the three months was up! Or else your starving body would drive you to overeating again. The Belief that you absolutely MUST always eat less is also illogical, because that is not the only way to lose weight.

Whenever you take almost any preference and raise it to an absolute demand, you:

- frequently do yourself and sometimes others more harm than good;
- are quite unrealistic (because you can often fail to get what you demand), and
- are illogical (because your demand says that only one method can work and that there are no alternatives).

Therefore, a quick way to discover whether your Belief is likely to be self-defeating is to see if it is a preference or an absolutistic demand. To tell yourself that you strongly *prefer* something but that you don't HAVE TO get it is practically always sensible and rational. To tell yourself that because you want it, you absolutely MUST have it and will be destroyed without getting it is almost always irrational and crazy. If your desires are preferential, good. If they are dire needs, you'd better beware.

Let's now turn to an exercise in distinguishing Irrational Beliefs from Rational Beliefs. Go through each of the statements listed below, and figure out whether—and if so, why—you think they are rational or irrational. The answer key is on pages 47–50.

Exercise in Deciding What's Rational and What's Irrational

Let's look at some examples of rational and irrational thinking. These examples can help you learn to judge for yourself which is which, and why. You will thereby improve your thinking about your thinking. Start with the Three Key Questions:

1. Does it help me or hinder me over the long run to believe this? If it hinders me, what thought would help me reach my goals better and feel better?
2. Is my thinking consistent with the facts? If it isn't, what *is?*
3. Is my thinking logical? If not, what would make more sense logically?

Then work down the following list of statements. After reading each statement, decide whether it's rational or irrational.

1. I absolutely must become the richest person in the world.
2. I'd like to become the richest person in the world.
3. I cannot stand having wrinkles.
4. I do not like having wrinkles.
5. Everything I do is wrong.
6. I make quite a few mistakes.
7. Because I had such a tough childhood, I deserve things to be easier now.
8. I've been addicted to cigarettes too long to change.
9. People who fail are complete failures as human beings.
10. Sticking with my diet and exercise program is very hard. I can't do it because it takes too much time and effort.

"All right," said Alejandro. "By 'rational' you mean helpful *for me*— with my goals and values—depending on the situation I'm in. Right?" Alejandro was a newcomer at a SMART (Self Management And Recovery Training) self-help discussion group and had just heard the meeting's opening statement that outlined the ABC model. He was there because of immense credit card debt. "But doesn't it help me to have a laptop computer? A safe four-wheel drive vehicle? To dress well at work? And relax on nice vacations with my girlfriend and her kids?"

"Well, yes, those purchases *could* be rational. But I thought you said you were in all kinds of trouble from overspending."

"I am!"

"So you'd better compare the helpfulness of the huge debt—the new clothes, the vehicle, the latest computer, the trips to Acapulco, and so on—with the *unhelpfulness* of the huge debt. How does it compare?"

Alejandro answered with verve, "The debt is much worse than not having all those things."

"What the ABC model aims to teach us to do is look at, and think about, our lives over the long run. If your life is going to be very short, and if you don't have any responsibilities to loved ones who will continue to live after you kick the bucket, or if you really don't mind suffering later, then forget about the long run. But, if you expect to live to an average age, and if you don't like to suffer, then you'd better focus on the long run! As our colleague Hank Robb points out, the trouble with a philosophy of 'eat, drink, and be merry, for tomorrow we die', is that sometimes tomorrow comes and we're not dead!"

"So," Alejandro chimed in, "rational is helpful, or at least not harmful, over the long run rather than only the short run?"

"That's right. You might enjoy spending a lot of money on fine clothes *now*, for example, but it might not be so great later, when you're the best dressed person in the poorhouse!"

"Well, let's say I realize I'm harming myself over the long run, like running up the big credit card debt. The actual truth is I already know what's in my best interest. I just don't do it. I don't seem able to stop spending money. I just seem to feel that I MUST have whatever I want! What then?"

MUSTurbation Leads to Self-Abuse

Now we will show you the best way to get a handle on your thoughts that contribute to self-defeat, unhappiness, and disturbance, whether about aging or anything else. The phrases, "Look for your 'must'" and "Look for your 'should,'" are a great shortcut. Just about all real emotional disturbances and self-defeating actions stem from one main root, which fortunately people can do something to change. That root is demandingness.

The basic demands fall into three categories—I MUST, You MUST, and It MUST—those "musty" voices inside your head! For each, there is a corresponding desire or preference, as indicated in the following chart.

The Three Demands	The Three Desires
"**I** absolutely MUST do well and be approved of by others *or else it's awful, I can't stand it, and it makes me a worm if I fail!*"	I WANT to do well and get others' approval, but if I don't, I don't. It won't be the end of the world, and I'll remain a fallible person who sometimes doesn't do well and gets rejected."
"**You** (other people) SHOULD act right and treat me fairly *or else it's awful, I can't stand it, and it makes you a worm!*"	"I'd LIKE you to treat me well and act right, but even if you don't, it's not *awful*, and it doesn't make you a *complete villain* and *totally damnable*."
"**It** (life conditions) HAS TO be, NEEDS TO be the way I want it—namely comfortable and fair—*or else it's awful, I can't stand it, and there's no use living!*"	"It's highly DESIRABLE if life conditions are favorable and fair to me, but they don't HAVE TO be so, and clearly I *can stand it* and still be reasonably happy if they aren't that way."

You can use the Self-Help Form below to list and analyze your thoughts. If you use it, you can

- identify your own unhealthful negative emotions (C's, Consequences);
- look for your underlying demands ("musts" or "shoulds") that spawn these disturbed feelings;
- change those demands to desires; and then
- see *and feel* the differing results when you demote Irrational Beliefs and promote Rational Beliefs.

David, a client of mine (Albert Ellis's), easily understood the ideas from the Self-Help Form. "OK," he said, "if I 'Look for the 'must' and 'Look for the 'should,' I can get to the bottom of my self-defeating attitudes quickly. Once I know my demand, then I'll know the corresponding desire that probably would work better for me *if* I truly believed it and didn't still believe the demand. Right?"

"Right. *If!* You had better dispute the demand and replace it with a desire."

"So if I'm driving myself crazy about something, the main thing to do is look for my root demand and change it to a desire?"

REBT Self-Help Form

A (ACTIVATING EVENTS OR ADVERSITIES)

- Briefly summarize the situation you are disturbed about (what would a camera see?)
- An *A* can be *internal* or *external*, *real* or *imagined*.
- An *A* can be an event in the *past, present,* or *future.*

IB's (IRRATIONAL BELIEFS)

D (DISPUTING IB's)

To identify IB's, look for:
- DOGMATIC DEMANDS
  (musts, absolutes, shoulds)
- AWFULIZING
  (It's awful, terrible, horrible)

- LOW FRUSTRATION TOLERANCE
  (I can't stand it)
- SELF/OTHER RATING
  (I'm/he/she is bad, worthless)

To dispute ask yourself:
- Where is holding this Belief getting me? Is it *helpful* or *self-defeating*?
- Where is the evidence to support the truth of my Irrational Belief? Is it *consistent with social reality*?
- Is my Belief logical? Does it follow from my preferences? Is it really *awful* (as bad as it could be?)
- Can I really not *stand* it?

C (CONSEQUENCES)

Major unhealthy negative **emotions**:

Major self-defeating **behaviors**:

Unhealthy negative emotions include:
- Anxiety   • Depression   • Rage   • Low Frustration Tolerance
- Shame/Embarrassment   • Hurt   • Jealousy   • Guilt

E (EFFECTIVE NEW PHILOSOPHIES)

E (EFFECTIVE EMOTIONS AND BEHAVIORS)

New healthy
negative emotions:

New constructive
behaviors:

To think more rationally, strive for:
- NON-DOGMATIC PREFERENCES
  (wishes, wants, desires)
- EVALUATING BADNESS
  (it's bad, unfortunate)
- HIGH FRUSTRATION TOLERANCE
  (I don't like it, but I can stand it)
- NOT GLOBALLY RATING SELF OR
  OTHERS (I—and others—are
  fallible human beings)

Healthy negative emotions include:
- Disappointment
- Concern
- Annoyance
- Sadness
- Regret
- Frustration

"Yes, you train yourself *out of* MUSTurbating and *into* preferring, instead."

"Also, I had better stop awfulizing and claiming I can't stand it?"

"Correct. You *challenge* your Belief in awfulness. You can do that by trying to find proof that anything in the universe is ever absolutely 100 percent bad. You can also do that by seeing that your exaggeratedly calling bad things utterly awful *gives* you a disturbance and rarely helps you cope with whatever the hell it is. So, instead, you give the situation a realistic rating of badness, not horror. Similarly with disputing the idea that you *can't stand* the adverse situation. Almost all the time you already are standing it, so you definitely *can*."

"I change my Belief to 'I *can* stand it, even though I still don't like it'? Because then I'll have more chance to cope with it better?"

"That's right."

"Well, I guess what I'd better do now is learn how to do all of that when I'm having trouble!"

David did learn how. He did do a great deal of therapy homework. He read REBT pamphlets and books and he filled out Self-Help Forms. My clients often tape-record their therapy sessions, and David listened to each tape, making copious notes. He kept his appointments, even arriving early so he could review his notes from the previous session. He referred several friends and relatives to me or other REBT practitioners. So, David definitely was far ahead of the game. A very good start. In REBT, we're not interested in mere lip service, but in rooting out deeply-rooted habitual self-defeating responses. So, REBT involves work and practice outside therapy sessions.

But, I noticed after a few weeks, David didn't really "get" it. In the real world, at the scene of the crime, so to speak, he didn't change. His self-defeating reactions remained the same. David still regularly enraged himself at his co-worker, Fred. He still gave himself high blood pressure dizzy spells, as well as "nervous stomach" attacks as part of his irritable bowel syndrome. His primary care physician had tried every test and medication in the book and was getting fed up—she had made the referral to me! But there was more.

If David remained another five years at his firm, he could retire with full benefits, which he very much desired. But, due to his anger, he vacillated among undesirable alternatives. One day he'd almost impulsively resign from his job—he had had his letter of resignation in his computer for almost a year when I met him! Another day he would phone in sick. Yet another day he'd simmer in his juices until he finally got to sleep at night. Sometimes he would get the image of bopping Fred on the head. He'd tell me, "That *is* one of my options." However, David had refrained from that option for almost a year, loathed violence and had no history of it, so the bopping scenario's probability seemed low. My preference was to see it go to zero.

David talked a good talk, and he even walked a reasonably good walk—but he didn't walk vigorously and far enough. He really did learn the *right words* to dispute his Irrational Beliefs. He really could *discuss* how to strengthen Rational Beliefs that promote optimal living. He had good motivation. He grasped most of the REBT ideas. In his therapy, he did large amounts of written homework. The doing, the work and practice, is "where it's at" in REBT. David was doing. He was working and practicing. But he still didn't "get it." He didn't change his emotions and his actions. He had what we sometimes call "intellectual insight," as contrasted with "emotional insight." I moved to Plan 2.

I decided that group therapy might help reinforce his Rational Beliefs and get David to take constructive action. He did join a group, but was a very difficult customer. David was one of the champion awfulizers in the therapy group. He insisted that his co-worker, Fred, bothered him continually, didn't shut up for a minute, screwed up their work so badly that David usually had to do it over for him, and made him—David—furious. No use telling the boss how rotten Fred's work was, because the boss was Fred's father and never would get rid of him. So, David ranted and raved to everyone who would lend an ear— especially the members of his group. He insisted he *couldn't stand* Fred and was probably going to have to take an early retirement even though he loved his computer work and it would be much better to wait five years, because he'd then get a much higher pension. He often felt (thought) that he *couldn't stand* another minute of working with Fred and he just HAD TO, damned well HAD TO, quit.

David admitted, when his therapy group got after him, that working with Fred really was not *awful*—it was just bad. And he obviously could stand it—as he had for the last few years. He hadn't died of working with Fred—not yet at least—and he enjoyed most of his work despite Fred's stupid chit-chatting and his screw-ups. He *could* stand what he didn't like about Fred, the group pointed out to David—and got him to see that he could.

Only lightly and temporarily, however. For every time Fred went back to his screwing up—which seemed to be what he was best at— David realistically saw Fred's failings, and went right back to awfulizing about them. So the group assigned David one of REBT's emotive-evocative exercises. He was to state one of his main Irrational Beliefs on a cassette recorder and for several minutes dispute it forcefully. He would then bring the tape for the group to listen to and critique.

David agreed, and for the following group session, brought in a recording. Its printable nuggets included, "Fred is an impossible *idiot!* I *can't stand* his constant yakking! Something's got to be done to stop him! It's *awful* and unfair that he even has the job. It's *totally unfair* that I have to work with him! I'll have a heart attack if this continues."

The group members agreed that these were juicy examples of irrational thoughts. Using REBT, David disputed these Irrational Beliefs fairly accurately—but mildly. He said in his disputing that he did not like Fred's yakking, but could stand it. That nothing had to be done about it, though doing something would be preferable. That working with him was highly inconvenient, but hardly 100 percent bad and therefore not *awful*. That, yes, it was unfair that Fred was even hired, and worse that David had to work with him, but that unfairness often existed and therefore should exist, though preferably it wouldn't. And that he would not have to give himself a heart attack but could only feel very displeased about Fred's screw-ups.

Good! The group found David's disputes fine, very rational, but said in much too mild a fashion. It didn't sound as if David truly believed them. Good content, but done in a namby-pamby style. On the ball, but not *really* forceful and convincing. The group asked David to do the tape over and make his disputes more vigorous, more convincing.

He did the tape over, and actually did it one more time, and then still another, until the group agreed that his disputing of his Irrational Beliefs was truly powerful and convincing. In his final version of the tape, which the group endorsed, David said, "I CAN, I damned well CAN stand Fred, though he's really obnoxious. No matter *how* unfair it is that his father hired him and of course won't fire him, it's merely unfair. Unfairness like this SHOULD and MUST exist because it does. It clearly does, and I can't change it. All right, but I *can* change me and *my* awfulizing about unfairness! I can change *my* whining about it. And I will!"

Not only did the vigor of David's disputing satisfy the group, but it worked beautifully for him. He gave up his awfulizing about Fred, viewed Fred's screw-ups in a sane but humorous light, and easily decided to go on with the job for several more years until he earned his maximum pension.

If, like David, you keep solidly upholding Irrational Beliefs and only lightly parroting rational ones, you too can use forceful disputing technique to help yourself. Record your major Irrational Beliefs, try to vigorously dispute them, play your disputes to critical friends or relatives, and listen to the critiques. If necessary, do your tape two, three, or more times, until you and your listeners agree that your disputes are forceful and convincing. In this way, you can get yourself to understand, and to really *believe*, your anti-awfulizing arguments.

Sample Answer Key

The sample answer key to the "Exercise in Deciding What's *Rational* and What's *Irrational*" from page 38 is provided below. In each case, we have given sample answers to each of the Three Key Questions, which are:

1. Does it help me or hinder me over the long run to believe this? If it hinders me, what thought would help me reach my goals better and feel better?
2. Is my thinking consistent with the facts? If it isn't, what *is?*
3. Is my thinking logical? If not, what would make more sense logically?

1. I absolutely must become the richest person in the world.
   Key Question #1: This Belief is irrational because it could make you anxious, hostile, and depressed, which would probably hinder your efforts to make money.
   Key Question #2: It is also irrational because it is inconsistent with reality. You do not HAVE TO become the richest person in the world. There is no law of nature to that effect, and the facts are otherwise.
   Key Question #3: The statement is also irrational since it is illogical. Just because you strongly prefer to become the richest person in the world, it does not follow logically that you MUST. And just because there are some desirable aspects to being the richest person in the world, it hardly follows that it has no undesirable features.

2. I'd like to become the richest person in the world.
   Key Question #1: This Belief is rational since it could motivate you to work hard to realize your goal. If you fail to reach your goal, then you will feel disappointed, but not depressed, hostile, or anxious.

Key Question #2: This Belief is also rational since the only claim about reality it makes is that you have a desire, which you do, to become the richest person in the world.

Key Questions #3: This statement has an underlying premise, that you think it would be good to become the richest person in the world. Your desire to become rich follows logically from your belief that it would be good if you did.

3. I cannot stand having wrinkles.

Key Question #1: This Belief is irrational since it will make you anxious, defensive, and depressed about your present and future wrinkles.

Key Question #2: If you have any wrinkles, are you or are you not alive? If you could not stand having wrinkles, then you'd be dead. If you have no wrinkles, then we can wait to see whether you die after you get any wrinkles. The statement is irrational.

Key Question #3: Inability to endure having wrinkles does not follow logically from the fact that you don't want to have them and that society may prefer wrinkle-free people over wrinkled ones. Irrational.

4. I do not like having wrinkles.

Key Question #1: With this Belief, which is rational, you will not like having wrinkles, but you will accept yourself with them and go on to live an adequate life. This Belief does not cause you a problem.

Key Question #2: This Belief is also rational since the only claim about reality it makes is that you have a dislike, which we assume is true, for having wrinkles.

Key Question #3: This statement has an underlying premise, that you think it would be good to be unwrinkled. Your dislike of being wrinkled follows logically from your belief that it would be good if you weren't.

5. Everything I do is wrong.

Key Question #1: Irrational. This thought is unlikely to be very helpful to you in trying to cope with life's problems.

Key Question #2: Irrational. It would be extraordinarily unlikely that everything you did was wrong.

Key Question #3: Just because some things you do are wrong, it does not follow that all things you do are wrong. If everything you did was wrong, what would be true of your thought itself "Everything I do is wrong"? It would have to be false!

6. I make quite a few mistakes.

Key Question #1: Probably rational. If you make quite a few mistakes, and don't want to, you might work to improve your performance or switch to another activity. The statement would become irrational if you believed, underneath, "But I MUST NOT make this many mistakes!"

Key Question #2: Probably rational. We assume you do make quite a few mistakes, so you are simply telling it like it is. The number of mistakes you make is large or small, depending on the standard you are using and whether you have objectively counted your number of mistakes.

Key Question #3: Your statement may be "logical," depending on the standard you use, which is arbitrary.

7. Because I had such a tough childhood, I deserve things to be easier now.

Key Question #1: With that Belief, you may make yourself depressed, hostile, and whiny, which may be detrimental to you because you will not work to make things easier for yourself now. So, irrational.

Key Question #2: Irrational. If you "deserved" things easier now, they would already be easier. You may think you deserve something, but the facts do not agree.

Key Question #3: Irrational. To be coherent, this Belief would require some premise such as "A bad childhood entitles a person to be treated more favorably later," which is manifestly absurd.

8. I've been addicted to cigarettes too long to change.

Key Question #1: Irrational. Hardly a helpful attitude, if you want to stop smoking.

Key Question #2: If someone were going to chop off one of your toes every time you smoked a cigarette, you would stop smoking. Therefore, we could prove that your statement is factually incorrect.

Key Question #3: It can be hard to stop smoking, but does it logically follow that after a certain number of years, it is impossible?

9. People who fail are complete failures as human beings.

Key Question #1: This Belief will make you arrogant and mean to others, and depressed and anxious about yourself. Irrational.

Key Question #2: How would we prove or disprove failurehood? A person would have to have failed at every single thing in the past, and in the future, for us accurately to say he or she is "a failure." Impossible, and irrational.

Key Question #3: Your statement is irrational because it is an illogical overgeneralization. Yes, people fail at many things, but "being a failure" implies they will always and only fail at everything. Unlikely.

10. Sticking with my diet and exercise program is very hard. I can't do it because it takes too much time and effort.

Key Question #1: Irrational, of course, since it will hardly help you reach your goals if you believe this statement.

Key Question #2: Again, we could probably get objective agreement that it's hard to stick to your diet and exercise program. But, with a gun to your head, you would do so. If it took 25 hours a day to stick to your program, then, yes, it would be factually true that there was not enough time for you to do it.

Key Question #3: Irrational. Just because it's hard does not prove "too hard."

What Rational Beliefs can you formulate to replace each statement above that originally expressed Irrational Beliefs?

5

How Do You Get to Carnegie Hall?

Doing it the hard way is always easier.

Murphy's Paradox

The answer to that old question from vaudeville is "Practice, practice, practice!" Different question—"How do you get to optimal living?" Same answer—practice, practice, practice! It takes hard work and practice to break old, self-defeating habits and to learn new skills to reach for optimal living. This point is one we return to in this chapter because it's so damned important. It's also contrary to the teachings of most forms of therapy and self-help. Most therapists preoccupy themselves with giving you insight. So do most self-help books. Most of them believe some version of this: If you find out how you originally became neurotic, if you find out who screwed you up, if you find out what your traumas were and what Adversities did you in, well, then you're going to be OK. Insight will magically change you. Lots of luck on that one! Sad but true, the fond hope that insight will cure you has almost no basis in fact.

Insight is not what it's cracked up to be. The more solidly a type of counseling or therapy or self-help is founded on the idea that insight is the real answer, the more abysmal its track record at helping people. This is true whether the people are rich or poor, educated or not, old or young, model citizens or criminals. So why do so many people cling to the hope that insight into the origins of their problems will end those problems? We offer our ideas on this puzzle a little later. For now, let's look more closely at the kind of insight we think it will be *useless* for you to pursue. This will help you contrast that type of insight with what works—and *takes* work and practice.

If you believe *at all* in the magical properties of insight, you can keep yourself stuck in the past. You can keep yourself hooked on methods that go nowhere since they never address basic causes of your current feelings and actions—your *current* attitudes and Beliefs. If you're an older person, belief in the magical, curative properties of insight is potentially even more self-defeating than it is for younger people. Why? Because you don't have as much time—our most valuable resource—to fool around. Waiting for insight to work its magic gyps you out of the chance to change now, so that you can enjoy the rest of your life more.

Penises and Cigars

Let's say you procrastinate, or you feel afraid to ride in elevators, or you are shy, or you smoke, or you feel terrified about aging. Or you have some other tough problem. Can you honestly say that knowing where your bad habit started is going to change it? Take smoking. It's a good example of how silly it can be to rely on insight to change you. Almost all smokers who want to stop are fully aware of how and why they started smoking. Usually people start smoking to fit in with peers, to look older, to relax when they are tense, to enjoy themselves, or to satisfy curiosity. Does insight into the origins of their smoking habit make the habit go up in smoke? Does it make the habit easier to break? Very, very rarely. We won't say *never*, because such a case may pop up someday. We've never heard of one. But it *could* happen.

For some good laughs (while you continue to smoke), consider Freudian "insight." You go to an insight therapist, you want to stop smoking, and over time you learn that the cigarette symbolizes a penis. Oh? Here it can get sticky and the insight therapist has a menu of options.

Option 1 is the "insight" that cigarette smoking has something to do with repressed homosexual strivings. When someone asked Freud, a heavy cigar smoker who had many bouts of cancer of the mouth and finally died of it, what he thought his cigar smoking symbolized, what did Freud reply? "Sometimes a cigar is just a cigar." The insight option didn't work even for Freud! In any case, the penis-homosexual interpretation sounds quite old-fashioned and can get overly complicated when the would-be nonsmoker *is* gay. Or is a woman. Do gay would-be nonsmokers have repressed *heterosexual* strivings? And what about smoking lesbians? Enough already! Evidently silly though the pure form of the Freudian theory about insight may be, in diluted form it remains the basic theory held by most therapists.

At this point, let's go, as the diluted or deluded insight therapist often does, to Option 2: Cigarette smoking "shows" adolescent strivings to be an adult, or "shows" adolescent rebelliousness. Perhaps that *is* where and why the person's smoking habit began. After all, most would-be nonsmokers started smoking as teenagers or younger. So what? Will that "insight" end the smoking habits of a middle-aged CPA, teacher, or farmer who has trouble stopping? Unlikely.

The insight therapist has many other options, all derived from the same basic Freudian theory that your upbringing and your current circumstances *make* you do what you do and feel what you feel. These options go along these lines: You started smoking for whatever reason—peer pressure, parental example, whatever—and you know it's a bad habit. But, you "can't" stop smoking due to poor self-image. Or low self-confidence. Or fear of success. Or fear of failure. Or a need to punish yourself. Or for unconscious reasons. And guess what? A great deal of tracing back to get insight into the answer is going to be required. And if you find the answer and continue to smoke? Usually that means you didn't get the correct insight. Or, you did get the correct insight, but you are refusing to accept it and work it through. And why is that? Well, much more insight therapy will be required to find out those answers. Get the picture?

Oh, we admit we may be parodying insight therapy just a little. The fact remains that insight therapists, and insight self-help methods, base *everything* on your finding the right answer and then somehow getting better due to having found the right answer. Some popular self-help methods, such as John Bradshaw's, combine insight—your parents didn't love you enough and that is why you are miserable now—with crybabyism. In the crybaby insight approach, you wail and scream and weep and damn your parents and get in touch with all the horrors of your childhood (some of which probably never happened). You hug your teddy bear and get support from other "walking wounded" crybabies—until you feel exhausted. Quite a workout! Methods like those claim to drain off your anger and hurt. What these and other drainage methods do, however, is give you more practice in focusing strongly on your Irrational Beliefs and so producing your disturbed feelings. It would be just about infinitely better for your mental health, as well as preferable from an aerobic viewpoint and easier on your vocal cords, to work out at your local health club.

Simple, But Not Easy

We agree that finding "the answer" is great, but we think the answers are usually fairly simple. If, for instance, you have retired from work and feel bored and somewhat depressed, it's not because of your childhood. It's not because of your parents. It's because of what you are telling yourself and doing *now* about retirement. It's because you lack meaningful activity. You need to get off your bottom, not to explore the past to work through alleged traumas (courtesy of your parents). Or let's say you are vastly overweight and would like to slim down, what is the answer there? Eat less and exercise more. That's *it!* A very simple answer, but not at all easy to carry out. And that, we think, is the appeal of therapy and self-help methods that trace your life back to incidents that supposedly made you the way you are, and which, if correctly detected, will lead you to change. Most humans *want to* believe that change will be easy. We easily assume that we really shouldn't *have to* sweat, to work and practice and discipline ourselves to change our bad habits. We *make ourselves* fall for all kinds of magical methods and easy answers, because magic is easier than work. Even though any adult knows that learning how to do magic tricks takes a great deal of work and practice, still we want to believe in magic. The famous magician, Harry Houdini, who lived early in this century, enjoyed debunking mediums at séances by exposing how they do their tricks. He sadly concluded that the motto of mediums was, "People *want to* be deceived. So, deceive them!"

But you don't have to make a habit of deceiving yourself. Instead, you can learn and use this Rule for Optimal Living:

Rule #8: WORK, WORK, WORK, AND PRACTICE, PRACTICE, PRACTICE

It takes work and practice to change how you think, feel, and act. This is the most important "insight" you can ever have.

Habits are *supposed* to stick and it's *supposed* to take effort to up-root or modify them. If you learned how to do something, such as drive a car, and between trips forgot how, think how inefficient that would be. Or what if you forgot how to speak your primary language and had to relearn it. Again, quite inconvenient, to say the least. Optimal living is a skill. Like carpentry. Like playing the violin or speaking a foreign language. You can learn how to do it. Given your natural talents, how far you get in a skill depends on how much you practice. So, to get to Carnegie Hall, to live optimally as you age, you start with your natural talents and your natural deficiencies. You figure out a plan, and then you work and practice, practice, practice! If you want to learn or improve a skill to overcome a problem and to enjoy life more, no amount of insight will work—without practice. Gaining insight into your past is one of the best ways to avoid having to practice pushing your ass to change in the present.

Three Stages of Insight Into Overcoming Neurotic Problems

Of course, insight can be true. You can see correctly how your current problem started. You can also see how you keep your current problem going now. These two insights, while important, don't by themselves lead to change. The important third accurate insight is that change takes work and practice.

What do we mean by seeing "correctly" how your current problem started? Let's say that your father terrified you with stories about the big, bad wolf—*which you believed*—and that's why you presently fear large dogs. Or your sacred mother taught you (and unlike many kids, *you believed it*) that you absolutely MUST be liked by people, and that's why you are now shy. This is a Stage I insight. It refers to what happened in your life in the past and it includes the idea that you learned something from what happened. These *histories* of your phobia or your shyness may be accurate—though they may not. You can see that your fear and avoidance of large dogs is a phobia, not a reasonable fear. You completely acknowledge that very few large dogs are dangerous and that it is self-defeating for you to be afraid to go to the park for fear of meeting a large dog. This kind of insight about the unreasonableness of your phobia or your shyness, and their historical origins, is OK as far as it goes. It gives you a good story to console yourself with as you continue to avoid large dogs and people! The key here is that you *believed* something your parents told you. You accepted or invented—back in the past—an Irrational Belief.

You may also achieve a Stage II insight. You fully see that your main Irrational Belief is "I *can't stand* anxiety," which keeps you from going for walks in the park to overcome your fear of dogs. You may even admit that you are going to have to withstand your fear repeatedly, without avoidance, to unlearn it. Does your anxiety now go away? No. Same thing with your shyness. Remember David's anger at Fred that we discussed in the previous chapter? Even after David saw that he was enraging himself by telling himself that Fred MUST not act the way he does, and even after David saw why the "must" was irrational, he mostly remained enraged. To change, you need a Stage III insight.

Fear of Fear Itself

One of our clients, Alan, came for therapy because he was afraid to visit his mother in her nursing home. When he visited her, he first felt sad that his once dynamic mother was nearly a complete invalid after having been felled at 70 by a stroke. Strokes ran in their family. Especially when he visited his mother, Alan felt afraid about *his* possible fate. When he would enter his mother's room, he'd begin to feel as if the walls were closing in on him. His heart raced, he felt dizzy, he thought he'd faint or have a stroke himself. Then he'd abruptly end his visit to his mother and put off returning. As time passed, Alan's panic symptoms would begin as he entered the nursing home. Still later, his heart would begin to race and his head to swim as he drove to the nursing home.

Alan had had "insight therapy" for some months for this problem. The therapist told Alan his panic attacks stemmed from repressed anger toward his mother that he must have had as a child. This anger, according to the story, was popping out now that his mother was helpless and he was in command. What about the fact, Alan asked the insight therapist, that he felt no anger toward his mother, only love, sadness and concern? Answer: repression. But what about the panic attacks?, he asked. All he felt was abject fear that he might be getting ready to have a stroke, not anger at his mother. Answer: all you consciously feel, *right now*, is fear. In time, your true feelings of anger and self-punishing guilt will reveal themselves. Alan came to see that these "insights" were sheer nonsense. Certainly they were unhelpful, in that Alan had understood them yet his panic attacks were increasing, not decreasing.

After months of therapy, Alan had gained a rich store of reflections about his childhood, feelings about his mother's invalidism, and a nonsensical theory about the origins and meaning of his panic attacks. He had all this, *plus* his panic attacks! Alan decided to seek a more solution-focused form of therapy. He did some research on the Internet and switched to Rational Emotive Behavior Therapy.

REBT (and the other cognitive-behavioral therapies) see panic disorder as largely stemming from your catastrophic interpretations of your feelings and physical responses. Alan started by being aware of the painful sadness and concern he felt for his mother. He would notice the physiological activation of his body, which is a normal part of emotions. Given that strokes ran in his family and that his beloved mother had had one that incapacitated her and would likely leave her totally dependent, Alan misinterpreted his bodily reactions. He thought his feelings and physical reactions were deadly danger signals. That increased his anxiety. He then thought the increased anxiety was greater evidence that he was possibly having a stroke. Eventually, Alan would hyperventilate and cause himself a number of other very uncomfortable feelings he thought were signs of a stroke.

At A (Adversity), Alan's mother had a stroke and was in a nursing home. At B (his Belief system) Alan had the Rational Belief, "This is sad and unfortunate, but these things happen and I can stand it." At C (Consequences), Alan had the healthful feeling of sadness and concern. But at B he also held the Irrational Belief, "Like my mother, I might also have a stroke. That would be *terrible*! I *couldn't stand* it if I did." So, at C, he also felt severe anxiety and panic.

As a result of his healthful concern for his mother as well as his unhealthful anxiety, Alan experienced at C bodily reactions, such as hyperventilation, and he made *them* into another Adversity. Then, at B, he first had some Rational Beliefs, such as "I don't like these reactions, but I can live with them." But he also had some Irrational Beliefs at B, such as, "How *terrible*! I *can't stand* feeling this way. Maybe I'm going to have a stroke like Mom did. What if I vomit and then suffocate?! Oh, no!" Then he felt extreme anxiety about his anxiety, panic about his panic.

This is what people often do. They take their disturbed feelings (C) and see them as a second Adversity (A2). Then, they awfulize about this second Adversity at B2 and produce another Consequence (C2), horrors about horrors! In REBT, we call C2 secondary symptoms that result from Irrational Beliefs (IB2s) about their primary symptoms of disturbance (A2).

Alan learned to get over his fears by disputing two Irrational Beliefs. The first was his Irrational Belief that it would be *horrible beyond belief* if, like his mother, he had a stroke. His second IB was that it would be *disastrous* if he had an uncomfortable panic attack. After Alan had done some disputing, I encouraged him to visit his mother frequently, no matter how uncomfortable he felt, to *prove* to his nervous system and habit system that his catastrophic interpretations were unrealistic. That is, *would* he faint? If he did faint, would it be *terrible* beyond words? *Would* the walls close in on him? *Could* he stand the intense discomfort of the panic attack? *Would* he have a stroke?

Alan bit the bullet. He repeatedly carried out his homework. He forced himself to visit his mother while convincing himself that (1) his fears were *not* overwhelming, but merely highly unpleasant, and (2) he *could stand* fainting if in fact that happened. (It didn't.) He thereby reduced his exaggerated fears and allowed himself to rebuild a loving and supportive relationship with his mother.

What stops you from working toward long-term objectives? Answer: doing the work is frequently uncomfortable. This brings us to the next Rule for Optimal Living:

Rule #9: PUSH YOURSELF

It's usually better to push yourself, uncomfortably, rather than waiting to feel comfortable, before doing what you know would likely be best for you to do. If you want to live optimally, you had best train yourself to tolerate higher levels of frustration. *High frustration tolerance* is basic to optimal living. Where reality—including your own behavior or that of others—is "wrong," that is against your interests, it unfortunately has the right to be that way. It is fine to dislike these aspects of reality. However, you preferably will refrain from damning the universe for unkind fate and from damning yourself or others as persons, for unacceptable or obnoxious behavior. Instead, push yourself—uncomfortably—to change what you can change: Stage III insight.

You have now learned the three stages of optimal "insight." These three REBT insights, which are distinctly different from how people usually think of insight, are:

1. How you *think, including your underlying Rational and Irrational Beliefs,* is the biggest factor in how you feel and act.
2. No matter how, when, or where you started thinking some Irrational Belief, *you* are responsible for still doing so now.
3. Through work and practice, you can change how you think, feel, and act.

The Shortest Route Has the Steepest Hills

The more you work and practice—assuming you are reasonably on the right track—the more progress you usually make in changing your habits for the better. That is why we say, "The shortest route has the steepest hills." Another way to put the same idea is this: the so-called easy way to do things often ends up being harder in the long run. Working hard today often leads to things being easier tomorrow. This brings us to the Tenth Rule for Optimal Living:

Rule #10: DO AND FEEL

No matter how frequently you voice Rational Beliefs, without acting on them, without consistently and strongly feeling them, they will remain unconvincing.

Most of the time you tend to know that a lightly held Belief is hardly as motivating as a strongly held one. Like the rest of us, though, you may sometimes *lightly* hold a Rational Belief, "I don't have to have whatever I want. I don't have to spend to the limit on my credit card." At the same time, you *strongly* hold an Irrational Belief, "I MUST have what I want even though my credit is exhausted!" What can you do to make your Rational Beliefs stronger? How can you train yourself to embrace them and act on them when the chips are down?

Here's a form you can use to examine Irrational Beliefs that interfere with the work and practice necessary for you to change your habits. For each such thought you jot down, you can learn how to get at the underlying demand and challenge it. In each case, the goal is to end up with a helpful desire that *promotes* your happiness.

How To Help Myself To Do SelfHelp Homework

The steps in getting off your duff and getting on with life are:

1. Ask, "What did I tell myself to stop myself from doing the homework?" These are your Irrational Beliefs. Write them in column #1.

2. Ask, "How does believing this *hurt* me? How is it unrealistic or illogical?" Then, answer those questions. Write your answers in column #2.

3. Ask, "What would be a more helpful, realistic Belief?" Write those answers in column #3.

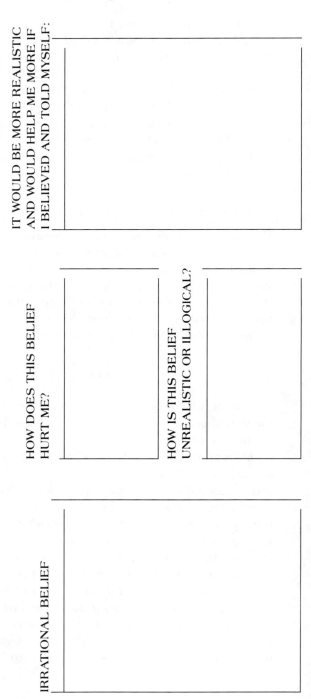

IRRATIONAL BELIEF

HOW DOES THIS BELIEF HURT ME?

HOW IS THIS BELIEF UNREALISTIC OR ILLOGICAL?

IT WOULD BE MORE REALISTIC AND WOULD HELP ME MORE IF I BELIEVED AND TOLD MYSELF:

Jane, a widow in her 70s, tripped at church and broke her arm. By the time she got out of the cast, she had lost so much strength she couldn't steer her car, which had no power steering. She went to physical therapy, and then the YWCA for daily, prescribed exercise. Though she felt frustrated at how much work it took and about her slow progress compared to her younger days, she kept telling herself to stick with it. She told herself that what she had to gain, namely being able to drive her car, was well worth the work.

As we already pointed out, there are three major Irrational Beliefs that lead to most human disturbance:

1. I MUST perform well.
2. You MUST treat me nicely and fairly.
3. Conditions MUST be nice and easy for me and not give me too many hassles.

The first "must" is very powerful and deadly, and it results in much human disturbance—self-downing. When you really put *yourself* down, and not merely the poor behaviors that you may often do, then you feel anxious, depressed, worthless, inadequate, and defensive. You may avoid situations where you could "fail." We deal with many aspects of this Belief throughout this book. If you vigorously dispute it and its numerous offspring, you will feel immensely better and usually perform much more effectively.

The second and third "musts" that we zero in on in this book, along with their many subheadings, can lead to two varieties of self-defeat. "You MUST" can lead to anger, rage, fury, and violence. "Life MUST" can cause low frustration tolerance and self-pity. In some ways, these two "musts" overlap and are part of the same process. When you demand and command that other people absolutely MUST behave much better than they do behave, you are really expressing a low frustration tolerance attitude. It is similar to demanding and commanding that *non-human* conditions MUST be fair and easy for you. In one case, you MUSTurbate about human conditions, and in the other case you MUSTurbate about non-human conditions. Either kind of demand works the same way—poorly! It often defeats your purposes to demand that conditions—*human or otherwise*—must be the way they aren't—nice and comfortable and fair for you, when they often are *un*nice, *un*comfortable, and *un*fair. Not that you should not want good behaviors from people and good conditions from the world. But to childishly demand that you MUST get what you want is thoroughly unrealistic, as well as illogical. The mere fact that you truly desire something very much hardly means that people or the world MUST give it to you. It would be nice! But that kind of niceness frequently doesn't exist.

Anger and rage at other people for not doing what you command that they do is therefore a form of low frustration tolerance (LFT). It is also a form of LFT to demand that the world, the economy, the political system, the ecology, and so on, obey your wishes. When they do not obey you, then you damn them for not giving you the ease and comfort that you demanded.

There are, in a sense, only two major forms of emotional disturbance. In the first form, you demand that *you personally* MUST do well and be approved by other people, or else you are a *worthless, deficient individual*. In the second form, which has two categories, you demand that (a) *people* and/or *(b) things* absolutely SHOULD be the way you want them to be. If they are not, the world is a *horrible* place to live in and the people who inhabit it are *the scum of the earth*.

LFT, then, is a major cause of human disturbance. This is true when it takes the form of intolerance of others for not being entirely devoted to you and not giving you what you want. It is also true when it takes the form of intolerance of conditions that absolutely SHOULD and MUST be exactly the way you desire them to be. It's extremely important for your emotional well-being to accept yourself fully with your wants and failings and never put yourself down for your failings and inabilities. At the same time, realistically and logically accept that people will often act the way you prefer them not to act. Similarly, accept that conditions and things will often frustrate you and deprive you of what you want. You will then be much more likely to succeed at what you are doing and to get what you really want. What we call unconditional self-acceptance (USA) is one of the most important characteristics that you can add to your life. High frustration tolerance, or accepting other people and the unfortunate things that you would like to change but for the moment cannot, is the other solid foundation of emotional stability.

The Self-Pity Trap

There's no *easy* way to solve your emotional problems and deal with practical problems more effectively, but the next basic Rule for Optimal Living is *simple*. It is:

Rule #11: THERE'S NO GAIN WITHOUT PAIN

No pain, no gain. Heard that one before? Yes, for the very good reason that it is true and crucial to living well.

Let's now target the self-defeating attitude that can undermine every resolution to buckle down and add quality to your life. It can defeat your desire to live fully and to have more of a ball in the process. This attitude and the feelings that stem from it are self-pity. Self-pity is one of the dangers of older age—and of *any* age. A self-pitying attitude easily turns molehills into mountains and complaints into catastrophes. It ruins your chances to cope gracefully with bad things you cannot change.

Self-pity as an emotion is feeling sorry for yourself. It is the projection of a "poor me" image. How do people create it? How does it differ from low self-esteem, which is a "bad me" image? How do you fight self-pity and replace whining with winning?

Feelings of self-pity stem from LFT—low frustration tolerance. In self-pity, you feel sorry for yourself. You whine about how hard conditions are. And how unfair and uncaring people are. And how you—superior being *or* inferior schlemiel—*deserve* things to be easier. Unfortunately, conditions and people are what they are. If you rationally preferred that conditions were easier and people were more fair and caring, then, what would happen when they were not? You'd feel healthfully frustrated and displeased. That would be OK, because those negative feelings would probably motivate you to cope with tough reality as best you could. Self-pity and whining, on the other hand, stem from "musts," from the low frustration tolerance (LFT) attitude *toward* difficult realities: People SHOULD be caring and fair to poor me! Whine, whine, whine, or feel hurt, hurt, hurt, or hate, hate, hate when they're not! Conditions SHOULDN'T be *this* hard for poor, poor me! Whine, whine, whine, or feel hurt, hurt, hurt, or hate, hate, hate when they are!

Self-Pity and Self-Downing Don't Help You But Sometimes Help Each Other

When you suffer from low self-esteem, as opposed to self-pity, you give *yourself* low ratings of worth. You put yourself down, because you don't have the achievements or the approval you believe you MUST have to be worthy. You dislike yourself; you may even hate yourself; but you do not *pity* yourself.

Yet we humans are talented screwballs, and we can damn ourselves at one time and pity ourselves at another time. So damning yourself, putting yourself down, can combine and interact with self-pity. Let's say you start with "I MUST achieve perfectly, or else I'm an inadequate, inferior person." And, surprise, you fail to achieve perfectly! That "makes" you a failure. Let's say you also believe "Things MUST be easy or else it's *horrible* and I *can't stand* it." Then your boss or your partner asks you to do something difficult. Can you see what often happens if you *already* view yourself as a failure, an inadequate person? Yes! You may begin to whine and feel terribly hurt about how horrible your boss or partner is for asking failure-in-life you, to do such a difficult thing! The two "musts"—I MUST achieve perfectly" and "Things MUST be easy and fair for me"—interact. You feel bad about yourself *and* sorry for yourself. It can get worse.

If you devoutly believe "Things MUST be easy and fair for poor little me," how do you think you will *do* at things? Usually not so hot. You'll goof off and procrastinate, moan about them and resent them, do them at the last-minute, or otherwise not put in the work required to do them well. Your boss or partner may point this out to you disapprovingly. At that point, what happens if you also devoutly believe "I MUST achieve greatly and be approved of or else I'm worthless"? Then you devalue yourself, you down yourself, you depress yourself about your unworthiness. To an unworthy slob, tasks seem much larger and harder than they are, and you may pity yourself about them. You may complain about how conditions shouldn't be so hard and unfair to a poor slob like you!

If you pity yourself, you victimize yourself. You make yourself grouchy, whiny, martyred, and depressed. You focus on how life sucks (as it SHOULD NOT), rather than on what you can do to accept an unfortunate situation or change it for the better. Not that there isn't some truth to pointing the finger. Blaming others and life circumstances, however, gets you nowhere. Blame is quite different from looking for the conditions that got you to this point, and then *deciding* to do, and *doing,* what you can to get beyond those conditions or to cope with them.

Unproductive Complaining, Valid Complaints

Complaining about bad circumstances *can* be helpful—if it motivates you or somebody else to do something about the situation you're complaining about. For example, it's often good to assert yourself and do what you can to bring crummy conditions to the attention of whoever can do something to change them. *Often* useful, not always useful! Is it sometimes *un*productive to complain? Of course, but how can you distinguish between *productive* and *unproductive* complaining? In a later chapter on assertiveness training we will answer that question.

An example of unproductive complaining that led to *very* suboptimal existing, to maximal self-pity, and almost to non-existence, is Bill. Now 48, he lost his aerospace job three years ago when the need for his specialty dried up. For a while, he did look for another job, but nothing turned up. He "couldn't" move—his wife, Jenny, had a good job and the children were still in school. He refused to look for another kind of job or get new training and felt bitter and depressed. "I can't start over at my age," was his refrain. He became so depressed about how he was too old to start over, that when a headhunter contacted him about a job possibility five miles away, Bill blew it off. He started saying that he hated life and couldn't face an endless future of hardship. He wished he'd just die and get it over with. It was then that Jenny referred him for counseling.

While Bill did at times condemn himself, those times were infrequent and relatively mild. For the most part he viewed himself as an okay person who was a victim of intolerably uncaring and harsh circumstances. Thus, most of his depression was self-pity. It stemmed from low frustration tolerance: "Conditions MUST be fair and not too hard." His therapy had many components, but what we would like to illustrate here is the use of the Three Key Questions to dispute the low frustration tolerance, self-pitying attitude. In Bill's case, the basic refrain was "It SHOULDN'T be this hard to start over" and "I'm too old to start over." In our sessions, we referred to those and similar ideas as the "I can't" attitude. Bill learned to dispute his "I can't" by asking the Three Key Questions:

Key Question #1: Bill asked himself, "Does it help me or hurt me to hold this I-can't attitude?" The answer was "It hurts me." So then he asked himself, "What would be more *helpful* for me to believe?" The answer he finally arrived at: "It's quite difficult for me to start over at this age, but it's more difficult in the long run *not* to start over."

Key Question #2: Bill asked himself whether his specific Belief, "I *can't stand* the hassles of starting over," was true or false. An honest answer, he admitted, was that it was false. Though he stubbornly considered sticking with a false answer, I (Emmett Velten) appealed to his sense of fair play to persuade him to consider *why* it was false. Why? What facts might show his Belief was false? For one thing, Bill realized that he had "stood" everything in life that had ever happened to him. Up to that point, at least! In Bill's case, he had stood job loss several times and it would be pretty surprising if he keeled over from job-hunting or training for something new.

Key Question #3: Bill asked himself whether "I can't" logically followed from "It's difficult, I don't like it, and I wish it were different." It did not follow logically, of course. It followed illogically! Even where the answer is clear, you can help yourself greatly, as Bill did, by inquiring into the logic of your self-defeating Belief. As soon as you ask yourself how logical "I can't" is, you can see that "I can't" does not follow from "it's difficult." Besides, "I can't" *makes it* almost impossible to do what *you think* you can't and thereby paralyzes you.

I showed Bill how the logical analysis of "I can't" would work. "Let's say you very much preferred to succeed at something. Would it logically follow that *therefore* you MUST succeed?" I asked Bill. After some discussion, he agreed, "No, just because success would be beneficial it does not logically follow that success is utterly necessary." I then showed Bill how to break those ideas down into major and minor premises, and conclusions.

	Logical	Illogical
Major premise	All people are mortal.	Success is good.
Minor premise	Elvis is a person.	I would like to succeed.
Conclusion	Elvis is mortal.	Therefore, I MUST succeed.

"So," I then asked Bill, "how would you apply this to your Belief that you 'can't' start over?"

"The major premise," Bill said, "would be something like 'Starting over is bad' or 'Starting over is hard'. The minor premise would be something like 'I don't want to start over'. And the illogical conclusion I've been reaching is 'Therefore, I can't start over.'"

"Exactly! Another way to logically analyze your Belief that you can't start over could be something like this: 'Starting over has its definite bad points. Therefore, *everything* about starting over is bad—in fact, is *awful!*'"

"That's pretty stupid," Bill interjected, "because you don't know as a fact that everything about starting over is bad. Starting over probably has some good points."

"Such as?"

"Well, I suppose it could be a challenge. It might get my brain cells to working again. Maybe if I got out and did something, the exercise and the change of pace would cheer me up some. Also, I might even like doing something different."

I then explained to Bill that after you dispute an Irrational Belief by asking the Three Key Questions, you do a follow-up. You do it by asking yourself: "OK, if my Belief is irrational—unhelpful, unrealistic, and illogical—what Rational Belief would make more sense?"

Bill answered, "Starting over is difficult, and I wish I didn't have to. But there's no evidence it's *awful* and *unbearable*. It might even lead to some good things."

"But it's so easy to feel sorry for oneself," Bill later pointed out.

"Yes, easy in the short run, but much harder on you in the long run. And it's especially easy to think that on top of middle age and *its* hassles, you SHOULDN'T also have to face something totally uncalled for. In your case, it was your job phasing out before you were ready to retire. How uncalled for! How unfair!"

"It *is* unfair!"

Bill, of course, was correct. What happened to him was not "fair." But self-pity hooks you on how reality SHOULD NOT be and has *no right* to be. Self-pity leads you to decide that it's totally impossible to be happy *at all* when circumstances are that *horrible*. The cold truth, of course, is that the grim facts of life have no obligation to be different from the way they are. They don't need our permission to be the way they are. Sometimes you can change things for the better. Up to this exact point, however, when things are rotten, they are rotten. You can't change that fact and seriously pitying yourself will make things worse.

Bill liked the version of the Serenity Prayer used by our colleague, Hank Robb. We call it the Rationality Prayer: "Let me seek the serenity to accept life as I find it, the wisdom to see what would be good to change, the courage to act, and the determination to follow through."

Five Forms of Self-Pity

Self-pity is a major form of LFT, and it is common in older age. Many of us actually did do better when we were younger. We had more energy, enjoyed things more, were more active, made friends more easily, got along well at work, and did various other things that we are less prone or less able to do now. So, older age has more frustrations of certain kinds than youth or middle age. We'd better feel healthfully sorry or disappointed about its limitations. To upset ourselves about them, however, almost always means we drag in a passel of "shoulds" and "musts." Consider, for example, some of the common forms of self-pity:

What I envy in others. As you get older, you may have more to envy in others than when you were younger. For they may be healthier, richer, more agile, and have more social support than you have. That is unfortunate, and you are not going to be very happy about it. But if you have feelings of self-pity, they come from the demand, "I SHOULD have the advantages that they have! How *awful* that I am deprived! Life is very unfair—and it absolutely MUST NOT be!"

What I used to be. As you go on far into age, you may accurately compare yourself to what you used to be, and find some real gaps and deficiencies. Instead of sorrowfully accepting these drawbacks of aging, but being happy about being alive and having capacity for enjoyments, you could pity yourself. For instance, you could tell yourself, "I SHOULD have the advantages that I had in my younger days. It's unfair that growing older has so many disadvantages. They SHOULD NOT exist—especially for poor, poor me!"

What I should have done. No doubt, you neglected to do many desirable things when you were younger, and now it may be too late to do some of them. Maybe they would have turned out well—and maybe they would not have. As you grow older, though, you may self-pityingly tell yourself, "I SHOULD have done more. I didn't take advantage of my opportunities. What *an idiot* I am! I neglected to do many things that would have certainly turned out beautifully had I done them. Now it's too late. Poor, poor, pitiful me!"

What others should do for me. As you grow older, you may well lack companionship, money, health, and other things that you once easily had. You'd better regret those lacks and losses, and do your best to make up for them if you can or to replace them with other things if you cannot make up for them. Instead, you may self-pityingly insist, "Because I am older and less able, people SHOULD treat me much better than they do. They SHOULD take pity on me and go out of their way to help me. Old age SHOULD be a time in which people favor me, because of my limitations, just as I have favored some others when I saw that they were in need of help. But I'm not getting the help and respect that older people NEED, and this is *terrible!*"

How others should repay me for what I've done. As you grow older and are less able to shift for yourself, you often remember the special things that you have done for others—especially for your children or other relatives. You are healthfully sad and disappointed that they are too busy or neglectful to give you some of this kind of help. Instead of being suitably assertive and acceptant, you could take this to a demanding extreme. You could pity yourself by believing, "After all that I've done for them, they absolutely SHOULD do some things for me that they are not doing! How *completely unfair!* They MUST NOT be that way. What a *rotten world* when people that you have been kind to and helped don't help you when you are less able to help yourself. How *horrible!* I feel so hurt!"

Self-pity in all its forms is common in older age, to say nothing of middle age and younger age. Notice that every form of self-pity includes a healthful desire that people consider your handicaps and do something to make up for them. It also includes a very childish demand that things absolutely MUST NOT be as bad as they are, when you can do little or nothing to stop them from being that way. Whenever you feel real self-pity, look for this obvious or subtle demand, challenge and question it, and turn it back into a preference. You may then still feel sorry and disappointed, but you will not feel *horrified*, at some of the common disadvantages of aging. You may also have more productive energy to enjoy life and to do what, if anything, you can do to make your situation better.

6

Ageism, Not Age, Is the Problem

No matter how often a lie is shown to be false, there will always be a percentage of people who believe it to be true.

Law of the Lie

We define ageism as harmful attitudes, feelings, and actions directed at people because of their age. What, if anything, can you do about the ageism you may encounter at work or elsewhere? How can you cope with it rationally? Here's what Carl did about it. At 61, Carl had no interest in retiring. He was passed over for a promotion for the second time, again in favor of a much younger person. In the laser printer tray at his office, he found an interesting email message printed out from his supervisor to the Personnel Director. The message said that Carl hadn't been chosen because he was going to retire in a few years anyway. Carl decided to sue. It took courage—over the months of the legal action—for him to continue to work with the people he was suing. He kept a daily log of incidents and information that he saw as supporting his case. How did he find the gumption to take these actions? Carl said he had figured, "Enough is enough! If black people hadn't started protesting, they'd still be riding in the back of the bus. Same thing with women and voting—they had to agitate. *Somebody's* got to have some intestinal fortitude! It might as well be me."

You do not have to do anything about ageism, of course. You can even pretend it doesn't occur. You can look the other way when you see it, or say to yourself, "Why make waves?" You can accept all the negative stereotypes about age and "act your age" in playing the role of a senior citizen. If you are young or middle-aged, you can tell older people to act their age, and you can discourage them from being active and adventurous. You can view age as a horrible decline from desirable youth rather than as a part of life. You have those options. However, it's hard not to become prejudiced against yourself if you don't flatly oppose other people's prejudices against you. If you sit on your duff while others get discriminated against, then someday you (and your duff) will face the same fate.

One of the rules of good mental health is to unconditionally value and accept yourself and to act in your behalf. When you settle for second class status, you break that rule. Second class? As an older person? If you have any doubts, read Pat Moore's remarkable book, *Disguised: A True Story*. She shows how the same actions, by the same person, in the same settings, but one time effectively disguised as an old woman, and the other time a young woman, elicit dramatically different responses from people who would probably feel aghast if they saw their behavior. *Disguised* is similar to John G. Griffin's 1962 book, *Black Like Me*. Griffin cosmetically changed his skin color from white to black. What happened? Surprise! He received very different and much worse treatment than when he was white.

Would you like to look younger? Most people would answer yes without hesitation. Expensive goods and services claim to keep you young or even to reverse the aging process. We would never fault anyone for using medically proven ways, from sunblocks to facelifts, to delay indicators of your age. It's your business. But remember: you *are* as old as you are. If you are prejudiced against yourself or others for looking older, self-revulsion lies in store for you no matter how many face lifts you get. You will feel happier and care less about your age, if you project a vigorous, interested and interesting attitude toward others. You'll probably also come across as younger. The same thing will likely be true if you dispute common ageist Irrational Beliefs. These include, "I MUST *be* young or at least *look* young to be OK and happy" and "My life is over if I'm old—I'm no use to anyone."

Myths of Aging and Their Underlying Irrational Beliefs

What are some common, harmful myths about aging? Many of our readers are likely to be baby boomers born between 1946 and 1965. If you are, then as you read these myths, think how each will apply to *you* someday. In the not too distant future! We've written these myths in the first column of the following worksheet (pages 74–75). There's space for you to add other myths. Each myth is either false, such as "old people can't change," or simply a matter of opinion. An example of the latter is "young people are good looking; older people are ugly." A couple of the myths are "should" statements, such as "people should act their age." Study each of these myths.

Then, in column two, think about and write down Irrational Beliefs you think could underlie each myth or worsen its effects. Irrational Beliefs are those that:

1. hinder you in the long run;
2. are inconsistent with facts; and
3. are illogical.

Recall that Irrational Beliefs will have a "must," "should," "got to," "have to," or "absolute need" at their heart. They may also have awfulizings, I-can't-stand-its, and damnings of oneself, others, and conditions.

In column three, write down your rational rebuttals of each myth. Your rational rebuttals will reflect Rational Beliefs. The latter are those that help you over the long run, that are consistent with facts, and that are logical. At the end of this chapter, you can find sample rational rebuttals. Remember, if you hold, or if society still holds, these myths when you are older, you may be hampered in having as active, vigorous, and full a life as you would like.

So, you'd better consider acting against ageism. Act against it if you dislike the way older people are sometimes treated, *and* if you realize that such treatment isn't going to go away by itself. In fact, discrimination may even get worse, because prejudice against minorities often increases as their numbers increase. If you know *you* won't like being discriminated against, then, yes, you'd better consider acting in *your* behalf.

To Do or Not to Do Something about Ageism

What are your options? They may include asserting yourself, organizing, and joining interest groups, such as American Association of Retired People (AARP). Your options also include protesting, boycotting, and selectively supporting politicians and businesses with favorable records *(buy*cotting). You can take legal action. You can consider militancy such as that carried out by the Gray Panthers. Already there are some laws against bigoted employment practices. Older people have begun to organize in their behalf. AARP has over 32 million members and advocates for those who don't plan to die young and who want equal opportunity in life, regardless of their age. Other advocacy organizations include the National Council on Aging, the Older Women's League (OWL), the National Alliance of Senior Citizens, and the National Council of Senior Citizens. All these organizations advocate for older people at the legislative and social levels.

An important part of countering prejudice against older people is to develop a framework for making decisions about what, if anything, you want to do in situations reflecting ageism. One way to do this is by systematically thinking ahead about the pros and cons of possible actions, and the pros and cons of inactions. A concrete method to do that is to fill out the following Cost-Benefit Analysis for yourself.

Sue Their Butts?

This is not a litigation handbook for consumers or a pep talk for older people facing discrimination. Showing you, for example, how to combat workplace discrimination through legal action is very important, but beyond our scope. The organizations listed above are resources you may want to consult. Call legal referral agencies or your local bar association. More important is to find the strength and develop the fighting spirit to pursue the legal angles of action against discrimination, if you decide to do so. Oh, yes, we admit that if you sue their butts for age discrimination it may not change their hearts right away—or ever. But it can change their behavior! You can learn how to cope with prejudice psychologically whether it crops up in government, jobs, families, public services, or in that most important place of all—within yourself.

Myths of Aging/ Irrational Beliefs/ Rational Rebuttal

Myths of Aging	Possible Irrational Beliefs	Rational Rebuttals
Younger is better; older is worse.		
Old people can't change.		
The young are our future; the old are our past.		
Younger is better looking; older is ugly.		
Youth is for learning; age is for remembering the past and forgetting.		
Youth is exciting; age is dull.		
You should act your age.		
Youth is the time for education, careers, romance, sex, adventure; age is for rocking chairs.		

Myths of Aging/ Irrational Beliefs/ Rational Rebuttal (Continued)

Myths of Aging	Possible Irrational Beliefs	Rational Rebuttals
Youth is health; age is disease.		
Young people are individuals; old people are all alike.		
Youth is active, effective, confident, living productively, smart; old is passive, fumbling, unproductive, stupid.		
If you aren't going to be living that much longer, then there's no use trying to do anything to make life better.		
It's normal to feel depressed when you're old.		
Age is nothing but decline.		
Sex and romance are embarrassing among older people.		

Cost-Benefit Analysis

Advantages/ Benefits of *Option 1*

Short-term advantages

For yourself	For other people
1. _____	1. _____
2. _____	2. _____
3. _____	3. _____
4. _____	4. _____
5. _____	5. _____

Long-term advantages

For yourself	For other people
1. _____	1. _____
2. _____	2. _____
3. _____	3. _____
4. _____	4. _____
5. _____	5. _____

Disadvantages/ Costs of *Option 1*

Short-term disadvantages

For yourself	For other people
1. _____	1. _____
2. _____	2. _____
3. _____	3. _____
4. _____	4. _____
5. _____	5. _____

Long-term disadvantages

For yourself	For other people
1. _____	1. _____
2. _____	2. _____
3. _____	3. _____
4. _____	4. _____
5. _____	5. _____

Cost-Benefit Analysis

Advantages/ Benefits of *Option 2*

Short-term advantages

For yourself	For other people
1. _____	1. _____
2. _____	2. _____
3. _____	3. _____
4. _____	4. _____
5. _____	5. _____

Long-term advantages

For yourself	For other people
1. _____	1. _____
2. _____	2. _____
3. _____	3. _____
4. _____	4. _____
5. _____	5. _____

Disadvantages/ Costs of *Option 2*

Short-term disadvantages

For yourself	For other people
1. _____	1. _____
2. _____	2. _____
3. _____	3. _____
4. _____	4. _____
5. _____	5. _____

Long-term disadvantages

For yourself	For other people
1. _____	1. _____
2. _____	2. _____
3. _____	3. _____
4. _____	4. _____
5. _____	5. _____

Speaking of legal action, how did the legal case turn out for Carl, who started off this chapter? Carl won his case. Besides damages, the court required his company to institute employee orientation for all employees, regarding age discrimination. It also required employment ads to say the company especially welcomed applications from older workers. Its orientation sessions for new employees discussed age discrimination. The employee handbook stated that the following practices were illegal:

- mandatory retirement;
- age discrimination in hiring and promotion;
- inequality in training opportunities and fast-track development programs based on age.

As you approach the age at which you could receive Social Security, don't buy the notion that you have nothing more to do and learn, no new challenges. That notion will restrict your using the law to protect you from being stuck on a career plateau. It could leave you without updated training, to drift into obsolescence on the job. It could give you an enticing golden, heave-ho handshake when what you want is a promotion.

What Goes Around, Comes Around

Let's now tackle one type of low self-esteem, namely *self*-prejudice about aging, your aging. It is bias against yourself *for* growing older and for showing the visible effects of growing older. This bad attitude— ageism—accounts for much of the fear and loathing many people feel when they think of themselves getting older someday. The worst kind of ageism is the ageism older people themselves buy into. It is self-inflicted ageism. It's self-hating elderliness. Often, you held the same attitudes toward aging and older people when you were younger. What goes around, comes around! Eleanor Roosevelt observed, "No one can make you feel inferior without your consent." Well, don't consent. Can you enjoy life more if you accept yourself and are not prejudiced against your future? Yes. Hardly controversial, but *how do you carry it out?*

Many therapies and self-help books advise you to make long lists of your positive characteristics, as a way to build self-esteem. That can help, but it usually will not ward off wormhood for long. Why not?

Because your *rating scheme* is still in place. Whether they are real negatives or merely characteristics *defined* by society as negative, what happens when you stop listing your positives and notice your "negatives" again? You go back to feeling worthless.

Our colleague, Hank Robb, cogently points out: *"If* Little Jack Horner sat in a corner, eating his Christmas pie. And *if* he put in his thumb, and pulled out a plum, and said, 'What a good boy am I!' Then what will Jack say, sticking with that logic, when he pulls out one of life's many lemons?"

The following example of ageism with both *self*-downing and *other*-downing shows how to use the ABC model for disputing the old Beliefs and building new ones. Let's turn to Jennifer, 47, and her gray hair, which she preferred not to color. Here we will use not only the A, the B, and the C of Rational Emotive Behavior Therapy, but also the D, the E, and the F.

A. *Activating Event or Adversity.* The grocery checkout boy asked Jennifer if she had her senior discount card (for people 60 and older). Jennifer thought, "This means I look much older than I am!"

B. *Self-defeating Beliefs.* I SHOULDN'T look old! That's *horrible!* It shows I'm over the hill. That *dirty little so-and-so,* how dare he say something like that to me in front of everybody in the checkout line!?

C. *Consequences.* Unhealthful negative reactions. Embarrassment, rage, depression.

D. *Disputing.* MUST I look younger? Even if my gray hair does make me look older, is that truly *horrible?* Do my age and my appearance make me *worth less* as a person? Is he really *a villain* for making a mistake?

E. *Effective New Thinking.* I *wish* people wouldn't think I'm older than I am, but no law of the universe *requires* them to be right about my age or to think I'm younger than I am! All that happened was that the checkout kid was trying to be helpful and he was wrong about my age. Hardly a capital offense! I'm choosing not to color my prematurely gray hair, so I'd better accept that some people will think I'm older than I am. I'd also better work hard at accepting *myself* no matter how old I look OR how old I am!

F.　*New Feelings.* Calm, amusement, occasional minor displeasure but not depression about having graying hair.

The Battle of the Beliefs

Flora knew that her two daughters had severe problems, one with her marriage to an alcoholic and the other with a teenage son who kept stealing. Flora also had two competing Beliefs. She paid lip service to one of them. The other had deeper roots and more often governed her activities and emotions. Flora rationally told herself that her daughters had enough problems of their own. She couldn't expect them to be too close to her even though she had recently lost her second husband and had no other close relatives apart from them. So at one level she accepted their neglecting her. But this acceptance was superficial, not deeply felt. Much more strongly, she clung to the Irrational Belief that they absolutely SHOULD see her more and spend hours on the phone with her. Furthermore, they were *rotten, ungrateful children* when they did not. She kept telling herself occasionally, without force, that her daughters' behavior was quite understandable in view of their own difficulties. Much more often and forcefully, however, Flora said to herself, "How *can* they ever treat me like this? I NEED their support and they won't even give me a little of it. What ingrates! I don't *deserve* this *horrible* treatment!"

Flora's Irrational Beliefs easily won out, and she resented her daughters for hurting her so cruelly. Only when I (Albert Ellis) helped her very strongly and persistently work at her Irrational Beliefs and change them from demands to preferences, was she able truly to accept her daughters' behavior. She was able to fully understand their "neglect" and still stand by the one with the alcoholic husband and the other with the teenage delinquent. In fact, she felt good about helping them. The more she helped them, the more she constructively built her life and lived better with her widowhood.

One of Flora's homework assignments involved using DIBS, a system for disputing Irrational Beliefs and changing them to Rational Beliefs. She completed a DIBS worksheet each day on each of her key self-defeating Beliefs:

- I *can't stand* neglect.
- Neglect is *horrible* beyond words.
- My daughters are *bums* to treat me this *horrible* way.

To use DIBS, you write out your answers to the following questions. After you've written out what seem to be effective answers, review them forcefully a number of times. It can help strengthen your conviction if you say your rational answers aloud. (If unrealistic shame and shyness are also a problem for you, you can do this exercise—aloud—in public.) Below is a sample DIBS worksheet, as completed by Flora.

DIBS: Disputing Irrational Beliefs

Question 1: *What Irrational Belief or self-defeating thought do I want to dispute and surrender?*

I can't stand the fact that my daughters don't treat me the way I want.

Question 2: *Does this Belief help me or hinder me?*

It hurts me, it defeats me, it makes me feel miserable. It leads me to resent and almost hate the people I love, my own children, who have their own problems and could use their mom's support.

Question 3: *Is this Belief factually true? Is there evidence against it?*

No. Obviously, I am standing it—and haven't died of it yet!—though I definitely don't like it and wish it were different. So, I can stand it. In fact, at work I stand neglect all the time, for instance when my supervisor cancels our weekly supervision hour, which is a waste of time anyhow. I'm happy about that neglect!

Question 4: *What alternative, effective Rational Beliefs fit with the actual, factual evidence?*

Well, I <u>can</u> stand neglect, though I don't like it, and it's scarcely awful. If my daughters are neglecting me, then they are, so it's nutty for me to imply that this can't be so when it is so! And my daughters are human beings, with many many good qualities—they are hardly horrible children at all. Though, I must admit, they are far from perfect.

Question 5: *What are the worst things that are actually, factually likely to happen to me if the Adverse situation continues?*

Well, if my children continue to neglect me, I'll be deprived of contact with them—contact initiated by them, that is. I'd be the one calling long distance to talk with them—a minor expense and inconvenience. Their continued neglect would mean they are continuing to have their own problems, which would be most unfortunate.

Question 6: *What constructive things could I do if the Adverse situation continues?*

I could involve myself in other activities instead of focusing on the lack of contact with my daughters. I can contact them—rather than focusing on their treatment of me—and offer sympathy and understanding, and if they ask for any, I could offer them advice.

Our Culture Is Kind of Crazy

Many, probably most, *personal* ageist Irrational Beliefs that you might hold, other people hold, too. So, what about *cultural* expectations for aging, especially the not so great expectations? Negative expectations and cultural stereotypes about aging have very powerful effects. One research study exposed older people subtly to very slightly negative words about aging, which were embedded in a list of other words. To a startling degree, many of the subjects (later in the experiment) behaved in ways reflecting cultural stereotypes about older people—such as walking more slowly. Similar groups of older people exposed to similar lists, without the negative age-related words, did not show the "aging" behavior.

Negative stereotypes about aging—if you believe them—can *contribute* to your decline. Firmly held negative stereotypes about ourselves, others, or anything else, can:

- prevent us from noticing contradictory evidence. For example, if you believe yourself to be "a failure in life," then you may not even notice your successes.
- lead us to discount contradictory evidence. Again, if you "are" a failure in life, you may attribute successes to luck or to someone's feeling sorry for you.
- lead us to *search for* additional negative evidence. Again, as a "failure," you may admit to some success, but add, "Yeah, but I failed at_____."
- create evidence to support the negative Beliefs themselves. For example, if you "are" a failure, then there is no use trying. If you do not try, say, in a college course you are taking, then you may manage to do poorly in it. Voilá! The evidence, you then say, *shows* that you are indeed a failure.

Our society harbors many myths about aging that research has debunked. If you look at healthy people in their own communities, not nursing homes, and if you study them over time, you may be in for a surprise. You do not find the marked deterioration in mental and physical capacities found in earlier studies of *cross sections* of Americans at different ages. Deterioration of all your capacities is not a biological "must." Studies over time have also found that withdrawal from society and decline in social activities was abnormal, rather than the normal pattern of old people.

One task of anyone who doesn't expect to die young, and who wants to enjoy the longer lives most of us will live, is to tackle ageist beliefs. Tackle them, whether they are entirely yours, shared by no one, or whether television, newspapers, movies, and government promote them. Then create a new constructive mental map for the adventures you can have throughout your life as you (of course) age.

Emotive and Behavioral Ways To Change Yourself

We have been emphasizing "cognitive" (thinking) ways of changing your disturbed and self-sabotaging feelings. They are probably the best ways for most people most of the time. Why? Because you largely create your unhealthful feelings about the prospect or the reality of aging, as we have been noting, by your grandiose and unrealistic demands.

- I absolutely MUST perform well.
- I MUST have other people to treat me properly.
- I MUST NOT have to work too hard to make conditions the way I want them to be.

These demands are illogical—for it does not follow that because you greatly want something you are automatically entitled to get it. If you give up these illogical demands, you will considerably reduce your upsetness and be ready to enjoy yourself much more—in spite of whatever real limitations and handicaps of aging you undergo.

REBT, however, holds that thinking, feeling, and behaving are closely related. They do not usually exist by themselves, and they strongly influence each other. I (Albert Ellis) clearly stated this in my first major article on REBT at the American Psychological Association Annual Convention in Chicago in 1956. From the start, therefore, REBT has been the pioneering cognitive therapy, and has led the way to the cognitive-behavioral revolution in psychotherapy that got under way in the 1970s. It is also, to use the apt term of Arnold Lazarus, multimodal.

It uses a wide variety of thinking, feeling, and behavioral methods, and is heavily integrational.

To make it easier to teach and more practical, we simplify the ABC model. In doing so, we make it sound as if events, thoughts, and feelings/behaviors are entirely separate from one another. In reality, they are not. The psychological processes of the ABC's—including events—are complexly interrelated. If you change your actions, for example, by acting *as if* you believe something or feel something, this often does lead to unintended *real* changes in your actions, feelings, and thoughts. If you change your feelings with chemicals, it may clearly influence how you think. If you change your thinking—for instance by focusing strongly on a recent injustice you suffered—you will (whether you know it or not) modify your biochemistry; and this may contribute to changes in your actions, too.

Chess playing illustrates the interaction of thoughts, emotions, and behaviors. *Thoughts or evaluations* (I see this as a good chess move and I like it) almost invariably accompany and interact with *feelings* (happiness or elation at considering or having made this "good" move). Thoughts and evaluations also accompany and interact with *actions* (the beginnings of muscle movements, making a move, increased or decreased respiration and heart rate). Similarly, feelings (pleasure at making and thinking about this "good" move) lead to thoughts (What a good player I am for making it). Feelings also lead to actions (getting ready to follow the move with other "good" moves). As well, actions (making the chess move) lead to thoughts (That's a great move! I'm glad I made it!) and feelings (pleasure or elation). If you change your evaluative thoughts about a chess move, your feelings will change. If you devoutly believe you absolutely MUST make the best move possible, you will feel differently in anticipation of your move, and after your move—depending on the other player's response—than if you only *prefer* to make the best move.

Activating Events, so-called objective reality, also depend on how you think, feel, and act. How you, as an individual, think, will lead you to perceive, notice, remember, and predict reality somewhat differently from how other people do. Your unique way of thinking will influence you to feel and act differently from others. Your emotions and moods will also influence how you perceive "factual" reality. Further, when your Beliefs and emotions change, your perceptions of reality may change. You may notice and remember different Activating Events from when you were in a different mood. For example, if you think you absolutely need total love and support from others, your memories of childhood events may differ wildly from those of your brother or sister who—treated about the same—does not care much about love and support.

REBT does not assume that disturbed behavior and emotions simply "come from" how you think. Rather, we assume that for most people, the easiest to learn and most effective way to change their disturbed feelings and actions is to first change how they think. Nevertheless, from its start, REBT has used action homework exercises to help people build their social skills. REBT has also always strongly emphasized forceful, vigorous methods. These include the use of real-life practice, staying with uncomfortable situations until discomfort lessens, risk-taking and shame-attacking exercises, role-playing, and of course humor—such rational humorous songs.

To combat ageist Irrational Beliefs and myths, you can use several of REBT's popular emotive and behavioral methods to supplement and back up your rethinking techniques. One of the most effective of these is the combined thinking-feeling-action method of Rational Emotive Imagery (REI).

Rational Emotive Imagery

Let us take the case of Joseph, 75, who had been an excellent athlete for most of his life but was now slowed down by age. Retired from his work as an accountant, and having much more time than ever to indulge in golf, tennis, and other sports, he was, he thought, tragically handicapped in these pursuits. His handicaps were a bad back, a heart condition, and a proneness to tire easily that he had never before experienced. Joseph was exceptionally prejudiced against himself for his "feeble" condition. Especially when he had to stop at nine holes of golf or after an hour of tennis, he considered himself to be "a pitiful old man." He pretended to his friends and relatives that he was much more active in sports than he was.

I (Albert Ellis) told Joseph, "Yes, people generally do become less physically capable at exercise and other activities with older age. Most people, however, slip into a sedentary lifestyle in middle age. After decades of inactivity, it's no wonder they can't do what was easy for them to do in the past when they were more active. So," I went on, "maybe you can gradually build up your level of physical activity—very gradually, to reduce medical risks. Then you may recapture some of your lost physical vigor."

Joseph said none of this applied to him at all, since he had remained active as he'd aged. He cited golf as one of his major declines. He had played golf a lot over the years, and now his playing was going to pot. So, his problem was due to old age, not lack of practice, he told me. To make matters worse—much worse—Joseph prided himself on his ability to maintain a stiff erection. Now, though his fifteen-years-younger wife, Madeline, was as interested as ever sexually, he had intercourse with her only about once a month. He was thoroughly ashamed of his inability to have intercourse two or three times a week—as he'd done for many previous years. Joseph did not buy the fact of sex decline, which we discuss later in chapter 12. It was difficult to say which he took worse, his athletic or his sexual decline. Both bothered him immensely. He felt much more embarrassed about his sexual "failings," however. He had had a recent full physical—everything was in the normal range for his age. But he had not breathed a word to his internist about his erectile problems.

It was not difficult for us to ferret out Joseph's main self-defeating Beliefs that led to his ageist prejudice against himself. He stoutly believed that he absolutely SHOULD be as good athletically and in his marriage bed as he had been for many years, that it was terrible that he was not. He also believed that it was shameful if his friends knew about his recent lack of prowess in sex and athletics, and that he had to do his best to hide it from them.

Joseph was angry at some of his friends who had taken less good care of themselves physically but who somehow were much better at sports than he was. He ranted and raved at the *horrible*, unfair conditions of old age that left him so weak when he SHOULD function like a young man in spite of his years. Why? He took good care of himself. So Joseph had all three of the major "musts" and demands that make people horrified about aging:

- I MUST perform better at golf and sex.
- Other people MUST NOT outdo me or put me down for my deficiencies.
- Life conditions SHOULD let me easily get what I want and what I used to be able to get.

Using the Three Key Questions and other methods, Joseph disputed his Irrational Beliefs and was able to reduce them to some extent. He seemed to accept his athletic and sexual limitations and disturbed himself less about them. Yet, whenever he saw younger men who were as good at athletics as he once was—and presumably much better at intercourse than he—his progress evaporated. When he saw that he could not now keep up with them, he went back to his dysfunctional Beliefs and started to depress himself again.

Particularly at his 76th birthday party, Joseph upset himself extensively when he felt tired after a few dances. He had to rest for a while when everyone else—including the younger men and some men older than he—seemed able to dance for hours. Also, later that night Madeline was eager to have intercourse, and he wasn't able to make it. That really hurt! Aging was a miserable problem and he would never, never get used to it and be able to bear it!

To teach Joseph how to use Rational Emotive Imagery, I gave him typical instructions. In REI, instead of thinking about positive things and using positive imagery, you do just the reverse. You begin by imagining something quite negative.

"Close your eyes," I said to Joseph, "and imagine vividly that you try to play eighteen holes of golf on a Sunday afternoon, but that you can barely manage nine holes. In fact, by the sixth and seventh holes you are already petering out, your legs are hurting, you are losing your breath. The men with whom you are playing are remarking on how tired you look, and how you are puffing. They joke about how you're just not what you used to be and that your tennis game is becoming pretty bad, too. They say maybe you'd better give up sports and rest a lot more in your old age. Can you vividly imagine that you're doing badly and they are making critical comments about how poor you've recently become at golf and other sports? Vividly imagine it, and tell me when you clearly picture this."

"Oh, I can easily imagine it," said Joseph. "I always do! I can just see it happening. It does happen often."

"Good. Vividly keep it in mind and tell me how you feel. How do you honestly feel about being so poor at sports and about their making negative comments about you?"

"I feel down. Low. Really depressed. Like aging has got me and I'll never be effective as I used to be in sports—nor in almost anything else."

"Good! Feel depressed. Feel low. Feel down. Get in touch with these feelings. Feel as depressed and low and down as you can possibly be. Feel it, feel it, feel it! Really depressed!"

"OK. I really do. I feel quite depressed."

"Fine. Get in touch with it. Feel it. Feel depressed, depressed, depressed. And now, now that you really feel it, keep the same image. Don't change the image. Keep imagining that you are failing at golf, that you cannot do what you easily did when you were younger, and that others are noting it and making comments on it. See it clearly. Feel what you feel."

"OK, I do. I feel it."

"Good. *Now* make yourself feel, feel with the same image in mind, *only* sorry and disappointed about what you are doing, sad and disappointed, just sorry and disappointed about what you are doing. But not depressed, not really depressed. Just sorry and disappointed. You can change your feelings. You control your feelings. You can change them and make yourself feel, with the same image, sorry and disappointed, most sorry and disappointed about what's happening, but not depressed. OK: do it. Change your feelings."

Joseph tried to work on his feelings and change them, but at first had a hard time doing so. I kept encouraging him, telling him that he could really change them, and after about two minutes, he said that he had done so.

"You're now really feeling only sorry and disappointed? Not depressed, but only sorry and disappointed, which are healthful feelings, instead of depressed, which is an unhealthful feeling?"

"Yes, I think I managed it. I did it."

"Great! Open your eyes. How did you do it? What did you do to change your feelings from depression to just feeling sorry and disappointed about what's happening?"

"Well, I told myself that it was really bad, my golf game and their comments about it. It was bad to be older and less able. But it didn't mean anything about me as a person. *It* was bad, but *I* wasn't bad. It was too bad that I played this way, but I could live with it and still enjoy playing."

"Fine! That was really good. You saw, rightly, that it was not good, your golf game, but that you were not a no-goodnik for playing badly. It was too bad, but not awful."

"Yes. I saw that it was not a final horror. I could still play. Even if they made fun of me, I could take it and still play."

"Excellent. Now that will work. What you did will work to make you sorry and disappointed about your playing, but not depressed. You would be telling yourself some rational statements and still feeling bad, but only healthfully bad."

"Yes, I am."

"Good. Now I want you to do the Rational Emotive Imagery as a homework. It is a training process. I would like you to do it every day for the next twenty or thirty days. It only takes a couple of minutes to do it. If you do so, you will train yourself—when thinking of grim things like aging and being handicapped—to feel healthfully sorry and disappointed and not unhealthfully depressed. So imagine this same thing every day, for the next twenty or thirty days. Let yourself, at first, if you really feel it, feel depressed, indeed very depressed, as you just did. But only for a few seconds. Then work on your feelings of depression, which you can always do, and change them to feeling just sorry and disappointed.

"Use the same coping statements you just used to change your feelings, or use a number of other similar coping statements that will occur to you. Such as, '*Tough* that I can't play golf or play tennis as well as I used to, but it's not the end of the world!' Or, 'Maybe my golf and tennis are not as good as they used to be, but I can still enjoy them, though perhaps not as much as I did before.' And 'Even if I were bad at *everything*, I can still accept myself and enjoy life as much as possible.' Use these and similar coping statements and train yourself to feel healthfully sorry and disappointed, day by day, until you automatically begin to feel that way when you imagine this 'dire' event. At the end of ten, fifteen, or twenty days, you will probably automatically feel disappointed and sorry, and not depressed, if you keep doing the Rational Emotive Imagery regularly."

Joseph agreed that it was a good idea to do so.

"Yes, most people come to feel the healthful negative feelings automatically after a while. They train themselves to feel them. Then, when they imagine the bad event, or when it occurs in real life, they are ready with the healthful feelings of sorrow and disappointment, instead of the unhealthful one of depression. Now will you do this once a day, for one or two minutes, as a self-training process?"

Joseph said he would do so.

"Just in case you forget to do it or procrastinate on doing it, we can give you reinforcement."

"Reinforcement?"

"Yes, what do you like doing, some pleasure you really enjoy, and that you do almost every day of the week?"

"Let me see. Oh, yes. Reading the morning paper."

"Fine. Hereafter, for the next twenty or thirty days, only read the newspaper *after* you have done the imagery and changed your feelings. Make the reading of the newspaper *contingent* on doing the imagery. OK?"

Joseph, laughing, said he didn't plan to have to delay very much in reading the paper.

"Fine. And if you still have difficulty doing it, you can enact a penalty every day you don't do the imagery."

"A penalty? I can't think of one."

"I can! For instance, if bedtime arrives on a certain day and you have neglected to do the Rational Emotive Imagery and to change your feelings, what penalty could you use? What unpleasant thing could you do that you usually avoid doing? What unpleasant thing?"

"Well, how about putting my room in order? I usually keep it a mess, because it's a pain in the butt to take the time to fix it up."

"Fine. Every day you don't do the imagery, and bedtime arrives, you stay up for an hour and force yourself to put the room in order. If it gets too tidy, you can put your wife's room in order or go door to door in your apartment complex!"

Laughing, Joseph agreed. "That's fair. I'll do it."

Joseph did Rational Emotive Imagery on his feelings of depression about golf and tennis for fifteen days. He found that he automatically started feeling sorry and disappointed rather than depressed about his sports limitations. He also became much less prejudiced against himself for suffering from these limitations. We used the same method for Joseph to de-upset himself about his problems with erections. Once he no longer felt disturbed and embarrassed about his problem, he agreed to visit his urologist for an exam and medication review, as I had originally asked him to do.

You can do Rational Emotive Imagery on your own if you use the following method. Take one of the things that you feel most distressed about—such as the limitations of and the prejudices against aging— and vividly imagine some bad thing happening to you in that respect.

Imagine yourself being handicapped by the aging process. Imagine yourself looked down upon by others for being older. Imagine any other highly unpleasant and unfortunate occurrence that you have experienced or that you *could* experience. Vividly imagine it happening, and put in some gory details about its happening, details that will usually contribute toward making you depressed, panicked, enraged, or self-pitying. Let yourself imagine this unpleasant thing happening until you really feel quite distressed about it. Get in touch with your disturbed feeling: let yourself feel it, feel it, feel it, until it really grips you. Then, when you feel most upset, change your feeling to a *healthful* negative feeling, such as sorrow, disappointment, frustration, sadness, regret, displeasure, or determination. Make sure that the *healthful* negative feeling is very pronounced, and that it overcomes your disturbed, self-defeating feeling.

Then, ask yourself how you changed your unhealthful feeling to a healthful one. The answer will normally be: you changed your Beliefs about the grim happening from an Irrational Belief to a rational one, from a "must" or a demand to a *preference*. You told yourself a rational coping statement instead of an irrational, disturbing one. You could also relax, or meditate, and thus distract yourself from your self-defeating feeling. This kind of distraction, however, will not make you bring on a healthful negative feeling. When bad things happen to you or you think about their happening, you'd better have feelings. You'd better not merely distract yourself by relaxation or some other method. For when you have a healthful negative feeling about something very unpleasant, you have a much better chance to change it or cope with it. Your feelings motivate you to do something constructive. Therefore, you'd better feel and even feel strongly when bad things happen, and not merely deflect or turn off your feelings entirely.

If you use Rational Emotive Imagery and really work at it for ten, twenty, or thirty days, you will most likely make progress, as Joseph did. You will probably begin to feel automatically sorry and disappointed about the real or possible event, rather than feeling devastated, depressed, and hopeless about it. Along with your new healthful negative feeling you will start internalizing, and keep for good, a rational, optimal-living philosophy of life.

There are two more benefits to overcoming prejudice against yourself because of your age. First, you can learn to stop rating your worth as a person on *any* basis and develop USA—unconditional self-acceptance, a skill crucial to happiness. Second, once you accept and value yourself, aging warts and all, you can deal more constructively with society's and some people's ageist prejudice against people getting a little older.

You now have many optimal living tools for coping with ageism, whether yours or somebody else's. If you consistently use those tools, you will have more time, energy, and savvy for dealing with, and minimizing, some of aging's many *other* possible Aggravations.

Now let's look at some sample responses to the harmful myths about aging we listed above. Think about them, compare them to your answers, and revise your responses where it seems useful.

Myths of Aging/ Irrational Beliefs/ Rational Rebuttal.

Myths of Aging	Possible Irrational Beliefs	Rational Rebuttals
Younger is better; older is worse.	I HAVE TO be young! It's *awful* to age.	Being alive is better! The key to happiness at any age is attitude.
Old people can't change.	Old people HAVE TO act exactly like young people. They HAVE TO be young people.	People can change themselves, if they want to, at any age.
Youth are our future; the old are past.	You MUST be young to have a future.	We can learn more from the past than from the future.
Younger is better looking; older is ugly.	You MUST be good looking.	Beauty is in the eye of the beholder.
Youth is for learning; age is for remembering the past and forgetting.	You MUST be young to be able to learn.	If you use it, you don't lose it. People can learn at any age.
Youth is exciting; age is dull.	I NEED excitement.	Many studies have shown older people are happier, on the average, than younger people. Now, that's exciting!
You should act your age.	It's *awful* not to and shows you are a bad person.	I'll act in my own best interests.
Youth is the time for education, careers, romance, sex, adventure; age is for rocking chairs.	All major activities of life MUST be done when you're young.	That's an old-fashioned way of thinking. You can do these things as long as you are alive.

Myths of Aging/ Irrational Beliefs/ Rational Rebuttal. (Continued)

Myths of Aging	Possible Irrational Beliefs	Rational Rebuttals
Youth is health; age is disease.	Everything about age is *horrible*.	Old people respond to medical care as well as young people. Older workers take fewer sick days than younger ones.
Young people are individuals; old people are all alike.	You HAVE TO be young to be noticed and worthwhile.	Older people are more likely to step away from the crowd. It is the young who try to conform to each other.
Youth is active, effective, confident, living productively, smart; old is passive, fumbling, unproductive, stupid.	You MUST stay youthful, or else.	Age is what you make of it. How you act depends on your attitudes.
If you aren't going to be living that much longer, then there's no use trying to do anything to make life better.	I HAVE TO have a long future ahead of me for my life to be valuable.	Even if my life were ending next week, I can choose to give my life meaning—life is more fun that way.
It's normal to feel depressed when you're old.	Being old is *awful*.	Depression stems from one's belief system and other factors that can be changed.
Age is nothing but decline.	I MUST not change or decline.	If I decline, I will adapt to it.
Sex and romance are embarrassing among older people.	Sex and romance MUST not occur beyond a certain age.	Maybe they are embarrassing to you, but to me they are enjoyable.

7

Unconditional Self-Acceptance (USA)

To err is human, but it feels divine.

Mae West's Observations

Oh yes, we the authors have experienced several of the ravages of older age. Dr. Ellis, pushing 85, has a little more excuse than most of us do, of course, including yours truly (Emmett Velten). Nonetheless, I got started pre-maturely with an irrationality about aging—and practically did myself in—at quite a tender age. Too bad this book was not available back then!

Emmett's Baldness

My dad was bald and I can't say I ever thought much about it until about age 17. I remember someone who sat behind me in my high school senior homeroom saying, "Emmett's getting a bald spot!" I pretended not to hear. But yes, I *had* already noticed a creeping northerly trend on my forehead. But my rearhead, too! That night, mirror in hand, bathroom door locked, I surveyed the recession. There *was* a definite thinning. Oh God, I thought. Oh God!, I *prayed*.

I tried a number of primitive, pre-Rogaine remedies, and endured the expectable "horrors," some of which were a little amusing—but only a little—even at the time.

- Someone told me that an iodine compress applied to your scalp will stop the balding. It didn't. It did lead to my having a red scalp that became a subject of lively speculation and merriment for my schoolmates.
- When I registered, at age seventeen, for my *first* year at The University of Chicago, there was a dividing point in the gym where older student volunteers separated the sheep from the goats. They looked at me and said, *"Returning* students go *that* direction!"* I replied that I was a first year student. Their disbelief was hard to miss. I could imagine their wondering, "What will he look like *four years* from now!?"
- Having been strapped into the dentist's chair, the hygienist asked me my age. I replied 20. Though she struggled briefly to prevent it, her eyes rose to my hairline.

I felt horrified at my pre-mature balding. My dad told me that bald men had more male hormones. Bah! I didn't care. I wanted more hair, not hormones. He cited Betty Grable, I think it was—the famous movie actress and pin-up girl—who said at a USO benefit during World War II that bald men made better kissers. Puke! I wanted hair! Not only was my disability *horrible*, but also something hilarious, though not to me. Only to rude, crude, hairy others. The fun poked at me, I have now known for decades, was often good-natured. It most probably would have been short-lived had I gracefully rolled with it rather than acting as if I were being poleaxed. That was high school. College, a more civilized setting by far, wasn't too bad. Once in 1960, fellow baldie Adlai Stevenson spoke on campus. He repeated his quip about how the hairy young men (alluding to John Kennedy) were apt to take over. Had I been old enough to vote, it would have been Stevenson all the way!

As I finally reached the age when *some* men were balding, my horror began to fade. This, however, was because the context of the Activating Event changed. I was no longer the only bald person my age. The change at A, rather than my making a philosophical change at B, led to less horror at C. Had I known how to use REBT disputation at the time, I could have questioned the helpfulness of my Irrational Beliefs *about* A. I could have questioned their factual basis and their logic. I could have changed my Beliefs to rational ones, to the effect: "It drives me crazy to tell myself it's *horrible and awful* that I'm bald. It would be better to believe, really believe, that it's too damn bad, but hardly *awful and intolerable*. And it's simply untrue that I *can't stand* it. Hell, I am standing it every live-long day!"

Albert's Deafness

Let's say you are older and your hearing has declined enough that you could use a hearing aid. Let's even say you *require* a hearing aid, as I (Albert Ellis) do. And you very much dislike the inconvenience of wearing a hearing aid, as I do. OK? Now, if I only *disliked* the inconvenience and *wished* I did not have to undergo it to be able to hear better, how do you think I would *feel* about wearing the hearing aid? How would I act? Would I or wouldn't I get the damn thing and put up with wearing it?

In all likelihood, if I disliked wearing a hearing aid, and I do, but *liked more to hear clearly*, I'd get the hearing aid and wear it. I'd feel *displeased* about having poor hearing and having to wear the hearing aid, but I'd accept reality and do it. My beloved, my friends, Romans, and countrymen and women would never have to bug me to get me to wear the blasted thing.

But let's now say that you *absolutely* despise wearing a hearing aid. You think it's *awful*. You *can't stand* fiddling with it. You believe that having to wear one shows you have defects you SHOULDN'T have. And let's say you think that if certain other people—younger people, for example—see you wearing a hearing aid, they will be less likely to talk with you, which could detract from your chances for conversation. How do you think you'd feel about wearing the hearing aid in *these* cases? Right! Off the goddam wall! And you wouldn't wear it. As best you could, you'd pretend to hear even though you missed a lot of the conversation.

I have worn a hearing aid for about eight years. I am not in the least ashamed of being seen wearing it, nor of asking people at times to speak louder because I have low hearing. I gave up feelings of shame many years ago, when I was using philosophy and my early methods of REBT to overcome them. I regret it when I do stupid things or am seen by others as doing them, but I am not ashamed and do not put myself down for doing them.

So, shame is no problem with my hearing. I also feel no shame that my hair has been progressively thinning for about twenty years; that my face is clearly wrinkled; that my gait is infirm; and that I have various other characteristics of an older-aged person. I am sorry about having them; but not in any way ashamed.

Hearing is still a problem, however, because of my remaining low frustration tolerance. My hearing aids—and I've tried several of them—just do not work well enough. They definitely improve my hearing, and I would have a difficult time, particularly with my low-voiced clients, without them. But I still have some trouble hearing; and I also have trouble with the hearing aids themselves. They whistle; they have defects; they have to be fairly regularly fixed; their batteries mysteriously run down when I have just replaced them. I once even lost expensive aids when the guards insisted that I remove them when I was going through a security check at the Barcelona airport, and somehow they never got back into my pocket.

So, I have trouble, trouble, trouble with hearing aids. I hate the time it takes to go through this trouble and feel quite displeased about it. But I remind myself about the much *greater* trouble I would experience if I had to live without hearing aids. I gracefully put up with the disadvantages of having hearing aids so that I can reap the real rewards of having them. So they're a real bother—too damned bad. But not awful.

These particular personal examples may not be exactly earthshaking, but they are some of the things people dread about growing older. Now that we have shown you a couple of our episodes of age-related self-defeat (and self-help), let's get back to yours. What realistic alternatives do *you* have to self-rating and self-downing?

Escape from the Self-Esteem Trap!

Let's look at how to escape from the low self-esteem trap and from feelings of inferiority and worthlessness, whether related to your age or anything else. Aren't you supposed to have high self-esteem?, you may ask. Answer: No, if you do have high self-esteem, you are likely to also have low self-esteem. You are likely to feel, quite often, defensive, anxious, down, and angry. Not convinced?

The key problem with self-esteem is that if you rate yourself, you will *berate* yourself. Perfectionism (or SHOULDhood about achievement and approval) leads to low self-esteem. Low self-esteem is different from self-pity. The latter stems from a whining attitude about the fact that other people and circumstances are not fairly treating poor you, poor noble—but martyred and misunderstood—you.

Why is self-rating on any basis other than being alive so bad? It defeats most of us mere mortals because we rate ourselves on some basis, usually achievements and approval. If you are fallible and imperfect, as all humans are, you don't do outstandingly well at most things. Your performance may be mediocre or even poor at quite a few. Therefore, if you make your worth depend on how you do, you often will feel *down* about yourself. Or, defensively, you will "see" yourself as doing well, when you do poorly. The same applies if you rate your worth according to what others think of you, because some people *won't* like you. Self-rating usually gives us many undesirable results. These can include generous helpings of anxiety, depression, defensiveness, blaming others, refusal to accept responsibility, and fear of taking risks and trying new things.

You're still not safe even if you do very well and many people adore you. Why? Because you could slip. You could come across people who do *better*. Your outstanding accomplishments could lose importance and pass into the dustbin of history. Those who approve of you now may later not care about you. This happened to me (Emmett Velten) when I got to college, where I was only average, academically. My "worth"— largely based on academic success in high school—went kerplunk!

There are several ways to drop the self-rating game and go beyond self-esteem to self-acceptance. First, you can see that self-rating makes most of us feel like losers. It often gives poor results—it's impractical. Unconditional self-acceptance (USA) works better. If you think, for instance, you will be worthless when your body sags with age, you'll feel increasingly anxious, depressed, and threatened as you grow older. You might then be afraid to exercise publicly, for instance, for fear that others would see old, sagging you.

Second, you can stop rating yourself, but continue to rate your *traits* and *acts* according to how they help or hinder you, by seeing that self-worth is definitional. Because it is, and because you hold that definition now (no matter where it came from), you *could* redefine your worth with no strings attached. With unconditional self-acceptance, you can feel better and enjoy life more. One way to see that self-worth is a definition, is to reflect on the people you know well who are well liked and yet feel relatively worthless. Many of them! And think of Adolf Hitler—a person with exceptionally despicable behavior, but who in all likelihood thought very well of himself.

Third, you can stop rating yourself and damning yourself by realizing the impossibility of knowing and properly weighing *all* your characteristics in order to reach a composite score. Besides, if you could get an accurate composite score, all things, including you, change. In a couple of hours, you'd have to do it all over again. And again, and again. You'd have little time for doing anything else.

Fourth, you can see that "self-worth" is an overgeneralization based on only *some* of your traits out of the scores that you have. Rating yourself based on *some* traits is a somewhat arbitrary decision. It's a decision that may lead to self-downing and to your bypassing chances to improve *how* you do. In addition, you could be inaccurate in rating the traits in question. You could be, say, rather stingy, but pat yourself on the back for your generosity.

We can summarize some of these points about unconditional self-acceptance in the Twelfth Rule for Optimal Living:

Rule #12: ACCEPT AND FORGIVE YOURSELF UNCONDITIONALLY

Healthy people are usually glad to be alive and accept themselves just because they are alive and have some capacity to enjoy themselves. They refuse to measure their intrinsic worth by their extrinsic achievements or by what others think of them. They frankly choose to accept themselves unconditionally. They try to completely avoid rating themselves—their totality or their being—and they try to refrain from labeling themselves. They attempt to enjoy life rather than to prove themselves.

Shame-attacking Exercises

Audrey was an excellent example of someone who had high self-esteem, but it was highly conditional. High self-esteem *sounds* very good. Many articles and books tell you how you can achieve self-esteem, but they are dangerous and misleading. For self-esteem, or *conditional* self-acceptance, is one of the greatest disturbances known to woman or man.

Audrey had it all, for she was, from her teenage years onward, a quite beautiful, very intelligent, socially adept, and athletic person. She was at the top of her class in most respects. She was popular with both sexes, and her parents and relatives were proud of her achievements.

She had self-efficacy. She knew that she excelled at important tasks, both in and out of school, and she had confidence that she would keep doing them well.

Unfortunately, Audrey did not have *un*conditional self-acceptance. She accepted and liked herself only *because* she did well and most other people favored her. This conditional form of self-acceptance made her feel good most of the time—but not in times of real crisis. Despite her general confidence and good track record in achievement and popularity, Audrey feared she might not make it and she had a number of panic attacks. She had severe anxiety attacks when she almost failed to become the valedictorian of her class in high school. The same panic, with bouts of depression added in, happened when she lost the tennis championship of her athletic club and when she was passed over for an important job promotion.

Audrey was strikingly attractive and knew she could count on her looks to dazzle almost anyone. Yet, even her looks could fail her—given her Belief that she HAD TO look better than anyone else. Once when she was at an AIDS benefit at a five-star hotel, truly glamorous and dressed to kill, Audrey became very miffed and hurt when her grand entrance went unnoticed. Diana Ross had just passed through the lobby! So keep in mind that the better you do and the better you look, someone does and looks even better. If your self-worth is contingent, back to worm-hood your ego will go. Besides, as you do better, you tend to get promotions, go on to advanced training, and attend swank benefits, as Audrey did, where the competition will get stiffer and you won't compare so well.

On the whole, however, Audrey got through, became an outstanding teacher, married the most attractive and successful man in her social circle, and had two handsome and talented sons. So she wasn't exactly a basket case.

As Audrey reached the age of 50, however, things became much worse. Though she was as beautiful as ever, she had bought into our culture's cult of youth. So, she felt ugly. Arthritis of the knee stopped her great tennis playing. She took an administrative job with her school system and felt the loss of her adoring students and her approving principal. Her loving husband had an affair with his 30-year-old secretary and almost divorced Audrey.

All Audrey's conditional self-acceptance vanished and she became severely depressed. She had based her worth as a person on her youthful looks and accomplishments, and now most of them were gone. She was still a well-loved mother, but both her sons were married, had families of their own, and lived a distance from her. They no longer "needed" her.

Audrey's conditional self-acceptance hadn't always worked too well even when she was young and accomplished. It hardly worked at all when she was older and less accomplished in the ways she believed she SHOULD be—to be worthy. She had rated herself as "good" because she was better than most people at most things. When anything jeopardized her accomplishments, she panicked.

I (Albert Ellis) had one devil of a time selling Audrey the idea of *un*conditional self-acceptance. She said she could see its virtue. Nevertheless, she kept falling back on the "fact" that she had to be an outstanding wife, mother, administrator, and even tennis player. She also had to look no older than 40—tops. Only then could she truly accept herself. Her therapy group and I tried to help her accept herself merely because she was a person, a human, and not because she was an achiever, and at first we dismally failed. Her entire history, together with the teachings of our culture, led her to accept herself only conditionally. When the conditions of her life led to less achievement, less success, less acclaim, she had a very rough time of it.

Finally, my using with Audrey my famous shame-attacking exercises really made a profound impression on her and helped her choose unconditional self-acceptance. I created these exercises back in the 1960s. I realized that shame, embarrassment, or feelings of humiliation are the essence of much human disturbance, and particularly of self-downing. When people do a so-called "shameful" act, and especially one that other people put them down for doing, they say to themselves, first, "I am doing the wrong thing, and that is bad." That *could* be true.

They also say to themselves, "Because I am so wrong and because people disapprove of me for being wrong, I am truly a *rotten person*, a no-good, *worthless individual*." In other words, they not only put their behavior down, which may be the correct thing to do in their social group, but they put themselves down, and damn their entire personhood. Then they feel so low and self-hating that they are very likely to repeat the "shameful" act—for how can a "rotten person" act adequately and win others' approval?

Shame-attacking exercises encourage people to stop this type of self-defeating thinking and to accept themselves fully even if their behavior is bad and disapproved of. To do this exercise, you think of something that you consider shameful, foolish, ridiculous, or embarrassing—and then you *deliberately* do that thing in public. Yes, first you let yourself briefly feel quite ashamed of doing the "shameful" act. But then—this is a two-part exercise—you *work* on changing your thinking so you do *not* feel ashamed.

Now wait a minute! Don't do anything "shameful" that would get you in trouble or potentially cause you harm. For example, don't do something idiotic at work, walk down the street naked, or honk prolongedly when you come up behind a bevy of outlaw motorcyclists in traffic. Don't do anything that would harm others, such as slapping people in the face or picking their pocket. But you do, yes you do, something that you consider shameful and that most other people also consider shameful and would look down on you for doing. For example, you yell out the stops in the subway, on a bus, or on a train, and you stay in your seat. You yell out the time in a department store or supermarket. You wear one black shoe and one brown shoe. You walk a banana on a leash, and you feed it with another banana. You ask a stranger where Broadway is when you are standing on Broadway. You say to a stranger, "I just got out of the mental hospital. What month is this?" You wear underpants on your head.

The real point of these shame-attacking exercises is to do something foolish, crazy, and embarrassing—and *not* feel ashamed, foolish, crazy, or embarrassed. It's fine to feel sorry and regretful that some onlookers are possibly thinking that you are no good or crazy. But not, definitely not, to blame yourself or berate yourself for doing that "shameful" thing. Other people cannot really put you down without your permission. They can only try.

In REBT, we have developed shame-attacking exercises for thousands of people all over the world. Usually, they do them and feel at first somewhat ashamed or humiliated. But when they keep doing them, they often lose practically all sense of shame, and even greatly enjoy the process.

This is what happened with Audrey. She was at first afraid to do any shame-attacking exercises. All the other members of her therapy group did them and usually reported that they had benefited from doing so. Audrey was afraid that even if she did one among strangers, her foolish behavior would somehow get back to friends and relatives. Most of the latter were very conventional and probably would look down on her. "That would be good!" the group members kept telling her. "Let them look at you in horror! We're trying to get you to see that it really doesn't matter that much what anyone thinks of you. So let them think you're an idiot. You don't have to agree with them. That's the point of the exercise."

No dice. Audrey still refused to do a shame-attacking exercise. She solidly held to the Irrational Belief that she was only a good person when she succeeded at some project or when she pleased other people. At the very least, according to Audrey, she MUST NOT fail or get disapproved of. Meanwhile she kept panicking more and more at the thought that she was no longer, now that she was older, succeeding in exactly the same ways as she had almost always done before. Therefore, she was, she believed, no longer able to achieve self-esteem. She believed in REBT theory—only a little and lightly. She hardly practiced it at all.

Finally, her husband's affair with his secretary resumed, and he became rather blatant about it. Practically everyone in his office knew about the affair. Audrey felt terribly afraid that her 90-year-old mother would find out about it, and would blame her for having put up with it for over a year. She said that she wouldn't be able to stand it if her mother found out; she would absolutely die. She felt paralyzed.

At this point her therapy group insisted more than ever that she do some shame-attacking exercises. They showed her how ridiculous it was to horrify herself about her mother's or almost anyone's disapproval, and they persisted in pushing her to challenge her old way of thinking. To get them off her back, she finally agreed to go to Bloomingdale's, which is close to our Institute, and to yell out in a loud voice, "Ten o'clock and all's well!" She tried to do so and gave up twice, but on the third attempt managed to shout out the time in the store. To her surprise, practically no one paid any attention to her shouting, and one of the guards smiled in a friendly manner at her. She thought that he, of all people, would feel horrified and order her out of the store.

When nothing happened, Audrey got up the courage to yell out the time in two other department stores. She also yelled out a few stops on the subway. She saw, by doing so, that nothing terrible happened. Even when some people probably thought she was crazy, avoided all eye contact with her, and walked away from her, she was able to take their criticism and not put herself down with it.

In the next few weeks, Audrey did several other shame-attacking exercises and had the best weeks of her life. She saw that she herself was giving enormous power to other people and that she didn't have to. She graduated from the shame-attacking exercise with strangers to telling some of her friends, and finally her mother, about her husband's having an affair with his secretary. She saw that nearly all of them blamed him and not her. She got used to asserting herself even when it was likely someone would criticize her for doing so.

Her shame-attacking exercises impressed Audrey with the fact that her estimation of herself did not have to depend on conditions like success and approval. To solidify her commitment to unconditional self-acceptance, she volunteered to teach a class of teenagers at a local community center. She taught them social skills, and went out of her way to teach them some of the REBT principles of unconditional self-acceptance. Doing this, she sank those ideas more and more deeply into her head and heart.

"I can see," Audrey reflected, "that rating *how* I do at the things that are important to me is the way to go. I could still end up feeling bad, I guess, but I'd *better* feel bad when my actions aren't measuring up to my goals and values, right?"

"Yes. The bad feelings in that case would be healthful if they motivated you to change what you can change and to accept what you cannot change."

"Including how old I am. If I rate myself down due to my age, I'm needlessly hurting myself. Even if some people are biased against older people, I don't have to share that bigoted viewpoint."

"Right! You also can challenge the negative expectations and stereotypes about age that we sometimes aren't even aware of. So, if you told yourself you were worthless because you were old and gray, or old and wrinkled, or old and retired, what could you do?"

"I'd better start believing, 'I will accept and value myself *regardless*. I'm always worth the same amount to myself.'"

"Which is USA—unconditional self-acceptance."

Two Headaches Tonight

Marylou and Matt, who were 55 and 58 years old, respectively, presented a double case of self-rejection. They had a wonderful second marriage to each other after their first ones had miserably failed. Marylou's first husband had criticized her for practically everything she did, but she had stayed with him 22 years until she had got their two children off to college. Matt, a civil service employee, had never made enough money or had sufficient status to please his first wife, Judy. He had stayed with her mainly because she was a beauty who loved sex, but he had left her as his sex drive waned and her fault-finding increased. In accounting for his divorce, Matt was fond of paraphrasing the old saying that the loving he got was no longer worth the screwing he got! So, Matt paired off with Marylou, who never had been very attractive physically but had been a kind friend of his since college. Marylou, in turn, found Matt very uncritical and easygoing. For two years, they had a wonderful, mutually supportive marriage.

Except for their sex lives, which they both were ashamed of. Marylou, who had known Judy, Matt's first wife, knew that her body could not compare to Judy's and was certain she could never satisfy Matt as Judy had satisfied him in bed. Though in her prime years at 55, Marylou felt inferior because she could not match Judy's beauty and sexuality. She felt particularly ashamed and embarrassed by her sagging breasts and large thighs. At one time she had looked into the possibility of plastic surgery, but decided it would be better just to resign herself to living with her body as it was. Marylou's sexual ardor and orgasmic ability were hardly deficient, but again, would never equal what Judy's had been (according to Matt's descriptions). So she was ashamed of her body and ashamed of her "mediocre" sexuality.

For his part, Matt had suffered from a decreased sex drive even during his last few years with Judy, partly because of her backbiting and partly because of his prostate problems. He would have been happy to have little sex and much cuddling and love from Marylou. But he knew that she was putting herself down for not being up to Judy's level of beauty and sexuality. Matt, therefore, blamed himself because he was not able to prove to Marylou that his lack of sexual interest in her had nothing to do with any shortcomings of hers. He tried to convince her that his inadequacies would have existed, at his age and physical condition, with practically any partner. He kept reassuring Marylou that his "deficiency" was his problem and not any fault of hers. She, however, was so fixated on taking the blame for it, that she ignored Matt's reassurances.

Matt became so overdetermined to show Marylou that she was beautiful and sexy enough to arouse him more often and more fully, that his self-commands in this respect boomeranged. His core Irrational Beliefs were: "I MUST show Marylou I really care for her by getting better and firmer erections!" "I've GOT TO show her that she's really attractive enough to make me hot!" With these demands, Matt kept spying on his penis and its ability to rise up and stay up and—what do you know—his penis got stage fright! Matt's sexual anxieties interfered even more with his performance than did his naturally decreased sexuality.

As often happens in men who have erectile problems, a vicious circle developed with Matt. The more anxious he felt, the more he would dread trying to have intercourse with Marylou. The more anxious he was, the less well he did. The less well he did, the more anxious he was the next time around. Why? Because he kept telling himself how *awful* and *intolerable* it would be to fail, and how he was not really a man if he failed.

Left to his inclinations, Matt would have had sex with Marylou about once every two weeks and would have fairly thoroughly enjoyed it. However, his MUSTurbation-caused anxiety made him hardly capable of getting erections at all. When he did occasionally get them, he was so preoccupied with making them last long enough to bring Marylou to orgasm in intercourse, as he had had no trouble regularly doing with Judy, that he came very quickly and hardly enjoyed himself at all. After those "failures," as might be expected, Matt berated himself strongly for his failing. He began to hate the thought of having to try again in another week or two. Soon, months would pass before he attempted intercourse.

Marylou, meanwhile, kept assuming that it was all her fault—because of her sagging and overweight body—for Matt's failures and sexual withdrawal. In truth, she was as relieved as Matt to avoid sex, for fear of "proving" what a terrible partner she was—especially compared to Judy. Though the couple still were affectionate, warm, and cuddly, sex between them came to a complete halt. One of Marylou's friends insisted that they go for sex therapy, and the American Association for Sex Education, Counseling, and Therapy (AASECT) referred them to me (Albert Ellis). When they learned that I had written some twenty books on sex, they overcame their reticence and saw me for several sessions.

It did not take long for me to show Marylou and Matt that their double jeopardy performance anxiety about sex stemmed from self-downing. Marylou had internalized all her first husband's caustic criticism and became an expert—one of the best!—at *self*-damnation. As well, years of movie-going and TV-watching had helped her devoutly believe that when a man became sexually aroused with a woman it was almost entirely her youth, beauty, and sexiness that pumped up his ardor. Marylou's imaginings about Matt's and Judy's early sex lives thoroughly confirmed that view. Without at least half-equaling Judy's slimness and sex-inciting ability, Marylou defined herself as not a real woman—just a nothing. And if her orgasmic ability was merely okay, but not sensational, she as a person was far less than okay.

As for Matt, he believed that his physical condition was no excuse for sexual—erectile—failure. With his former wife, Judy, he had lost much of his desire because who wanted to go to bed with a barracuda? But he really loved Marylou and wanted to satisfy her as well as himself sexually. The more he had to get it up and keep it up, the less his anxiety allowed him to do so. He therefore put himself down, first for his sexual "inadequacy," and second, for his anxiety. A "real man" SHOULD be highly sexual and completely free of anxieties, and he was insufficient in both these "crucial" respects.

I used several regular sex techniques with Marylou and Matt. I first advised them that sex does not equal intercourse. There are many other, often far more satisfying and effective ways to enjoy sex. These include sensate focus, relaxation, and distraction methods, and use of arousing imagery. I described methods Marylou and Matt could use to communicate with each other and assert their sexual desires. I encouraged them to use what Masters and Johnson called sensate focus—to forget about intercourse for a while and pleasure each other's bodies to the point of orgasm in various noncoital ways. I showed them that they did not have to achieve climax together, but could focus on achieving it one at a time and thereby bring it on themselves without simultaneously worrying about pleasing their partner. I introduced them to guiltlessly using imaginative techniques and physical enjoyments that worked for masturbation but that they thought were "too selfish" for mutual sex play. I also explained to Matt that many men find that stuffing a soft penis into the vagina leads to its becoming erect.

These personalized methods of sex therapy considerably helped. What especially seemed to assist Matt and Marylou was their shamelessly employing various sex techniques to help each other become fully aroused and individually focused on achieving climax. Soon Marylou was able to get more fully aroused than she had ever been before and sometimes to come to climax three times a week. Matt never reached that peak, but was able to get a full erection and orgasm once a week by focusing on "selfish" methods of sex. He particularly liked Marylou's giving him oral sex for ten minutes while he fully concentrated on his own enjoyment. Then later Matt satisfied her with a combination of clitoral manipulation and vaginal penetration with his fingers. Relieved of the burden of bringing Marylou to orgasm with his sacred penis, Matt thoroughly enjoyed focusing on his own pleasure for ten minutes and then concentrating for another ten minutes to bring her to orgasm. Their "selfishly" taking turns tremendously increased the sexual enjoyment the couple found with each other. First one, and then the other, would concentrate fully on the other's enjoyment. Matt was pleased that he could bring Marylou to fulfillment such as she had never had before.

Most of all, however, my teaching Marylou and Matt unconditional self-acceptance was important in helping them calm down their mutual sex anxieties. When Marylou was able to fully accept herself with her far from perfect body and her "mediocre" sex arousability that was distinctly inferior to Judy's, she became much less fearful of displaying these "handicaps" to Matt. She then focused on pleasing herself and him to a much greater degree than she had ever had previously. Her body, surprisingly, responded, as her anxiety subsided, and she became in her mid-fifties, increasingly arousable and even eager to have sex.

Matt also accepted himself unconditionally with his somewhat aging sexuality and his prostate problems. When he no longer thought that he had to be a great Don Juan to prove his "manhood" to himself and to Marylou, he became less anxious than he had ever been. He didn't become a sex athlete but he did become distinctly more sexy. The cognitive-behavioral techniques used in REBT helped his sex life, but the profoundly philosophical method of unconditional self-acceptance (USA) helped him and Marylou even more. Sex was indeed much better, but living with greatly reduced self-downing and anxiety was the greatest development in this couple's lives as they approached older age.

8

Families and Finances

Having a detailed business plan doesn't guarantee success, but not having one guarantees failure.

First Rule of Business

"On the whole, I'd rather be an orphan," Claudia said with a regretful sigh, humorously mimicking W.C. Fields's voice and his quip, "On the whole, I'd rather be in Philadelphia." She wasn't pleased with several of her family members, but now no longer felt disturbed about them. Just three weeks earlier, Claudia had felt furious and hurt about the obnoxious behavior of those family members. At that time she had said with anger and hurt, "I wish I didn't have a family."

"Yes," I (Emmett Velten) had agreed at our first session, "but remember, people without families, orphans for instance, could upset themselves over *not* having families. People with perfect families can awfulize about *other* things! It's not the Activating Events themselves, like your obnoxious family members, that upset us, . . ."

"I know, I know," Claudia quickly replied. "It's our judgments about them." Claudia had run into the Albert Ellis Institute's Web site, http://www.rebt.org, which had led her to me to work on her problem with her family. She had also studied several pamphlets about REBT I had sent her after we had scheduled our first appointment.

"And what is your judgment that disturbs you?"

Claudia thought for a moment and replied, "My brother and sister-in-law and husband SHOULD NOT be the way they are! In fact, I upset myself about them even when they are nowhere in sight. So it's not them, it's me."

"That's right," I agreed. "Although they do their very best to *help* you upset yourself by acting the way they do."

Claudia laughed bitterly and agreed that her brother and sister-in-law were very proficient at that sort of thing, and her spouse wasn't that shabby at it either. What had they done?

Claudia and her brother, José, had alternated for about fifteen years having the family's Thanksgiving celebration at their homes. There were other sisters and brothers, but Claudia and José were the eldest, and now that their mom and dad had both passed on, headed the family. They both had large, spacious homes. The Thanksgiving dinner was a big tradition for the extended family, with as many as 40 or 50 people attending, most of them bringing dishes. While Claudia and José lived about 120 miles apart, in Tucson and Phoenix, so did most of the extended family. So it all worked out, until the previous Thanksgiving. Claudia's husband, Ruben, had made a facetious remark that Luann, José's wife, had taken the wrong way. In the ensuing months, this had led to remarks and incidents on Luann's part, which Ruben had taken the wrong way. The remarks had gone back and forth, like tennis balls, until the present, when it was Claudia and Ruben's turn to host the Thanksgiving dinner.

A new phase of hostilities had begun at the family's picnic on Labor Day—not nearly as big a celebration as Thanksgiving. Claudia's sister-in-law, Luann, had let it be known that she no longer felt welcome or comfortable in Claudia and Ruben's home. This had got back to the latter soon enough. For his part, Ruben had lost no time in spreading the word that he did not want someone in his home who did not feel comfortable—and who couldn't take a joke! José, Luann's husband, had then construed Ruben's "couldn't take a joke" comment as insulting. He had phoned Claudia and Ruben and left a voice-mail message that he and Luann deserved an apology, and until they got one, the two couples would have no further contact. He had also phoned various family members to give them his and Luann's version of events, as well as somewhat uncomplimentary interpretations of Ruben's motivation in insulting Luann, and Claudia's motivation in not setting him straight. When *those* family members had eagerly relayed this material to Claudia and Ruben, Ruben had disinvited José and Luann from the Thanksgiving gathering. Claudia had thought her husband had gone too far with the disinvitation, but she could see his point. Then came the shocker. José and Luann issued a *competing* Thanksgiving invitation to all the family other than Claudia and Ruben! Same day and same hour, so that each person invited could attend one and only one of the happy events.

That had been Claudia's family-related Adversity. At C, as an emotional Consequence, she felt very angry and hurt. What were her relevant Irrational Beliefs? The main ones were:

- My brother, that idiot, how can he (translation: he SHOULDN'T) let this happen and do this to us and our family?
- After all I've done for Luann, I can't believe she would (translation: she SHOULDN'T) do this to me, personally!
- And my husband! Why did he have to tell them (as he SHOULDN'T) they weren't invited? He could have just let it all blow over.

That had been Claudia at the first of four sessions. Angry, hurt, bitter. However, she strongly wanted to return to good terms with her brother and sister-in-law and to heal the rupture. She also hoped the combatants, including herself, could learn to act a bit more sanely and forgivingly in the future. So she worked on herself and her part in the family fracas, with the hope that she would feel forgiving and rational enough to do what she could to produce a peace treaty. What if she weren't able to do that by Thanksgiving? Well, she could at least accept—without horrifying herself—the uncharming way things were working out. She could also continue her efforts to influence everyone to forgive and forget and bury the hatchet.

By her fourth session, Claudia had effectively disputed her "musts." As a result, she felt regret about what had happened. She had gotten it into perspective, even a somewhat humorous perspective, as witnessed by her W.C. Fields remark. Claudia accepted that families, and family members, do have their bad features and feuds, as well as their strong points. She had unconditionally accepted her brother, her husband, her sister-in-law, and even herself, as highly fallible. And highly funny! Inspired, she had phoned her brother and sister-in-law several times, and had had some heart-to-hearts with her husband.

The twin Thanksgiving celebrations took place, however, with the

Tucson branch of the family at Claudia and Ruben's and the Phoenix branch at José and Luann's. To Claudia's surprise, quite a few family members said they liked the twin celebration better than the old, alternating custom because they didn't have to drive as far. The last I heard, it looked like next year would see a variation on the "tale of two cities," with Thanksgiving lunch in one city, dinner in the other! According to Claudia, the principals in the family fracas now felt amused that they had taken themselves, and each other, so seriously.

Refusing to take serious things *too* seriously is important to good mental health. Humorous leavening of serious family issues can be quite a challenge, but it's worth a try if your relatives have the normal quota of redeeming features. Some common family-related Adversities, which can also be age-related, include:

- estrangement from family members
- having children or other family members who turned out bad
- neglectful or abusive family members
- not having a closely connected family any more.

What Is a Family?

Traditional families are alive and kicking—far from facing extinction as some media reports imply. Undeniably though, families have changed considerably in our lifetimes. Many readers can well remember when working mothers and divorces were rare, to say nothing of single-parent families. Times have changed, and several trends continue to change the characteristics of what people consider "family." For example, twenty percent of the baby boomers have no children. Another 25 percent have only one child. Overall, people have fewer children. Large numbers of people are reaching their middle years and will reach their elder years with no, or few, children to lean on. People live longer than they did several generations ago, and the death rate among infants and young children is very low. So, a giant wave of older people is moving this way! People are much more mobile now than even a generation ago. If you do have children or other biological relatives, most likely they are scattered across the continent and even across the world.

Then there's divorce and remarriage. Many couples have his children, her children, and their children! This can get complicated when it's multiplied by several marriages and divorces. Adults with adult children marry each other, get to be friends with the various in-laws (of the spouse and the spouse's children), and then the "children" divorce. Or their parents do. Often, one's emotional ties with these ex-in-laws remain. They *are* family.

Single-parent families, now common, once were a shameful scandal. Those who got pregnant without benefit of wedlock might be sent to homes for unwed mothers. Or might get shipped off to live with aunt Florence to have the baby. And they'd be dropped from school. Even as a mature woman, the late film star and multiple Oscar winner, Ingrid Bergman, almost had her career shattered by having a child out of wedlock in the 1950s. Probably the only thing that saved her was that she was European, not American! While men cannot have a child without someone's cooperation, there are increasing numbers of single-parent families where the single parent is male.

What once was almost unimaginable in our society, gay and lesbian couples with children whom they often adopt, are increasingly common. Until comparatively recent decades, interracial marriage was against the law. Now, large numbers of mixed marriages take place. More of the children of these unions are refusing to be racially classified for census or other purposes.

So families are much more varied than they used to be. Long gone are the days when your family was only your biological relatives and in-laws, and you had no choices other than marriage and divorce. (Even in the old days you could rid yourself of family members by quietly bumping them off, but it's not a recommended method.)

Many families now are adult-centered rather than child-centered. Individual independence, the smaller proportion of people with children, and other demographic and economic trends, are leading to smaller and farther-flung families. At the same time, these trends are producing extended families composed of fewer, often no, people who are biologically related to each other. Or even married to each other. In these new families, shared values and choice are as important as biology. You can now bond with peers rather than relatives, and commitment and choice are more important than blood kinship.

Can Your Family of Origin Be the End of You?

In a word, yes. A character in a play by Jean-Paul Sartre makes a remark Claudia could agree with: "Hell is other people." Sometimes true. Nobody's perfect, but there's quite a range of imperfection. There are others and then *there are others.* You may be one of those unlucky souls whose dear relatives themselves may be among the most adverse others. Yes, at A, the Activating Event, some of these beloveds behave poorly, giving you plenty of opportunity to express your Irrational Beliefs, and to disturb yourself at C, your emotional and behavioral Consequences. Some of these dear ones can be obnoxious, neglectful, mean, petty, back-stabbing, stingy, messy, or otherwise highly fallible and imperfect. You name it, and your or your mate's family members may do it. They haven't yet? Give them time. The possibilities are endless. Even when no one of your family members is a screwball of the worst sort, there are plenty of more ordinary stresses they can effortlessly provide. They can live too far away, for instance—often true if you are older and they're your children. And, *of course,* they can live too near. Your family can be too big or too small. Too sticky, too emotionally unavailable, too rich, too stingy. Too one way or the other.

Are you an older person who has grown children? If so, have you noticed that they still show certain annoying behaviors they established as youths? Sound familiar? Or, they could be the creative types and started their annoying behavior as adults, whereas their childhood records were unblemished. Very possible. But mainly, if they're human, they are, or have remained, *oh, so fallible!* Some of them turn out great, others OK, others not so hot, some very badly indeed, but even the best remain—*oh, so fallible.* It is preferable to accept this reality and not disturb yourself over it. Otherwise, you may make relationships unpleasant for you and for them.

Instead of acceptance of people's flaws, and staying with the people, what other choices do you have? One is non-acceptance, but staying with the people. This is usually a very poor choice. Another option is to become a hermit or a loner. Even there, you can be a contented hermit or a bitter one, depending on your attitude toward the people you left behind. Most people, of course, do not have the temperament for the life of a hermit or a loner. They want some contact with people. That's fine. To enjoy that contact, and not give yourself a stroke, you'd better accept humans with their fallibilities. If you *can* change their poor characteristics, go for it. Give it a good try. If you fail, don't wail. Instead, accept other people with their flaws even as they (perhaps) accept you, with your flaws.

Blame the Parents!

One of the pervasive ideas in our culture is that parents are just about wholly responsible for how children turn out. Especially when they turn out badly, blame the parents! (When our children turn out very well, we may graciously accept much of the credit.) Usually the mother gets blamed severely, but father gets blamed, too, for how little Johnny and little Janey turn out.

We disagree with that notion. For one thing, if it's 100 percent your fault your children turned out the way they did, who was responsible for how *you* turned out? *Your* parents. And so that line of reasoning would go, all the way back to Adam and Eve or to Fred and Wilma Flintstone, presumably. You can see that this line of thinking leads nowhere fast, other than to a world populated only by victims, who aren't responsible for anything they do. It would be an amoral anarchy.

Not that it isn't important to rear your children as best you can. Not that it wasn't also highly preferable that your parents would do a good job of parenting. However, your upbringing is an Activating Event or possible Adversity. How you now act and feel, as a Consequence at C, stems directly from B, *your* present Belief system, not from A, your upbringing. If your parents were ineffective, if they set bad examples, if they were too lax or too strict, that's definitely adverse. But it's not making you do what you do and feel what you feel *now*. The same applies if *you* made mistakes galore in rearing your children. Of course, at times, something had better be done about poor parenting to correct it or to remove the child from the home if he or she is being abused. Nevertheless, people's actions and feelings are their own responsibility. If your adult or juvenile child commits a crime, for instance, he or she did it. He or she is responsible for that choice, not you, no matter if you were a poor parent.

This blaming of parents by grown children is usually a mistake. Consider the following ideas. Different children from the same family may take very different paths in life. One will become an average citizen, the other a murderer, with about the same upbringing. Given excellent parenting, some kids turn out to behave disappointingly. Others turn out very well despite adverse childhood experiences. Society will get much better results, we think, by holding people responsible for their own behavior, rather than falling for sob stories and psychiatric diagnoses that let people off the hook. So, in our book, you can relax and let nature take its course with your grown children who aren't doing as well as they preferably should. Give them your opinion, but know that how they act is up to them.

Yes, some of the difficulties many people face as they age—but also their satisfactions—have to do with their children. But other difficulties (as well as advantages) can spring from *not* having had children. If you did not have children, you can expect good, bad, and indifferent results of that. The same is true if you did have children. Dealing with the good and even the indifferent results is something most of us can face OK. What about the worse or much worse situations? What do you do then? That's the time to do some detective work. Figure out, and rip up, your Irrational Beliefs about these scenarios. Then you may have more mental strength and opportunity to change them for the better. Failing that, you can accept unfortunate reality, and then continue to make the best life for yourself you can.

The Family Tree Ends Here

Connie and Mark, a couple one of us worked with recently, had no problems with each other, but shared a family-related depression. At A, their Adversity was that they had no grandchildren while most (but not all) of their friends did. They explained this Adversity in detail. Their daughter, Rebecca, a very successful career woman, had reached her mid-40s. Not only had she and her husband never wanted children and remained very happy without children, but they didn't seem to even recognize that they were "killing" Connie and Mark by remaining childless. Much less did they feel guilty and do something about it. They could at least have adopted—but no, Rebecca and her husband had zero interest in that. Below zero even. It got worse.

Connie and Mark's son, Mark Jr., was gay. This never bothered Connie and Mark—at least not while they entertained fond hopes that Rebecca would have children. The best case scenario—grandchild-wise—Connie and Mark pointed out morosely, was that Mark Jr. might adopt. He and his partner had never expressed any interest in that, but he had never definitively ruled it out, as the wretched Rebecca and her husband had done. So, without significant advances in human cloning, and soon, that was the Adverse Event at A that Connie and Mark were stuck with and depressed over, leading to C, their emotional Consequences.

You can probably guess the general nature of B, Connie and Mark's Irrational Beliefs *about* A, their grandchildless state. What "musts" and "shoulds" might they have held? What might their awfulizings and we-can't-stand-its have been? Did they feel inadequate as people? Did they put down their children? Let's work it out, A through F.

- **A.** *Activating Event, Adversity:* No grandchildren and no prospect of any.
- **B.** *Self-defeating Beliefs:* We NEED TO have grandchildren, like everybody else, if we are to be happy people. It's *awful* that we don't have grandchildren. Especially when everybody else shows us pictures of their grandchildren or talks about them, and we feel like *nothings*.
- **C.** *Consequences, unhealthful negative reactions:* Depression, embarrassment, (unsuccessful) attempts to lay guilt trips on their children.
- **D.** *Disputing:* Is it really true that we NEED grandchildren in order to be happy people? Where will our Belief that "we *can't stand* not having grandchildren" get us? How does it make us *inadequate people,* just because our children have no children?
- **E.** *Effective New Thinking:* We'd probably enjoy having grandchildren, and maybe we would be happier, but there is no evidence that we HAVE TO have grandchildren. We have two very fine and loving children that we're proud of—and that's a lot more than we can say of some of our friends who have grandchildren! While it's against our hopes, and disappointing, that we don't have grandchildren, it's scarcely horrible and awful. It's completely illogical to say that our worth as human beings depends on whether we have grandchildren. We had better work hard at unconditionally accepting ourselves, our children, and our grandchildless state.
- **F.** *New Feelings:* Occasional wistfulness about not having grandchildren, some disappointment, but no depression, no resentment, no guilt-tripping.

Here are two examples of family-related problems, Meg's and John's. As you study these, see whether you can think of any additional arguments *against* the relevant Irrational Beliefs.

Meg's Self-Help Exercise

A. *Adversity:* Meg's son committed a well-publicized crime.

B. *Irrational Beliefs:* People will think it's all my fault! How can I stand showing my face when people know this?

C. *Undesirable Emotional Consequences:* Shame, embarrassment, isolation

D. *Disputing:* Where is it written that I'm responsible for his actions? Do I truly NEED people to think the "right" thing about me?

E. *Effective New Thinking:* My son's actions were tragic, but his own responsibility. I am a separate person. If some other people think ill of me, so be it.

F. *New Feeling:* Regret.

John's Self-Help Exercise

A. *Adversity:* John's daughter never calls and asked him not to call her more often than once a month. He's done a lot to help her.

B. *Irrational Beliefs:* After all I've done to help her, how can she hurt me this way?

C. *Undesirable Emotional Consequences:* Deep hurt, anguish

D. *Disputing:* Is it true that she has MUST NOT behave unfairly even though I've treated her well?

E. *Effective New Thinking:* She has free will and therefore can act wrongly. I wish our relationship were better but I can get along in life as-is. I'll be friendly and positive when we do talk.

F. *New Feeling:* Sadness, resolve to enjoy other parts of life.

Rational Coping Statements

As well as using the Self-Help Form, you can come up with what we call "rational coping statements." Study these statements and repeat them to yourself many times, until they sink into your head. For example, in one of the illustrations in the Self-Help Form above, John arrived at the Effective New Thinking, "My daughter has free will and therefore can act wrongly. I wish our relationship were better but I can get along in life as-is. I'll be friendly and positive when we do talk." You can reinforce this Effective New Thinking by saying it aloud, emphatically, again and again. It can also help you to write down or put on a tape-recorder several additional rational coping statements, such as these:

- People, including my daughter, do NOT HAVE TO behave fairly, no matter how well I've treated them.
- Even nice people like my daughter have the right to be neglectful and busy with their own lives. If they didn't, they wouldn't be *able* to act the way they do.
- The fact that my daughter doesn't call me may not mean anything personal about me.
- Maybe I did something wrong with my daughter and that is why she is neglecting me. If so, maybe I can find out what I did and correct it. If I can't fix it, tough! That's the way it is.
- I'm NOT a bad father, and certainly not a rotten person, even if I did something to turn her off. At most, I would be someone who makes mistakes.
- I dislike my daughter's treating me so neglectfully but I can accept her with her poor behavior. She's NOT a *bad person*, but merely a *person who's acting badly in this respect.*

If you keep going over these coping statements you are likely to give up your feelings of hurt and anguish about your neglectful son or daughter—or about anyone else you have helped over the years and who is now neglecting you.

In disputing your Irrational Beliefs and in constructing your rational coping statements about your family-related issues, you can also try one of REBT's emotive techniques. One of those emotive options is this: You can work out several rational coping statements, such as those just listed, and then repeat them to yourself many times *very* strongly and vehemently. You can do this to show yourself that they are correct and will work. You also do it to show yourself that if you practice these statements repeatedly and powerfully, they will override the Irrational Beliefs that you may still have about your neglectful offspring or about other people. Remember that REBT is highly emotive as well as cognitive and that it frequently uses evocative-expressive methods to supplement its disputing of Irrational Beliefs.

Thus, if you have a child who greatly neglects you and you feel angry, hurt, and anguished about this, you can use the following kind of powerful rational coping statements. Strong, repeated use of these statements can help minimize your disturbance about your offspring's neglect:

- Yes, she is neglecting me and I think that is unusual and unfair, especially when I have helped her in so many ways. So it's unusual! Why the devil MUST she act normally? So it's unfair! Why the hell MUST she be fair?
- I really don't like being treated this unfairly, so I don't like it. I can damn well lump it and not upset myself about it.
- If I really did something to turn her off, well, I did it. She might still tell me what I did to offend her, and I probably could correct it. But she doesn't HAVE TO let me know what I did. She doesn't HAVE TO tell me anything! She is what she is, and I'd better accept that grim fact. Too bad! Tough! But that's the way she is and I may never be able to change her.
- So, maybe I can't change her. If I can't, I can't. I can still determine, really determine, to be a happy individual, no matter what she does and how she neglects me!

To sum up: If you are really upset about how you are being treated by family members, your own family, or your mate's family, try these steps:

1. Find your "musts," "shoulds," or other demands that are creating your upset.
2. Dispute your Irrational Beliefs in your head or preferably on a Self-Help Form.
3. Come up with Effective New Thinking as a result of your disputing and put it into rational coping statements.
4. Repeat these statements many times, and very vigorously, until you really believe them and keep holding onto them.

Now that you have learned ways to stop making yourself needlessly miserable over family- and age-related Adversities, let's look a little closer at another common problem faced by older people. Money. Too little, usually. Once in a while, too much (and too many outstretched hands).

Finances

It would be nice to have plenty of money for your "senior years," should you choose to retire. Wouldn't it, though? Yes, it would be nice, but for most of us who aren't going to win the lottery, it would be *work*—that is, working hard to get it and keep it. This book is not about specific investment and savings plans, which may leave you enough money for your senior years so you won't be homeless. There are plenty of such plans around, and quite a few of them probably work quite well—when implemented. But there's the rub! People tend to do themselves in by bowing to short-range enjoyments and not planning for the future. Again, that's human nature. It is also human nature to learn from your mistakes, to plan wisely, and to act in your own long-term interests. You can cultivate attitudes that can help you save or wisely invest your money and not blow it. You can develop a philosophy that will allow you to prepare for the future without the specter of being a bag lady or bag gentleman someday.

Because of retirement and fixed income, money issues disproportionately affect older people. We'll look at retirement in more detail in a later chapter. It's no longer mandatory, and though the patterns of retirement are changing, so that some people retire several times from several careers, and others never retire, retirement is common and will remain so. In fact, it's becoming more common. Rather than face dead-end jobs, more people are retiring earlier. That often means a reduced, and fixed, income. Living within a budget without bankruptcy is the key monetary issue for many older people.

Additional money problems you might have with respect to aging include these: How much money should you save? How much should you spend? On what? And on *whom?* Yourself, or someone else? Your offspring, for instance? Yes, you have the issue of the disposition of your assets. Some of these issues can result in conflict and guilt. What erroneous Beliefs might cause conflict and guilt?

Angela and Ed are examples of people who did not indulge themselves in guilt. Having just retired, they sold the family home in suburban San Francisco and bought a loft downtown in the theater district. This news got a chilly reception from their daughter Grace in Houston. A brief note from her arrived, saying she could not visit at Christmas after all. Later, Angela and Ed learned from their other daughter that Grace was angry that they had "wasted" part of the inheritance she thought she "deserved." Ed and Angela didn't agree, nor did they think they absolutely NEEDED Grace's approval. They regretted she felt the way she did, but they remained guilt-free and excited about the opportunities living downtown offered. They did not tell themselves they were bad, selfish people for their actions, despite their daughter's displeasure and immature way of showing it.

The sensible rule of thumb for optimal living despite money problems is to first learn to *de*-disturb yourself about the practical problem—usually lack of money. Why? Because if you do, you will have more energy left over to do something productive about your money problems or to enjoy yourself as much as possible whatever your money situation.

What is more, suboptimal, irrational thinking *creates* many money problems. If you aim to apply the principles of REBT to money matters, what are the neurotic reasons why older—not to mention younger—people have money problems? The two most important are problems of self-rating and of low frustration tolerance. Let's take a look at these two emotional issues, to see how they help you create and keep financial problems. Again, we are not giving you financial or investment advice in this book. We *can* show you how to detect and counteract your own suboptimal, irrational thinking that can help create financial problems for you.

To Have Self-Worth, I MUST Keep Up With, and Ahead of, the Joneses

If you believe you MUST have a lot of money and the things it can buy, to be a worthwhile person, then your goose is cooked. Why? First, let's say you do have the amount of money you believe you MUST have. You may still feel anxious. Why? You could lose the money through bad deals or a downturn of the market. You could encounter others with much more money than you. What happens to your self-worth then? Back to wormhood it goes! What happens when you have *less* money than the Joneses? You feel down, worthless, envious. Your ego takes it on the chin. You may feel depressed. You put yourself down and accept yourself as a human only when and if you perform well financially and other people admire or approve of you. You damn yourself tremendously when you are not accomplished and popular. Self-rating, giving yourself worth based on your success and popularity, can create a long list of emotional and money problems.

Let's see how some of these ideas might particularly apply to older people. They often demand that they SHOULD have made more money during their lifetime and SHOULD have saved more. They believe that because they have been around for quite a few years, they therefore SHOULD be at least as well off financially as the other people they know. Furthermore, they SHOULD be respected by all and looked up to by their friends and relatives for the substantial, even very substantial, amount of money and property they have. If they are not doing as well as they SHOULD in any or all of these respects, they often beat themselves up mercilessly. They may do so even when they have a reasonable degree of financial security and are likely to keep it till they die. Many—probably millions—of older people in our culture are self-hating because of their money "difficulties." Yes, even when they have few actual difficulties.

Moreover, the tendency to equate your self-worth with your financial worth is a major reason that older people may have less money than they think they MUST. People often rate their human worth on how well they keep up with, and even decisively pass, the Joneses. Rather than save a decent amount of money for their older age, hordes of people spend too much money during their lifetime by "having" to—*deciding to*—keep up with the Joneses. To keep up with those fabled Joneses and the latest trends and fashions, what may you do? You buy expensive cars or live in expensive apartments to show your friends and neighbors how "good" you are. You go on expensive vacations; you buy the latest stereo equipment and computers; you have to have all the latest styles in clothes—again, to keep up with the Joneses. And ahead of the Joneses! You push your children to attend expensive private colleges and private high schools, when state colleges and public schools would do just as well. You jet to Vegas to live it up in the latest colossal hotel, when you'd probably enjoy a camping trip. As fun as Vegas? Probably not. But when tomorrow and tomorrow and tomorrow *do* arrive, and you are broke, you may wish you *had* camped out *then,* so that you weren't involuntarily (and homelessly) camping out *now.*

The $30K Pickup

Speaking of Las Vegas, Jon's wife, Kathy, referred him for therapy because of a problem with gambling. By the midpoint of our first interview, I (Emmett Velten) could see that Jon didn't really have a gambling problem. His gambling wasn't compulsive, and very little of his and Kathy's income went to gambling. He had an overspending problem. In just the last few months, he had gone deep-sea fishing with friends he called "big shots," and had taken two trips to Vegas (with Kathy). He'd then bought a $30,000 pickup truck and a $7,000 laptop computer that he used infrequently. He and Kathy were members of the poshest country club in town, lived in the highest class gated community, the whole nine yards. You might be thinking, well, if they have that kind of money, more power to them. Let them enjoy it. But they didn't have that kind of money. They were in very serious debt because of Jon's overspending. He agreed that he was overdoing it, but he said he didn't seem able to stop.

I zeroed in on the $30,000 pickup truck. Kathy had told me over the phone that Jon would not use the truck at work (he was a contractor) for fear of getting a dent in it or getting it dirty. He would drive it to and from work, but at work he used another vehicle. He wouldn't let her or their son drive the truck, again for fear it would get marred. Jon agreed that the truck was a purchase they didn't really need, as he put it, "in the sense of being able to use it." So, I asked him what he had told himself to get himself to buy the truck or to justify his buying it.

"Oh, I guess I just feel I have to keep up with the Joneses," Jon explained, immediately stating the likely "must."

"And why MUST you keep up with the Joneses?"

After some discussion, Jon said, "I feel depressed if I don't."

"Because you're telling yourself *what* about not keeping up with the Joneses, for instance, by buying the 30K pickup truck?"

"Nothing," Jon replied.

After discussion, Jon said he still didn't think he was telling himself anything to depress himself. I asked him if he would try one of REBT's imagery methods, and he agreed.

"Close your eyes, and imagine in the scene I'm going to describe, that you *don't* own the 30K truck. Imagine you're at a construction site. Your friend, Randy, owns that truck, and he stops by the construction site for some reason. Yours is a battered, weather-beaten, older truck. Right? And the two trucks are parked side by side. It's lunch, and all the guys are admiring Randy's truck. Do you have that image in mind?"

Jon assented.

"What comes up for you as you see that image? How do you feel inside?"

After a pause, he said, "Embarrassed. Ashamed. I guess, depressed."

"And what are the thoughts that go along with those feelings?"

After a longer pause, he said, "Randy's better than I am."

"According to your Belief System, your B.S.! You *define* your worth as a human being, based on what you own, what you have. That kind of Belief System can end up bankrupting you."

In therapy, Jon worked to learn unconditional self-acceptance. He used real-life disputing, for instance, by talking with a couple of his "big shot" friends and canceling his participation in a lavish, upcoming fishing expedition. "I can't afford it" was his key homework phrase. When first we practiced in session his making that phone call, Jon could barely get the words out. Before long, though, he could say those words smoothly. He canceled other planned, and costly trips, including one to Las Vegas. When I pointed out that he could go gamble if he wanted at one of the casinos on Indian reservations near Tucson, he said he'd pass. He'd never had any real interest in gambling. What happened to the pristine pickup? The last I heard, Jon was—with regret—selling it. It looked as if he'd get blue book value on it, since it had scarcely been touched by human hand!

If you wish, later in life, that you'd saved earlier, that's fine. Wishing will give you feelings of regret and motivate you to do something about your lack of savings, such as beginning to save now. If you have a reduced income due to retirement, you may not be able to save much. You may not want to. Regretting your past actions and inactions is fine, too, even if it really is too late to do much if anything to correct that particular situation. Regretting your sins of omission and commission from the past can still help you focus on making the most of the present. How so? By seeing that if you focus on rational living right now, then tomorrow you will have less reason to regret what you did and did not do today!

As long as you do not turn wishes into demands, you'll be OK. For if you inwardly demand that you SHOULD have saved more money years ago, you may disturb and depress yourself. Wishing you had done something differently in the past, and regretting you did not do otherwise, does not mean you made a mistake. You may simply be looking back with the usual wisdom of hindsight. If you arrive at older age with less money than you would have had if you had saved rigorously all those years, you may suffer some deprivations and frustrations because of your choice to spend rather than save. Perhaps you can no longer get even a short-term loan because of lack of collateral. Does that mean you victimized yourself in the past? Not necessarily. Regrets don't equal mistakes, and neither regrets nor mistakes depress us. Our Irrational Beliefs do that.

I Want It. Therefore, I NEED It!

The first Irrational Belief that can cause you money problems is to assume that your self-worth equals your money, possessions, and lifestyle. We discussed that in the section above about Jon and his $30,000 pickup truck. But there is another key Irrational Belief that can give you money problems. It applies particularly to older people who have considerably less money than they could have had if they had handled their affairs more wisely. That emotional problem is abysmally low frustration tolerance (LFT). It stems from the third "must," namely, "I MUST have what I want, when I want it." Translated into the financial arena, it's the philosophy of short-range pleasure-seeking. It's loss of a future perspective. It's the refusal—because it's "too hard"—to save a comparatively small percentage of your income even though you know it can make a very appreciable difference by your old age.

Particularly in our own product-promoting society, you and practically everyone else are continually urged to buy cars, appliances, clothing, gourmet food, and a hundred other things you don't really need. You may often foolishly follow these urgings. You want these items, because you have a natural inclination for them. And advertising steadily prods you to acquire them. That's OK. Business people with services and products to sell have a right to try to make a living. You *could* just toss all those mail order catalogs in the trash. You *could* prepare meals at home. You *could* save money. No one forces you to buy what you want. Just you.

You convince yourself that you absolutely NEED what you want, even though you don't. You can comfortably live without it, but you make many purchases that you can ill afford. Because you absolutely MUST have, or think you MUST have, what is tantalizingly brought to your attention, what happens? You buy many items, or at least many more expensive items, than will fit within your budget, especially when you can do so on credit. Advertisers point out how "necessary" many unnecessary items are. Let's not blame them, for they are only using your desires to try to make a sale. *You're* escalating your desires into dire needs and selling *yourself* on them.

This brings us to the Thirteenth Rule for Optimal Living:

Rule #13: Live for Now *and* for the Future

Well-adjusted people tend to seek both the pleasures of the moment and those of the future and do not often ask for future pain to get present gain. They seek happiness and avoid pain, but they assume they will probably live for quite a few years and that they had better think of both today and tomorrow, and not obsess themselves with immediate gratification.

In Charmaine's Shoes

Charmaine explained that she had a closet full of clothes of the latest styles, going back several years. Shoes, too. Her friends referred to it as the Imelda Marcos room. Unlike Mrs. Marcos, Charmaine had a large debt and no savings. She sought therapy to figure out why she spent so lavishly on wearing apparel. "Didn't I get enough love as a child?" she asked.

I (Emmett Velten) explained the basics of the ABC model and how it focuses on the here and now, not the past. Charmaine, who was the director of a large agency, agreed that this really fit better with her style.

"But," I said, "let's assume the worst. Your parents didn't love you at all. Your stepsisters got everything, and all you got were switches and ashes and rags like Cinderella. OK? If that happened, that could be where you originally 'got' your strong preference to dress in the latest styles and look like a million dollars. However that may be, what do you tell yourself *now*, when you see an outfit that would look great on you, to get yourself to buy it? What do you tell yourself, even though you've maxed out many of your credit cards?"

"I want it," Charmaine replied with no hesitation.

"Wanting is fine. If you just wanted, you wouldn't be spending yourself into the poorhouse. You'd be saying, 'I want it, but it's too expensive. Too bad, but that's the way it goes.' You'd feel disappointed, but you'd go on your way without getting out the plastic. In fact, over time you'd build up the automatic habit of knowing that you can't afford such things, and you wouldn't even waste time and energy tantalizing yourself and disappointing yourself by window-shopping. So, you may be telling yourself something more than just 'I want it.' 'I want it,' . . . and . . . what? Is there a 'must' in there?"

"I've GOT TO have it! I NEED it for some special occasion!"

"That's right! A *true* need would be something required to stay alive.

Food, water, oxygen, that sort of thing. Not designer workout clothes and track shoes. You may tell yourself you need that outfit, but it's not true. You don't. And you don't need the additional debt."

One of the methods Charmaine and I used to help her learn solidly that a want is not a need, was "cue exposure." In it, the person with the cravings, in Charmaine's case, for gorgeous new items of clothing, goes to where those items are located. She window shops; she tries on outfits; she touches them, holds them, looks at them in the mirror. She builds her cravings up. But she doesn't buy anything. She disputes the "I've GOT TO have it" Irrational Beliefs as they come up. In their place, she emphatically tells herself, "I'd LIKE to have it, but I don't NEED to have what I want, and I cannot afford it."

A rule of thumb in these cue exposure sessions is to stick with each session until your initial level of craving has dropped by about 50 percent. You can use a mental measuring device often used in psychology—SUDS. SUDS stands for "subjective units of discomfort scale." It's like a thermometer, with 100 being the top of scale. One hundred would be the maximum in craving you could possibly have. Zero would represent a complete absence of craving *while in the presence of whatever it is you've been driving yourself crazy for*. If your lunch hour is only 30 minutes, you may not have sufficient time. Plan and carry out your cue exposure sessions as you would a minor military operation!

Charmaine, for instance, had been dying for an elegant, dressy raincoat temporarily located at Neiman-Marcus, but "calling my name." She had a serviceable raincoat that was fine on rainy San Francisco evenings for anything from the opera to jazz clubs. So, she didn't even bother with rationalizations about "needing" the one at Neiman-Marcus. No, she NEEDED it, she told herself, because it was just so gorgeous. Charmaine had "cruised" the coat several times during her lunch hour, pretending to be mildly interested in a couple of neighboring coats, but practically salivating to try on the object of her affections. She did not try it on, though, because she knew "My fate would be sealed!" In terms of SUDS, Charmaine rated that moment as 90. By the mid-point in only her third cue-exposure session at the store with the coat, her SUDS rating had fallen to about 20.

On her lunch hour, Charmaine did additional therapy homework by cruising Saks, Nordstrom's, and several boutiques that made everything else look like outlet malls. In each of these "exposure" *non*-shopping trips, Charmaine rated, using SUDS, how agonizing her cravings were.

For Charmaine, the predicted results came about within five exposure sessions. The cravings to buy the new items of clothing fell to a very mild level, far below the "I can't stand it" level Charmaine felt at first.

"It would be nice to have," Charmaine commented about the raincoat, "but it's not that big a deal. I can definitely take it or leave it. I can't afford it and don't need it, so it's a waste of time even to think about it." She reported that at times she felt bored or even slightly repelled by some of the gorgeous items she used to drool over and often purchase.

You may be a short-range instead of a long-range pleasure-seeker. You spend it now and you don't have it later. You either get yourself into continual debt or barely manage to get through financially even though you and your family have a better than average income. To make things worse, you may then whine about how *awful* deprivation is—*real* deprivation! You may frequently berate yourself for overspending. You may call yourself an "utter fool" instead of much more accurately designating yourself as a person who has acted foolishly this time, but not all the time. You will remain a person who can well use his or her constructivist tendency to act better next time. So you overspend, damn yourself for doing so, and convince yourself that this is your "nature" and that there is no way in which you can change it.

For Reasons Beyond Our Control

For either or both of two emotional reasons you could reach your older years with considerably less money than you might have had. The emotional reasons are (1) self-rating that leads to ego-related spending (keeping up with the Joneses), and (2) low frustration tolerance that leads to *short*-range pleasure-seeking and long-term deprivation. However, even without either of these emotional handicaps, you may have financial problems for a variety of practical reasons. You may have had a restricted income for much of your life. You may have had unusual financial requirements, such as those brought on by raising a family or putting yourself through school. You may have suffered from unfortunate conditions over which you had little or no control. These could include corporate downsizing, a recession, or increased taxes. A hurricane, earthquake, or flood could have knocked your local economy for a loop, leading to your going out of business.

For various reasons, then, your income in your older age may be limited—and even very limited. But again, the two emotional bugaboos that plague most people much of the time may rear their ugly heads. First, you may blame yourself and convince yourself that, in spite of poor social and economic conditions, you SHOULD have been wise enough to make more money and to save more of it. Since you haven't done what you unquestionably SHOULD have done, what does that make you? An *incompetent and worthless person.*

So you may have ego or self-rating problems, even when your poor finances are largely the result of conditions that were beyond your control.

Second, you also may have low frustration tolerance or discomfort disturbance *about* your financial limitations, even when they are almost inevitable and you could have done little to ward them off. You may be, especially in your older age, in tight financial circumstances, but still pay the rent, eat regularly, clothe yourself suitably, and have some money left over for recreation. You may insist, however, that because others have better finances than you and are not afflicted with some of your deprivations, you absolutely SHOULD have more resources than you do have. You may insist that your monetary limitations are *awful,* that you *can't stand* being deprived. You may then conclude that the world is a *horrible place* for not taking care of you better or for being harder than it SHOULD be. Even though you are getting by without any great financial discomfort, you may whine and scream that you absolutely SHOULD NOT be frustrated as much as you are. Thereby you make yourself resentful and horrified, rather than rationally disappointed, about your meager means.

Becky and Tom had just retired and lived in an attractive mobile home park. It was near a public swimming pool, golf course, and tennis courts, all of which Tom and Becky enjoyed. Their Social Security and small pensions easily covered living expenses, with some left over for fun and some tours in chartered buses with their church group. Their health was fine for their age. Yet, they felt unhappy, even depressed. They could remember having had the same feelings, less intensely, from time to time in the past. Now, however, their feelings of unhappiness were very strong and seemed to be continuous.

"Could it be boredom? Because we just retired?" they asked when they consulted me (Emmett Velten).

As we talked over their current circumstances, and got some examples of when the depressed feelings were strongest, I explained the ABC model. We began to look for a clear-cut Adversity. A juicy one, that seemed to propel both Becky and Tom into despair, was their neighbors' state-of-the-art, "blazing" personal computer. Graciously, the neighbors, another retired couple, had shown their computer to Tom and Becky, who explained to me that their computer was practically ready for the Smithsonian, that it operated at a snail's pace, and that its modem was badly outdated. Yes, they could surf the Internet, but only very, very slowly. Unfortunately, they had to live on a strict budget, which they were indeed doing, though they weren't used to it. They hadn't expected retirement to be like this. Back in their working days, they had had much more discretionary income. But no longer. What were Becky and Tom's Irrational Beliefs, which directly produced their depressed feelings?

Tom's "must" was "I SHOULD have made more money in life so that we could buy things like a new computer." As a result of this Irrational Belief, Tom concluded that he was a *failure in life, worthless as a person.* Becky's "must" was different. She believed, "It's *terrible* to have to do without these nice things. We SHOULD be able to have them, like we used to." As a result of her Irrational Belief, Becky, too, felt depressed, but it was a self-pitying depression rather than a self-downing depression, like her husband's.

Tom and Becky enjoyed a higher standard of living than the huge majority of the world's population. They were hardly on the streets of Calcutta. What made them miserable was not their standard of living. It was not their dislike of having to live with reduced income. It was their MUSTurbation about their reduced circumstances that left them "down in the dumps."

How To Smell More Roses and Smell Them Better

It isn't a question of making a mistake in buying the things you want. Your wants are your wants. The fact is that you usually enjoy the things you spend your money on. When you have few savings in old age, you may then wish you were richer, but it's not clear, just because you feel regretful then, that you have ever made a mistake. You enjoyed it while you had it. If you *did* make a mistake, then so you did.

The real question is how to balance the present against the future. It is rational to give *some* weight to the here and now, and to discount the future a little because of its greater uncertainty. We might die in the next 24 hours, and some of us will! Fortunately, most of us won't. We will live a long time. How do you try for the optimal balance between spending in the present and saving for the future? Again, it is beyond the scope of this book to offer financial planning. You may want to consult with a pro in that field. At the very least, consult resources in your library and over the Internet. Look at your current income and expenses. Look at how older, perhaps retired people live, and pick out some who have enough to meet their real needs, plus some creature comforts. Like Tom and Becky, in the example above. How much does it cost them to live the way they live? Using the advice of your financial planner or other reputable resources, you likely will be told what everyone already knows. If you steadily save a small percentage of your income over the years, it can make a big difference in old age. Develop your plan and stick with it. It will be easier for you to stick to your plan if you:

- Overcome low frustration tolerance, that is, the Irrational Belief that you *can't stand* frustration, unfairness, deprivation, delay, knowing that others have it easier than you, and lack of certainty.
- Stop rating your worth as a human being, whether in comparison to some absolute standard or to those ever-present Joneses.

What do you build in the place of low frustration tolerance and self-rating? You develop and strengthen Rational Beliefs, namely:

- I'd LIKE to have it easy, but I *can stand* frustration, delay, doing without, unfairness, and lack of guarantees.
- I'd LIKE to do very well financially, but if I don't, I don't. It is not written into the U.S. Constitution that I MUST do well financially in order to feel OK about myself. I will fully accept and value myself no matter what the values of my assets.

As you get older, you will most likely become more efficient at attaining pleasure and fulfillment. When you are young, you have often not developed the capacity for savoring and contemplating. So your pleasures are often snatched at hungrily, and then are gone without really satisfying. When you are older, your capacity to stop and smell the roses, to extract deep and leisurely gratification from experiences, will be greater. Therefore, a dollar saved today will, if you survive, give you more kicks later than a dollar spent today. It will have earned interest in the meantime, too!

Well, if what we have been saying is even partially true for you, the solution to many of your so-called financial problems is really the solution to your emotional problems about money. First, work on your ego or self-rating, and make sure that you do not put yourself down even if your present financial straits are largely the result of your past overspending and undersaving. Then train yourself to accept yourself even if all the Joneses of the world are far ahead of you. So now you know this, but perhaps in the past you neglected to look at it. You bought too many expensive things; or you bought the friendship of other people by spending a lot of money on them. All right, so you did. So you acted, in regard to money, downright foolishly. That never makes you a zero, a crumb, or a worm. Just a fallible human being who somewhat carelessly overspent and who in theory could have known and done better, but didn't. Too bad. You missed your chance to have a more financially secure older age. You were often unwise, sometimes a compulsive spender. Never beat yourself up or damn yourself for that incorrect behavior. Even now, you may still have time to learn from it and correct it. Whether you do or not, you are never a rotten person for your rotten financial behavior. Get that idea solidly into your head, give yourself unconditional self-acceptance (USA) in spite of your financial foolishness. Give yourself unconditional self-acceptance even if the Joneses are preening about being ahead of you. Do this, and you will eliminate many of your serious problems with money. You will also be able to start saving. For, as usual, the basic problem is rating yourself, your essence, your being. With USA you can conclusively lick that problem—and the many related ones that go with it.

Second, work on your frustration tolerance. Yes, you did not really NEED many of the expensive goods and services that you thought you needed as you were overspending and undersaving. You thought you couldn't live without them—but you were wrong. Well, it's too late to correct that now. If your present financial situation is a tight one and if you can barely afford the necessities of life, you still don't HAVE TO have what you want. Financial deprivation won't kill you. However, disturbing yourself extremely about your deprivations *may* help knock you off before your time. How? Excessive worry and anger can help weaken your immune system and other physical resources. Worrying and anger won't help. Except maybe to help give you needless pain, ailments, and disease. So you're now deprived and may be, financially, for the rest of your life. That's bad. That's rough. But not *awful, terrible,* or *horrible.* You can stand it, even though you will never like it. You can cut down your expenses, skimp, and even save a little. If you refuse to whine about how bad things are and how they absolutely SHOULD NOT be that bad, you'll have the inventiveness and creativity to figure out how to do more with less income. Living without some of the things you really want, and that you cannot now afford, is hard. Wailing about your monetary limitations is still harder—and won't decrease your deprivations. Plot and scheme financially and do the best you can with your meager income. By all means increase it if you can. But if you can't, you can't. Gracefully accept what you can't change. If you do, then you'll be in a much better position to get more enjoyment from life and possibly to reduce some of your monetary limitations.

If you want to pursue the REBT approach to money problems further, get the book by Albert Ellis and Patricia Hunter, *Why Am I Always Broke? How To Be Sane About Money*. This book discusses in depth the two emotional problems that actually encourage—indeed often push—people to have financial problems, and it has a chapter on money management and aging.

9

I Didn't Set the World on Fire

No experiment is ever a complete failure—it can always serve as a negative example.

The Futility Factor

Our greatest limitation as humans is a finite lifespan. We can *say* "It's never too late," but someday it *is*. We can *say* "There's always tomorrow," but then there *isn't*. The older we get, the less we can tell ourselves that someday we *will* do the great things we thought about doing. We just may not write the Great American Novel, save the world, become a star of stage and screen, or achieve a completely satisfactory long-term relationship. Someday you may look back and realize that you did not set the world on fire, and now you're almost out of matches and the wind is still blowing very hard! How do you deal with those disappointments?

For example, at A, let's say you realize you've not achieved all you hoped you would in your work or your love life. Do you depress yourself or make yourself excuse-ridden and defensive through your evaluative Beliefs at B? Or do you constructively accept the disappointments, as well as yourself (for your part in those disappointments)? Do you try to learn from your mistakes and then move on? Those are your choices.

Let's think about your tendency to put yourself down for not having done what you think you SHOULD have done in life and what you may now see as no longer likely or even possible—due to too much human fallibility and too little time. Your many "hopeless" achievements can include:

- never having found true love, career success, or financial security
- never having had children
- never having really used your talents and potential
- never having traveled.

Type A Personality or Desirelessness?

You have probably heard about the Type A personality. Such people are hard driving and often make themselves hostile, defensive, and depressed when they don't achieve what they believe they MUST. "Having" a Type A personality, which means having the "need" for achievement instead of the preference for achievement, has been implicated in everything from heart attacks to ulcers to writer's block. *Desires* for achievement, however, whether applied to work, love, leisure, or hobbies, cannot cause emotional disturbance, even if you don't achieve what you wanted. Unfulfilled desires cause disappointment and regret—if you hold Rational Beliefs, preferences, about those unfulfilled desires. It's the "must" that makes you miserable. *Demands* for achievement characterize the Type A personality. *Desires* for achievement will motivate you to keep striving for what you want. They can motivate you to accept yourself and get on with life even if you fail to achieve what you wanted.

Our culture is changing and there are reactions against not just the Type A personality, but also against the *preference* for achievement. As so often happens with people, once we determine that, say, our political viewpoint is incorrect, we go to the opposite extreme. Once we decide we are eating the wrong foods, we go to the opposite extreme of compulsively eating right. This has happened with some people in their reactions against the achievement orientation. In some circles, anyone who *likes* to work hard may get diagnosed as a workaholic! The reaction against the Type A personality's *demands* for achievement, as well as against rational preferences for achievement, may have stimulated the boom in conversions to "eastern" religions in North America and Europe. Desirelessness is often their spiritual goal. As this boom grows, it will be interesting to see whether people take it to the extreme.

Converts may end up striving to achieve *more* desirelessness than their neighbors, those bums. Back to the NEED for achievement! They may become Type A's in the pursuit of desirelessness.

Disappointments are a normal part of life, unless you are extremely lucky or else have no desires. Your children are just one of many possible disappointments living to an older age can bring. If you did not have children and wish you had (nearly one out of five baby boomers have not become parents), or did have them and wish you hadn't, you may feel some sadness about that. That is quite rational. You may not have achieved—so far—the right relationship for you. About that, you may feel disappointed and regretful. That's rational, too. You are not supposed to feel good about disappointments.

Depression and despair, however, are a quite different matter from disappointment. Maybe you never completed that Great American Novel you worked on for all those years. Maybe you can see that you are not going to succeed professionally the way you had aspired to do. Maybe you never found love, never traveled, never—whatever it was. Resolving these issues is sometimes called a mid-life crisis. An optimal mid-life crisis is to come to terms with the mediocrity of some part, or even many parts, of your life. Then, you move on. We will show you who have had big disappointments how to cope with them and then to move on. How to feel OK about yourself even though you fell short of what you had hoped you would achieve. How not to fill yourself with despair. How to stop seeing your life as a straight line, and begin to realize these are non-linear times. Longer life and better health open up all kinds of new possibilities for you.

A Million Laughs

After she'd retired, Carol saw on HBO a woman she'd seen perform many years earlier as a stand-up comic at a local comedy club. Known for her wit, Carol had long wanted to give comedy a try. She felt very depressed, thinking, "I'm too old to start now" and "If I were going to do anything, I SHOULD have started years ago."

Demands for achievements, like Carol's, as a way to acquire self worth, lead to a dire dread of making mistakes. They lead to fear of trying new things and taking risks. This can especially happen with older people. Why? Because older people are "supposed" to be mature (fully formed) and never, ever "old fools." The more you MUST have self-worth based on achievement, the less chance you have for happiness and, often, the less chance you have for achievements. You will feel better and do better if you view yourself as a fallible work in progress and focus on the benefits and enjoyments of *doing*, not only doing well.

Carol learned to dispute the Irrational Belief (IB) that her worth equaled her lack of achievements in comedy. She learned to dispute the IB that she SHOULD have used her talents more fully and was now a slob because she had not. She learned to dispute the idea that having "failed" to become a comic, as well as in other ways, she now couldn't be happy *at all* in life. Having accepted herself and the reality that she was not a stand-up comic, when perhaps she could have been, Carol's depression lifted. She began to think it *could* be fun to try comedy. She read books, she took a junior college class in humor. She met several times with a local rabbi who did some charity work as a comic.

The demand for achievement by the time you have reached your older years is hardly confined to people who have not accomplished anything. Many people view themselves as nonachievers when, in fact, they have had some unusual accomplishments but have not done anything that in their eyes is "outstanding." Like Benjamin. By the time he retired from his law practice at the age of 70, Benjamin was quite accomplished in the eyes of the world. He had built from scratch a leading law firm, which he started as a one-person practice. He had won many important cases. He was the president of the local Unitarian Church. He had devoted himself to his wife and had cared for her for several years before she died of cancer. He had seen all three of their children, two sons and a daughter, through law school, and now they were successfully carrying on his firm. He had written an outstanding textbook and was a revered teacher at a law school where he had taught for 30 years. Certainly, not a bad record; and one that everyone said Benjamin should be very proud of.

But he wasn't. He had dismally failed, in his own eyes, to do anything that he considered *outstanding*—such as be a judge of the Supreme Court in his state. Or, to be *truly* outstanding, to be appointed to the Supreme Court of the United States! At best, he said, he had been appointed to some minor judgeships that he considered practically an insult, and he had held them for only a short while. The real thing, his prime goal in life, he had missed; and his many other accomplishments, in the face of this loss, hardly counted.

Benjamin quickly grasped the principles of REBT and used them very successfully in his life. When one of his sons was arrested for drunken driving, Benjamin first felt exceptionally ashamed at his own failure to raise his son so that no delinquency of this kind occurred. He then used REBT to convince himself that, first, he was not entirely responsible for his son's behavior, and second, that even if he were partly responsible for it, that didn't make him a bad father and a bad person. Several people did severely criticize Benjamin when his son got arrested, but he was able to realize that their vilifying him for what his son had done was unjustified. He realized that no matter what they thought about him, he was able to take their criticism and not savagely berate himself because of it.

Benjamin still held to the Irrational Beliefs, "I really haven't done anything outstandingly well and therefore I'm sort of okay but I am not truly a worthwhile, thoroughly respected individual. I'm not bad but neither am I very good—as I definitely should be." He saw that he had made some serious political mistakes that had kept him from any kind of good judgeship, and he refused to forgive himself for making these "idiotic blunders." He disputed his Irrational Beliefs, "I SHOULD have spent much more of my time and energy pursuing a Supreme Court judgeship. I actually wasted a good part of my life pursuing other, infinitely lesser goals. I let the one life I'll ever have largely go down the drain. I can never really forgive myself for that." When he disputed those IBs, Benjamin came up with the same right answers. But they didn't stick. He really did not believe them.

I (Albert Ellis) finally helped Benjamin to use the emotive technique of reverse role-playing. We often use role-playing in REBT, to show people how to be assertive with difficult people, how to respond in a job interview, and how to do other things that they find trouble doing. These individuals play themselves and one of their friends or relatives plays the difficult person or the job interviewer. Doing this gives them practice in learning how to play the kind of a role they want to play, and it gives them more chance for good results. Such role-playing is often helpful, since a person can practice prior to the actual situation, and therefore do better when the real encounter or interview occurs.

The Best Defense Against Irrational Beliefs Is a Good Offense

Role-playing has many variations. The variation Benjamin thought would work for him requires two players and is called rational role reversal. One player's role is to express and stick to Irrational Beliefs. In this case, that player—the prosecutor—stuck to Benjamin's Irrational Beliefs. They were:

- I SHOULD be outstanding.
- I SHOULD have been appointed to the Supreme Court.
- It's *awful* and *intolerable* that I'm not outstanding and that I wasn't appointed to the Supreme Court.
- I'm really *a failure as a person* because I didn't achieve in life what I SHOULD have.

The prosecutor also expresses and sticks to additional distorted and self-defeating thoughts—again, Benjamin's—derived or inferred *from* core Irrational Beliefs. Among Benjamin's self-defeating inferences were such automatic negative thoughts as these:

- Nothing I do is right.
- I failed at everything.
- All I'll ever do is make mistakes.
- I'm a phony as an attorney and as a person.
- Everyone can see that I'm a failure.
- The only reason I have succeeded at some things is that people like my voice.
- I feel so depressed—that proves I failed, doesn't it?
- When my lawyer friends mention something about the Supreme Court, they are trying to rub it in.

The second player's role—defendant—is to argue fiercely against those same Irrational Beliefs and self-defeating thoughts. As you might guess, Benjamin needed no additional practice in irrational thinking. He had been practicing for years. Therefore, Benjamin's job in rational role reversal was to play the defendant—instead of his usual role prosecuting himself! Benjamin thought it would do him more good if he got a friend of his, Paul, to help him with this therapy homework, rather than do it in session with me. Since Paul was also a capable attorney and knew many of the details of Benjamin's life, he was well suited to play the role of Benjamin, the prosecutor.

   Before the first of the Great Debates, Benjamin and I first prepared a list of his Irrational Beliefs and other automatic negative thoughts, already listed above. Then we prepared a set of ways he could dispute and argue against his own Irrational Beliefs and automatic negative thoughts. Here were the guidelines Benjamin, the defendant, was to use in the Great Debate against Benjamin, the prosecutor (played by Paul):

- Does this Belief or thought help me or hurt me?
- If it hurts me, what Belief or thought might help me?
- Is this Belief or thought consistent with facts? Is there evidence supporting it?
- What alternative, effective Rational Beliefs or thoughts fit with the actual, factual evidence?
- Is this Belief or thought logical?
- If not, what Belief or thought would make more sense logically?

Naturally, in his role as the defendant, Benjamin would do everything he could to persuade Paul, the prosecutor, to give up the Irrational Beliefs and automatic negative thoughts.

The two debates Benjamin and Paul held had elements of a formal debate and a criminal trial, with Benjamin as the defendant and Paul as the wicked prosecuting attorney. The prosecutor, Paul, led off with a stinging indictment of Benjamin, appealing to Benjamin's own Irrational Beliefs. Paul went into damning detail about how Benjamin had failed to be outstanding in the field and therefore was an inadequate person, a failure in life, and deserved to suffer. Paul said Benjamin had really not accomplished anything outstanding in life, and had failed to become what he most wanted to become, a Supreme Court judge, and that therefore he was a worthless individual.

Paul did an excellent job of holding to Benjamin's own Irrational Beliefs. Benjamin would defend himself by trying to prove that he really had done some fine things in life even if he had not become a Supreme Court judge. "Besides," Benjamin thundered on a couple of occasions, "Where is the law that states that I'm a bad, worthless person if I didn't set the world on fire?"

As prosecutor, Paul also warmed to his task. When Paul's turn to reply came, he vehemently upheld Benjamin's own drastically negative view of his worth, and refused to give way. "Rot!" Paul would exclaim. "You're making up silly excuses! You're really an nonentity—a worthless pretender. A phony! You're guilty! You're a failure. And you know you are," the prosecutor accused.

As he later recounted the "trial," Benjamin told me he found his heart beating faster and he was starting to sweat as he put everything he could into finding loopholes and errors in the prosecutor's arguments. He really had to work to convince the jury that he could accept himself, even if he had failed to achieve greatly in life. The prosecutor always held his ground and refused to budge from the accusation that Benjamin was guilty and deserved no mercy.

These mock trials gave Benjamin some fine practice in strongly disputing his Irrational Beliefs. After several such debates with his friend, Benjamin's arguments *against* his own self-defeating view became more convincing. His Rational Beliefs felt much stronger. He was able to see that he had done some foolish things in going after the judgeship he wanted but that his worth as a human was not involved in these miscalculated acts. They did not prove him to be a worthless zero.

Largely as a result of these rational role reversal debates, Benjamin finally acknowledged that he could give himself unconditional self-acceptance (USA). He could do so even though he *had* acted quite foolishly in one of the most important goals of his life.

You too can use this REBT thinking-feeling method if you have an Irrational Belief about not doing something well or well enough during your lifetime, and if you keep flaying yourself for this lapse. Take your Irrational Beliefs in this respect and present them clearly to a friend or relative until he or she fully understands how you are blaming yourself and is well conversant with your irrationality. You might write out a list of your Irrational Beliefs for use by the "prosecutor."

Spend time preparing your defense. Remember, the best defense is a good offense. Go for the jugular. Think of every way you can to show how the Irrational Beliefs being used against you by the prosecutor don't hold water. Then let the other person, the prosecuting attorney, stick very strongly, very firmly, to your set of Irrational Beliefs, while you try to talk him or her out of them. Let your role-playing friend persist in stubbornly holding your irrational views, while you persist in arguing against them. If you get enough practice in doing this, you will tend to see how ridiculous your Irrational Beliefs are and how you can attack them when your role-playing friend is no longer present. Try this, if you will, with several different friends. Let them all stoutly maintain your irrationalities, and then do your best to talk them out of these self-defeating Beliefs. After doing this for a while, you may feel surprised at how *un*convinced you become of your own deadly ideas.

Once you stop putting yourself down for lack of sterling accomplishments, you can adopt a more helpful attitude about yourself. That new attitude can include the idea that, rather than being finished products, people of all ages are continually growing and developing. That attitude can help you continue to create and grow throughout your life, reaching new levels of wisdom, fun, and adventure.

Many people famous for their achievements are famous only for what they did later in life. There are, of course, exceptions like Judy Garland, Bobby Fischer, Mozart and Mendelssohn, who were child prodigies. An actor familiar to most readers from *Casablanca* is Sydney Greenstreet, who made his first movie, *The Maltese Falcon*, at 61. There are many other striking examples of this. In particular, there are many cases of "false starts," people whose early efforts are not of enduring importance and whose fame stems from what they did later. An example is George Bernard Shaw, who started out as a novelist. No one reads his novels today—hardly anyone ever did. People do read his plays, which came later. Gandhi and Mother Teresa changed careers in middle age and became world famous. Julius Caesar spent much of his life as a back room politician in Rome who held wild parties. He once cursed himself because, at the age when Alexander the Great had conquered the world, he had accomplished nothing of importance. His political enemies schemed to get rid of him and got him made military commander in Gaul—modern France. Gaul was the graveyard of many Roman generals, along with their reputations. Caesar, however, was successful as a general, and he went on to lead Rome. Dwight Eisenhower was *last* in his graduating class at West Point, yet he went on to command allied forces in World War II and to become President of the United States. History has many noteworthy people of whom it can be said, "If they had died before reaching the age of 40 (or 50, or 60), they would not rate a footnote." So, those who do set the world on fire sometimes do so later in life. Naturally, we are not arguing that you HAVE TO do something spectacular late in life. But your life isn't over yet.

This is only one aspect of a general problem. Namely, you sometimes don't really appreciate what you are good at, or what is good about what you do. With increasing age, it becomes more likely that you will discover where you can make a contribution.

There are some activities where a late start that results in outstanding achievement is quite unlikely. These include musical performance, original work in mathematics, chess (if you hope to become a grandmaster), physics, and computer science. There are, however, many areas where a late start is perfectly feasible and may have advantages: any literary or creative writing (novels, short stories, movie scripts, magazine production), entrepreneurship (such as starting a restaurant), photography, teaching, or publicizing. These are areas where the wisdom of accumulated experience becomes more important. Apart from these areas where you might expect to be able to make your mark publicly, there are also numerous areas where you can gain profound satisfaction without being well known. You can become a good cook or gardener, become an expert on the history of the locality where you live, or do well at and profoundly enjoy any one of hundreds of possible activities.

Aside from "setting the world on fire," there are many things you might like to do, or to have done, at some time in your life. You *can* do many of these in middle or older age. For instance, you can read the best novels. You can buy CDs of the best pieces of music. You can visit the one place in the world you would most like to have visited. If you list things you wish you had done during your lifetime, it may surprise you to see how many of them you can quite easily still do. Being older can bring the benefit of greater focus—doing the things that you most want to do in the remainder of your life, rather than just whatever catches your attention next.

There is another side to this. If you have been reading the great books, you may decide it is time for reading exactly what you most immediately enjoy—Joan Hess or Ngaio Marsh or Kinky Friedman or Joyce Porter mysteries, for instance. If you've kept up your Bach and Beethoven concert-going religiously, you may get more enjoyment from listening to Cajun music, the blues, or the Big Band sound. If you have always dressed in the latest styles, you may decide from now on to dress for sheer comfort—or partly for comfort and partly for personal, whimsical vanity. I (Emmett Velten) once knew a very sober woman of almost 70 who told me that before she turned 70, she was going to sky dive. The next time I saw her, I got to watch the video of her sky dive!

As a friend and retired physician, Ava Wolfe, put it: "Life can begin at 40, but also at 50 (the big five-oh), or at 65 when Social Security begins, or at 70 when you remarry. There is always chance for a new beginning. I feel I have lived several lives, some almost disconnected, as though I had been several different persons. Part of the fun of older age is to look back and see how they were connected, what each era drew from the prior ones and how it anticipated the subsequent ones."

Time Flies

As you age, you often *perceive* time to go faster. It also flies when you're having a good time and drags when you're not. Several other factors affect your perception of time. They include not just how much you *want* to do, but also:

- how well you tell yourself you MUST do
- whether you believe you MUST finish within a certain amount of time
- whether you believe the task SHOULD be easier than it is.

The older you get, the less time you have left to live. That's a given—not exactly welcome, but nevertheless true. Many people view it as a definite Adversity that aging leaves them less time to enjoy life and get things done. A typical self-defeating Belief you may tell yourself as you get older is that you have *too* little time left (and SHOULD have more), and that it's *useless* to continue to live fully. With those Irrational Beliefs you can demoralize or depress yourself, at C. This line of irrational thought can lead people to say "it's too late," when it really is not.

Jonelle was an extremely active retired woman with "too little" time. She had many commitments, which she enjoyed but believed she HAD TO complete. At times she would panic and find it impossible to get anything done when she thought about the decreasing number of years she had left on this planet. Fear of death? No way. Jonelle's Irrational Belief was that she MUST finish all her tasks, an impossibility since she continued to take on new ones. Had she believed "I want to finish them, but I don't HAVE TO," she probably would not have given herself the panic attacks and could have maintained her enjoyable involvements.

Jonelle alternated panic attacks with deep lethargy and depression. She believed that since she would die someday and all her projects would ultimately be unfinished (by her, at least), which she defined as *awful*, therefore "why try?" At times she'd waver toward depression and inactivity when she'd start thinking "I'm going to die anyway. *That* means I can't get everything done" (rational), "so nothing makes any difference anyway" (irrational). Many people bedevil themselves with variations on the same "must" theme held by Jonelle. They may believe, "I MUST have control and guarantees that no bad things will happen."

In Jonelle's case, this included unfinished business. Others may tell themselves they have to be sure nothing bad happens in such areas of probability and chance as these: economic setbacks, death of loved ones, relationships, mugging, inability to continue to drive, and difficulty accessing public transportation.

In therapy, I (Emmett Velten) taught Jonelle to ask the Three Key Questions of her Beliefs:

1. "Where does it get me to demand that I finish everything I ever start?" she asked herself. Answer: Depressed and frantic.
2. "And is it really true that I, or anyone else, actually MUST finish everything I ever start?" Answer: Of course not. If it were true that everything had to be finished, then there'd be a law of the universe to that effect and I'd have no worries at all on this topic!
3. "And is it logical to think that since it would be nice to see all my projects through to their conclusion, therefore I MUST do so?" Answer: Of course not. Necessity does not logically follow from my preferences.

Jonelle could see she was much happier with goals and objectives and things to do. But much unhappier if she told herself she MUST finish those things. The only way she could finish most of them was to refuse to take on new tasks and to drop some of her lower priority current tasks. She didn't want to do that. She felt happier when she was busy and involved. So she decided to focus on the fact that she was happier when she was keeping busy in meaningful activities. If she keeled over, which someday she would, too bad. "It was quite a ride, and I enjoyed it, while it lasted," as Jonelle put it. Jonelle also said that she had read somewhere, and thought it applied very well to her, that it was best to live each day with a blend of two ideas: 1. It's going to be your last day. 2. You are going to live forever. Well said.

But what about the *other* extreme—too much time? That can be an Adversity, too. Some retirees and empty nesters may piddle through the day at loose ends. They have too much time on hand, given what they want to do *during* the hours they have available. If they feel happy with that arrangement, great—no need for self-help there! But if they feel bored, unfulfilled, useless, or worse, then what? What's the answer? What stops them from doing more?

If you are prone to piddle, and you think you'd feel happier in a non-piddle mode, what self-defeating Beliefs might you hold that keep you piddling? The problem may be simply a misunderstanding. You may hold the erroneous idea that people are happier when they have nothing to do. Yes, but only for a while or when genuine rest is needed. Your body is built to be busy, your brain to solve problems.

Working On and On

Albert Ellis: Until thirty-five, I had a time neurosis. I realized that my days on earth would definitely be numbered and I wanted to make the most of them—particularly as a writer. I had already published a number of articles and had written as many as twenty—yes, twenty—full-length book manuscripts, none of which got published. I thought that I would write many more articles and books and I wanted to get as many of them finished by the time I died as was humanly possible. So I worked assiduously at my research and my writing, indeed worked on two or three articles at the same time, and rarely wasted any time.

I realized, however, that I was rather compulsive about my work schedule, and talked to my psychoanalyst about it. He was a good analyst, and not particularly Freudian, so I trusted him a lot and got some good ideas from him. His basic method of psychotherapy, however, was classical analysis, with much listening and not much talking. Though his interpretations seemed sound enough, they didn't help me overcome my time neurosis. So I thought about it, applied some practical philosophy to it, and came up with my own solution. I concluded that if I had a reasonably normal life span, I would have published a great many articles and probably several books by the time I died. I also concluded that even with a very long life span, I would *still* have about 50 books planned and schemed—and unfinished. Yes, fifty books unfinished. The more I thought about it, I could see that no matter if I lived to be the oldest person in the history of the world, I'd always have still more things I'd like to do and could have done. I'd never finish all my projects.

Well, what was so bad about that? So the damned books would be unfinished! I would still lead a happy and productive life and finish what I could. I could get myself vitally absorbed in my writing and other projects and would enjoy them whether I finished them or not. The world would not stop spinning because of my fifty unborn books. Besides, I would be dead and gone anyway, so I would hardly sweat about them!

That line of rational thinking soon finished off my time neurosis. I kept working hard to do as much as I could do, and still enjoyed the research, the writing, and the clinical work that I was then doing— uncompulsively. I gave up my *demand* that I greatly accomplish, and turned it back into a *preference*. That was before I originated REBT and realized the great value of preferences and the great *dis*value of demands. I clearly saw that difference, and put it into REBT, almost a decade later. So I saw strongly that however *desirable* my writing was, and however much the reading public might well benefit from it, it wasn't absolutely necessary that I do it *at all*. It was not necessary that I do it to the maximum or to the optimum. I would do my best—which, of course, was all I could do—and let the chips fall where they may. If, as I predicted at the age of 35, I did have 50 or more books in my head when I died, so be it. They merely would be unproduced—thought about, but never carried to completion. Too bad. The world would survive.

As I grew older and older—for I am now 84 and have some 70 books published or on their way—I solidly hold on to this youthful conclusion about work. I work just about every day of the week, including Sundays. I do therapy with individuals and groups and have some duties as president of the Albert Ellis Institute for Rational Emotive Behavior Therapy. I still travel throughout the county and the world to give lectures, workshops, and other presentations. I do my writing and research. But I gave up the desperation that I had when I was 35. I am not obsessive-compulsive about my work. I do not frantically engage in it. I feel absorbed in it, I thoroughly enjoy it, and at times I have to rush it somewhat to keep up with deadlines that I have agreed to. Finishing tasks is not necessary, only highly *desirable*. Finishing *all* my tasks would be truly impossible. Why? For one thing, I like to take on new tasks and challenges. The *process* of living, of loving, of working, is at least as important as the outcomes. So, with that philosophy, I remain quite productive and, I think, creative, despite my fairly advanced age. Largely because I am not desperate.

As *real* old age approaches, moreover, I realize more than ever that I will hardly last more than a few more years—especially since I have diabetes, somewhat high blood pressure, osteoarthritis, and several minor ailments. Nevertheless, I believe more and more that there is no reason that I absolutely MUST accomplish, certainly not that I MUST greatly accomplish. I do not *believe* that I absolutely have to finish my projects within a certain amount of time. I definitely don't believe that my labor MUST be easier than it is. That way of thinking leaves me freer than ever of my absolute "musts" and "shoulds." It leaves me free to noncompulsively, and enjoyably, work on and on.

No matter how old you are, if you are reading these words, we can be sure your life is not over. You have the right to do new things, take new risks, meet new challenges, experience new excitements. Who gives you the right?, you may ask. Answer: You do. You can exercise that right at any time as long as you live, and if you exercise it, you'll probably have more fun than if you don't.

10

Vital Absorbing Interests:
The Key To Long Life, and to Happiness at Work and During Retirement

The more studying you did for the exam, the less sure you are as to which answer they want.

Basic Law of Exams

People are purposive creatures. We think better, act better, and feel better when we pursue goals and objectives that we care something about. Those who "kick back," retire from all activity, and "take it easy," usually find that that way of life is not all it's cracked up to be. They feel they're missing something. They are! Sometimes they may feel that life has no meaning. They do not realize that you *create* meaning in life. They may say their days are boring, and wait for life to entertain them and lift them out of the doldrums. Instead, they would do better to realize, and act upon the realization, that you often get out of life what you put into it. If you put nothing in, you get nothing out—to lift a saying from the computer world—garbage in, garbage out. So: retirement. Should you or shouldn't you retire? And if you do, or don't, how do you have as enjoyable a life as possible?

People are problem solvers as well as problem causers. The ABC model is a tool to help you solve problems—but problems *related to* your goals and objectives. Your unique goals and objectives *define* your actions as self-helping or self-defeating. Your purposes in life *define* your thinking as rational or irrational. Your personal motivations and desires *define* your emotions as healthful or unhealthful. Does desirelessness really lead to happiness, the way some advocates of eastern philosophies say? We don't think so. If you have no desires, then, yes, you will have no demands. True enough, you won't have anything to MUSTurbate about if you have no desires. You also won't have any fun, zest, adventure, love, attachments, or—yes, they go with the territory— frustration, sadness, or grief. This brings us to the Fourteenth Rule for Optimal Living:

Rule #14: Commit Yourself

Most people tend to be healthier and happier when they are vitally absorbed in something outside themselves and preferably have at least one strong creative interest, as well as some major human involvement. They consider such commitments so important that they structure a good part of their daily existence around it.

Get Interested in Something

Not only do vital absorbing interests contribute to happiness and to being able to distract yourself from hassles and pains, but they may help you have better health and longer life. Research by Erdman Palmore shows that work satisfaction is the best overall predictor of longevity. This is one reason that retirement, when it means giving up your interests and social contacts, may shorten your life. Purposes that organize your existence and give you social ties are the chief factors in vital aging. Most people report greater satisfaction in life the more they feel satisfied by their work. They also report greater satisfaction in life, the busier they are—within limits, of course—with complex purposes and tasks of their own choosing to carry out. In other words, people feel more satisfied when they have vital absorbing involvements. It will be easier to have vital absorbing interests and maintain an independent lifestyle for as long as possible, when you view yourself, no matter how old you are, as acceptable, worthwhile, and valuable. You will likely be healthier mentally and physically, too. None of this will be possible unless you challenge the old view of age as a disease. Then you can exercise your options and create a new image of your choosing: old as fun, old as productive, old as romantic, old as vital, old as wise.

What are the attitudes and Beliefs you can cultivate to help you achieve involvements and commitments? How can you identify and *promote* thoughts and Beliefs that help your pursuit of vital absorbing interests? What can you do to *demote* the thoughts and Beliefs that hamper that pursuit of happiness? Let's look for some answers to those questions.

Albert Ellis: I have easily zeroed in on a number of vital absorbing interests for just about eight decades. I became absorbed in voracious reading—mainly literature, but also books on everything else under the sun—since I was five and a half years old. Then I made baseball and baseball statistics vitally interesting. At twelve, I determined to be a writer, wrote scads of essays, stories, poems, song lyrics, and whatnot. By age 28, I had finished no less than 20 book-length manuscripts—none of which, alas, was published! Nothing daunted, I continued to write, write, write until the present day, and have now published over 800 articles and 70 books.

At 19, I became absorbed in revolutionary activity and was a paid revolutionist for a while—a secretly paid member of a small group of revolutionaries. We were collectivists, and wanted a world revolution, but we solidly opposed the American Communist Party and the dictatorial communists who ran the Soviet Union. Witnessing communism in Russia, however, and Hilterism in Germany, I gave up my revolutionary activity within a few years. Instead, I devoted myself to freedom of thought and freedom of speech, without which many of my early publications in psychology would not exist. Because, from political revolutionary activities, I turned, instead, to sex and became one of the leaders of the sex revolution in the 1950s and 1960s.

At age 25 I became absorbed in love, marital relations, and sex, and became one of the world's leading sexologists and eventually the first President of the Society for the Scientific Study of Sex. At 30, I began a life of true devotion to the theory and practice of psychotherapy. At 43, I created the first of the cognitive-behavioral therapies, Rational Emotive Behavior Therapy, and have been doing it and revising its theory and practice ever since. Oh, yes: I nearly forgot: from the age of 15 I have been composing hundreds of songs and song lyrics, including more than 200 rational humorous songs.

Okay: So vital absorbing interests came naturally to me and in truth, you can't keep me away from them. Although I get involved in them spontaneously, I learned one important thing from involvement. When I was a youngster and suffered from kidney inflammations, I was hospitalized nine times between the ages of five and seven. My vital absorbing interest in reading considerably helped me focus on more pleasant things than my illness. During my later childhood and adolescence, when I steadily had bad headaches, my writing very nicely helped me get by. During the Great Depression, when my family almost went on welfare, my writing and my revolutionary activity kept me nicely afloat. At the age of 40, insulin-dependent diabetes afflicted me. Again, my work as a therapist and my (now published) writing helped me over any disturbance about my illness. Finally, since the age of 43, my devotion to theorizing and writing about Rational Emotive Behavior Therapy—and practicing and teaching it—for about 80 hours a week has helped me cope with many life Adversities. It now helps me handle the difficulties of older age.

Not only did I have the benefits of my vital absorbing interests since my childhood, but I also became interested in the psychology of human happiness when I was in my twenties. I realized that two things were frequently required before people could be truly happy and self-actualized:

1. Most people feel happier, actualize themselves more, and reduce their needless misery, when they stop their irrational thinking.
2. Most people feel much happier and withstand the unavoidable troubles of life more easily, when they acquire a vital absorbing interest in something they consider important. If they devote considerable time and energy to this interest for a good many hours a week, they tend to enjoy life still more.

When I saw how important was the achieving of a long-term vital absorbing interest, I described its value in my 1961 book with Robert A. Harper, *A Guide To Rational Living*. Its readers have sent me many hundreds of enthusiastic letters describing how they implemented this goal in their lives. Now I see that vital absorbing interests are even more important, in many ways, for aging people. For they usually face more limitations, ailments, and disabilities than they did when they were younger. If you feel vitally involved in some active, absorbing project, hobby, cause, or goal, then the tedium, boredom, and restrictions of your older age will almost magically vanish. Well, not magically. It happens because humans are born and reared so that when you pursue your purposes and goals, especially on a long-range basis, you often feel intensely involved. These feelings of intense involvement make your troubles seem lighter and your enjoyments greater.

Get a Life!

If you do not now have a vitally absorbing interest, the best advice we can give you is to find one. Take one (or more) of your enjoyments and build it up. *Actively* take it, or some aspect of it, and emphasize it, expand it. For example, if you like reading history, take some facet of it, say, the American Civil War—and concentrate on it. Read up on it. Write an essay—maybe a book—on it. Relate it to something else that interests you—perhaps Abraham Lincoln or Ulysses S. Grant or the emancipation of the slaves. Become an authority on some aspects of it. Interview historians who specialize in it. Speak about it to clubs and groups. Make it, in several ways, a big part of your life. Meet people in person or over the Internet who also have your interest. Almost any large city in America has Civil War clubs or round tables. On the Internet, you can find Civil War Web sites or chat rooms where you can meet people with your interests and where you can learn more about the Civil War.

The same will be true, in one form or another, of any interest you have or may have had in the past and want to rekindle—gardening, raising orchids, refinishing furniture, making stained glass, raising dogs or cats, putting together your genealogy, coping with specific diseases, keeping up with opera, country music, UFOs. You name it, and there are resources for it. Check out your library. Along with books and periodicals, most larger libraries now have computer work stations. Library personnel teach novices how to use the computer for research. Most newspapers have a daily or weekly section listing upcoming concerts, poetry readings, rock and gem shows, recovery meetings, and so forth. Take a vital interest of yours and expand it. Take some special part of it and work it up. Or get a brand new interest—new for you—and throw yourself into it. You may learn all there is to know—or want to know—and then discard it. Or you may remain enjoyably hooked on it forever. Try it. Experiment with it. It may become an intriguing, joyous part of your life.

If you are a very verbal person, continue or expand the amount of reading you do. Try kinds of literature you haven't experimented with before. If you are a scientific thinker, continue to solve problems and ask questions. If you like to play cards, look into bridge clubs, poker parlors, and the like.

Of course, there's the Internet, yes, the Internet. Just having a home computer and being on-line can completely transform retirement. If you are "too old" for a computer and yet you can afford one, you are seriously selling yourself short. You can easily communicate with people all over the world without paying long distance rates. You can access immense stores of knowledge. You can shop for just about anything—cars, homes, clothing, apartments, groceries, books, antiques, hotel rooms, tickets, and of course, friends and potential mates. You can easily find the lowest airfares, the most direct or most scenic or the safest route—door-to-door—for your next trip. You can buy and sell stock and tell the computer to notify you if your stock rises or falls beyond points you choose. You can read, and write, book and movie reviews. You can search for trivia, you can play games, you can place bets. You can design and print your own, personalized greeting cards. You can find Web sites to research your interests. You can use search engines to look for information about people and places and any interests you have. You can browse, you can cruise, you can surf the Net, and you will find endless stimulation and ideas. You can develop your own homepage as a way to advertise your interests, your business, or yourself. You can save a great deal of money by communicating with friends by email, rather than by snail mail or phone.

If you have never used computers, don't be intimidated by them. They are much more user-friendly, much simpler to use, than was true only a few years ago. They are fun and they open up an exciting world of information and communication. You need no technical knowledge, no training in computer vocabulary, or even typing skills, to get started. As soon as you see how much fun you can have using your computer, you will be hooked. Your motivation will carry your learning along rapidly, if you stick with it.

Commitment Is Therapy

In many ways, having vital absorbing interests insulates you against some of the pains and trials of life—such as knowing you will not be around forever or having very difficult diseases or handicaps. *Commitment* focuses your thinking, feeling, and actions. It helps you create a meaningful, passionate existence. Committed, absorbing interests can be abstract, such as political theories. They can relate to family, children, career, hobbies, games, sports, arts and crafts, or other projects. They can be traditional, untraditional, commonplace, unique. It depends entirely on you, your values, your interests.

Accidents Will Happen

Sometimes, by accident—even unwelcome, *real* accident—you may discover interests you didn't know you had. Interest in a topic may blossom in you, very much to your surprise, and despite initial dislike. That happened to me (Emmett Velten) in my interest in the topic of addiction. After I first moved to San Francisco almost two decades ago, the group private practice I moved there to join—I learned after about a month—was almost bankrupt. We had lots of clients, all right. But even more expenses. By the time the group collapsed about nine months later, I had been paid a grand total of $100! Had I checked out its balance sheet before leaving my previous secure job and life? No. Had I made a big, foolish mistake? Yes. Was I a very fallible human being? Unfortunately. Right away, I began to job hunt.

At first, I was looking for a position suitable for one of my great education, diverse talents, and in-depth experience. Strike out! (Grand visions of self are nothing if not shared by others—employer-type others.) Later, as the weeks passed, I was looking for just about any job in psychology that would keep me from having to live on the streets of San Francisco. Through making cold calls, I did at least get some informational interviews. One of those led to meeting someone socially who had heard of a job in a methadone clinic. I had little experience working with addicts, which was fine with me. The topic of addiction bored me. My interest in working with the addicts themselves was not just zero, it was well below zero. Since the same was true of my budget, I applied for the job. I was, after all, still interested in eating.

Soon enough, there I was, in my very proper suit and tie, sitting in the lobby of the methadone clinic, waiting for my job interview. The clinic was at the edge of the worst, most dangerous section of town, part of which I had had to walk through on the way to the interview. Considering what I saw after entering the clinic, it was definitely a community clinic. The lobby was bedlam. It was near closing time, and clients by the score were milling around, calling to their friends, waiting noisily in line, complete with crying babies. Several people had arrived at the clinic too late for their medical examinations to determine whether they could begin the program, and they were yelling at staff, who yelled back! I made my mind up rapidly to get out of there fast without being obvious about it. I stood up and did a good imitation of a person reading the various posters and warning signs along the walls, such as "Do not bring weapons into the clinic," as I neared the door. Before I escaped, the clinic director came out of her office to fetch me. I got the job.

I never stopped job hunting. Working in a substance abuse treatment clinic was even worse than I expected. Some of the staff were OK, and some of the clients, but the whole experience was very close to awful. Very close. For the first few months, I job hunted with fierce determination. Somewhere along the line, completely to my surprise, I began to get interested in the psychology of addiction. Within about a year and a half, I was reading avidly about addiction, theories of addiction, the history of addiction treatment, and the effectiveness of various treatments.

The psychology and treatment of addiction became one of my strongest interests and a consuming professional involvement. And it really did happen by accident. Were it not for my very big, very stupid mistake, I might never have had the chance to develop what became one of my greatest interests. I might not have been able to learn, first hand, that you don't have to be sure you don't make a mistake. Because, of course, you can never be absolutely sure ahead of time. But also, you can learn from mistakes. Mistakes can give you new, unexpected experience, from which you can grow. To be sure, avoid mistakes where you can, but *when* you make them, which you will, learn from them and be open to the experience that comes your way.

Liabilities Can Be Assets

You can sometimes combine a vital absorbing interest with a supplementary source of income, killing two birds with one stone. You may be able to work out of your home, which is hard to beat for the commute. In Rosa's case, she was already at home most of the time—not because of retirement, but disability. She had developed multiple sclerosis, a condition leading to fearsome debility. She could not escape being rudely reminded of the immensely inconvenient symptoms of her condition. However, she began to engross herself in researching and writing a book that told the firsthand stories of people in similar predicaments. She also read *So Desperate the Fight*, Warren Johnson's first-hand account of his coping with an extremely disagreeable, painful, and eventually fatal illness. Rosa wrote a book about her own coping with multiple sclerosis. Almost to her surprise, the book sold fairly well. Rosa was in business! Her publisher asked her to do a series of booklets, each addressing a different severely disabling condition. The money she earned in advances and in royalties from these projects dwarfed her Social Security disability income. More important than income, she gained tremendous satisfaction from her deep involvement in her writing projects and from holding out hope to others facing very adverse medical situations. What hope? To learn that through commitment, you can give meaning to your life, your experiences. You can lessen your suffering by focusing on your purposes and goals, and then pursuing them as well as you can. Along the way, you might even earn some income from them.

More Careers, More Retirements

Work is a wonderful opportunity—about on a par with relationships—for problems for people of any age. Several Adversities related to work can be especially pertinent for older people. They can have stresses at work younger people don't have, including age discrimination in hiring, promotion, and layoffs. Some employers get rid of the higher-salaried workers, who've been there longer and often are older, and then hire new, less expensive young people. Employers who do that are showing very poor judgment in choosing cheap labor over the *real* cost-effectiveness of accumulated experience, good judgment in complex situations, and fewer sick days a year. (Yes, younger workers do take more sick days than older workers.) So older people have practical problems at work and about work.

Irrational Beliefs, however, are the major cause of emotional problems about practical problems. For example, if you NEED success (to give yourself "worth"), you will give yourself trouble at work, about work, and when you contemplate retirement. The same "need" can also adversely affect your chances to enjoy retirement and new careers after retirement. The same thing happens if you define your worth as dependent on taking care of your children. Once they're gone, they take your ego, your self-worth, with them. And you may prolong your (and their) agony by trying to hold on to them or by taking care of them to their detriment after they grow up.

Retirement is a relatively new idea and practice in our society. The once common view was that older people knew their jobs *better.* They were the "old masters," who had real knowledge and wisdom about what was important and what was not. They could cut through the crap, get to the answers, and produce. President Franklin D. Roosevelt invented American retirement in the Great Depression partly to remove older people from the unemployment rolls and make jobs available to younger people. Now, the age mystique in our culture holds that people not only *want* to retire, which often is true, but NEED to retire (and get a well-deserved rest) as they wobble toward senility. Decline begins in earnest at 65. It wasn't that way in the past, and it doesn't have to be now. What happened?

First, you arbitrarily remove the people over 65 from the productive workforce. With nothing productive to do and lacking stimulation and challenge, they are bored witless. Being human, they may readily embrace the too-old-to-work mentality. They decline because they are supposed to decline, in the role of retiree. That role-related decline then "proves" that they "needed" to retire and "couldn't" continue to work. Ageist expectations can become self-fulfilling prophecies.

Yet many people do look forward to retirement and most expect to retire someday, though they are less eager about it as they get closer to that point. If they look forward to it, they do OK with it. In fact, studies of retirement typically do not show it to be a crisis, nor do most people become less satisfied with life, or depressed, after retirement. The same goes for the "empty nest." A number of studies suggest that women, on the average, are happier *after* the children leave.

People who want to retire may want to escape boring jobs. They may want opportunities to do new things, such as start new careers and pursue hobbies and interests. They may look forward to chances for fun, leisure, and travel. People who like their jobs and careers typically feel ambivalent about retiring. Then, too, there's the dark undercurrent of expectations about retirement. Don't many people kick the bucket soon after they retire—because they no longer have any purpose in life? What are the facts?

Those most likely to have a hard time with retirement, and whose health is most likely to suffer, are those who don't look forward to retirement, but still retire. Those who equate their worth with their jobs: My work = my worth; therefore, no job = no worth. Others who have trouble with retirement neglect to build alternative enjoyments and involvements for themselves after, or before, they retire. Exactly the same thing is true when that nest empties. The people who have a bad time with it are the ones who had an overspecialized view of themselves as possessing one and only one important role, parenthood.

If you are an older person and believe you MUST avoid making mistakes and MUST be successful to feel worthwhile and happy, those "musts" will tend to give you trouble at work and trouble about your career just as much as they did when you were younger. Those "musts" can cause you trouble about parenting and homemaking, too. About anything. About retirement, for instance. About the so-called empty nest. How so?, you may wonder. You may think that if you retire and the children leave home, you are then off the hook in terms of putting yourself down for lack of achievement. Far from it! With time on your hands, you may put yourself down *more* than when you were busier. You may be afraid to retire or to see your children leave home because retirement could equal utter hopelessness for achievements. If you did retire, and if your children did finally leave home, you might not enjoy yourself much because of those same "musts." If, like many people, you want to retire so that you can pursue another career, those "musts" could disrupt your plans. You might feel afraid to try new things, because you might fail and—if the "must" itself has not retired—that would be *awful*.

Should I or Shouldn't I? What If I Don't Like Retirement?

Greg was ambivalent about retiring, because he saw his worth as stemming from his work. He obsessed about whether to take an early retirement. At 62, he'd receive each month 75 percent of what he'd get if he waited until 65. He got stuck thinking, "What if I don't like retirement?" Instead of answering rationally, as he later did, "Well, if I don't, I don't. I'll then figure out something else to do," Greg would dramatically conclude, "Then I would have stupidly thrown away 25 percent of my pension! Fool!"

Even with those irrationalities, Greg could probably have made up his mind eventually—if money were the only issue—partly because his spouse had a good income. The larger reason he couldn't decide was his question, with its implied self-rating, "If I don't have my career, who am I?" Helped along by Irrational Beliefs, that line of thought led firmly to the dreaded answer, "Nobody!" Later, much later, Greg could reach a more helpful, factual answer, "A person who retired from one career."

A key to Greg's successful therapy was persuading him that if he retired and did not like it, he would be a person whose experiment hadn't worked out, not an idiot who got himself into a catastrophe. At first, he'd hold his head in his hands as he thought of the absolute awfulness of making what later might prove to have been a mistake. In time, Greg combated his self-rating and accepted himself unconditionally, mistakes and all. He made lists of his options and the steps for pursuing them in case he *didn't* like retirement and wished he hadn't done it. He began to feel a lot better, but definitely not flippant about his prospective decision.

Polls sponsored by AARP and the National Council on Aging have found that about two out of five retired people would rather be working. And the closer people get to 65, the more they'd prefer to continue working. Most people, including older people, do not want to stop working. They prefer a balance of work and leisure. If you prefer, or think you would prefer, to work full-time, part-time, all the time, or seasonally, what's to stop you from experimenting? If you would like to work as long as you are physically able, what's to stop you? You can make these decisions, and carry out these experiments, based on what you think might be fulfilling for you. You can do what you think would give you more control over your life. You can do what you think would contribute to society as well as to yourself. The choices are almost unlimited. Most people would like to have choice and control over whether to retire, when to retire, and how often to retire. For most of us, having choices and feeling in control increase our degree of satisfaction in life and help maintain our health.

According to futurists like Ken Dychtwald in his book, *Age Wave*, a new version of retirement will become much more common in the 21st Century. People may retire several times from several careers or never retire at all, and not just do these things later in life, but all along the way. Based on present trends, Dychtwald predicts that taking time off from work will become more common—to travel, go back to school, change careers, start a new business or a new family.

Some people, like Bertrand Russell, who won the Nobel Prize for literature, have a number of careers. Russell was a mathematician, then a philosopher. His writings in philosophy began to morph into social criticism, especially of marriage and morals, the political and economic systems, religion, education and the treatment of children, and many other issues. Often politically active, Russell became an ardent activist opposed to nuclear weapons. Very late in life, he wrote a couple of collections of amusing short stories, and they were widely read. He never retired. He worked for the causes he favored until he died, having almost reached 100.

Many fields of enterprise are broad enough that you can develop several careers within the same field, if that is your choice. Singer Linda Ronstadt, for example, first sang with a rock group with folk music overtones. Later she did more classic rock and remakes of earlier rock 'n roll hits. Still later she went through phases of Gilbert and Sullivan operettas, Mexican mariachi music, blues, and popular standards. In show business it can be risky trying something new when your fans expect something familiar. In each case, Ronstadt was quite successful in her new endeavors. Now semi-retired from music, she has adopted children and is studying photography. Stay tuned.

Not all risks and new endeavors turn out successfully, of course. Your efforts don't have to be successful for you to get satisfaction from them. And they definitely don't have to be finished. When Russell was well into his 90s, he continued his work in advocating for world peace and for nuclear disarmament. These were meaningful activities to him, and he threw himself into them even though he knew he would not live forever and would never know the outcome of his causes. This brings us to the Fifteenth Rule for Optimal Living:

Rule #15: TAKE RISKS

Emotionally healthy people tend to take a fair amount of risk and try to do what they want to do, even when there is a good chance that they may fail. They tend to be adventurous, but not foolhardy.

Changing Careers

The world of work has been changing dramatically in the last fifteen years. Very few young people have any notion of staying with one company until retirement. Many people have little notion of remaining in one career. Employers and workplaces have responded to some degree by allowing variations in work methods and styles, to entice or hold onto valued employees. New versions of work already exist. They include telecommuting and various versions of "home-officing." There's old-fashioned working at home, too. Then there is flex time, job sharing, shorter work weeks, hour banks, retirement rehearsals, flexi-year contracts, sabbaticals, project-oriented work, and temporary contract employment. Naturally, old stand-bys, such as part-time work, seasonal work, temping, and job retraining are still around. These options, and others you have yet to invent, may give you much more satisfaction than the old-fashioned routine of working until 65, then retiring forever.

The non-linear lifestyle will apply to work as well as retirement. It will likely become popular as more people, younger as well as older, have the option to choose new directions and new challenges many times in their lives. MUST you stick to the traditions of schooling while young, working and family-raising while adult, followed by a declining retirement? Does this new style of work and retirement appeal to you? What can stop you from experimenting with a new style? Let's look at what stopped one of my (Albert Ellis's) clients, Ariana.

Ariana had a double problem about possibly changing her career path at the age of 52. She had worked very hard to become a podiatrist at the age of 40. She had put herself through podiatry school by working as a substitute teacher, and for twelve years had made out reasonably well in the field. Friends and relatives admired her status in the medical field, and status was direly important to her. Now there was an oversupply of podiatrists in her region, and it looked as if Medicare was going to cut back and stop paying for many services that older people came to her for. To make things far worse, medicine in her region was coming under managed care. Managed care forced "gatekeeper" physicians to skimp on referrals, including referrals for podiatry. So the prospects of keeping up her independent practice were not good.

Fortunately, Ariana had some skills in managing computer networks, and by taking some courses she could upgrade her skills and quite probably make it in this new field. To do so, however, she would have to go back for some training, which she was tired of doing at her age. After all, she had already trained as a teacher and then as a podiatrist. So she did not want to go to the trouble of taking another two years of training. To be sure, she might well work for another 25 years as a computer expert. When I first saw her, though, she was stuck with several ideas. First, she thought it was unfair that she should have to enter a new field at her age. Second, she also thought it was unfair that there were too many podiatrists in her region. In themselves, these ideas were not deadly. What made them deadly and irrational was

Ariana's underlying "must." It was, "It SHOULDN'T be so unfair!" So she railed against these unfair conditions and couldn't decide what to do.

Moreover, Ariana had some degree of professional status in her community, because a podiatrist was almost a physician and her friends and relatives looked up to her for that reason. As a computer consultant, she was afraid she wouldn't have the same degree of status, and her self-worth might decrease. That would be *awful*, to lose the status that she had had for the past decade!

Ariana's Irrational Beliefs were fairly apparent after a few sessions of REBT. She believed that she MUST NOT have to go to the trouble of starting all over in the new profession. She also believed that she MUST NOT lose the status that she had benefited from for a number of years. Yes, it would be difficult for her to train for a new profession, but she saw it as *too hard* to do. And yes, it would be disadvantageous to lose some professional status—if that happened—but she saw it as meaning that she would be a *lesser person*. She believed that her friends and relatives might not look up to her in the manner that she absolutely NEEDED.

She also believed that managed care and other atrocities were *forcing* her to enter a new career. The more she thought about how *awful* and outrageous that was, the more she riled herself up. In truth, though, nothing was forcing her. Yes, podiatry was down, but she could choose to cut back her expenses. She could choose to deal productively with boredom and to add zest to her podiatry career.

Ariana started to dispute these Irrational Beliefs, but was having some difficulty doing so. She had a great sense of humor that she frequently used to entertain her friends and relatives. But she lost it completely, as people often do when they make themselves neurotic, when she contemplated some of her own personal problems. So I used one of the main REBT techniques—humor. If you view life with a sense of humor, it can help you, as it did Ariana, overcome Irrational Beliefs. In Ariana's case, humor helped her convince herself that her career difficulties and her possible loss of status in the eyes of others were *somewhat* important problems but that she was making them into a double disaster. I showed her how to view her possible change of career as a hassle, but not as a sheer horror.

Ariana could see—lightly—the possible joys of figuring out solutions to the computer problems she would meet with in a new career.

She could also see—lightly—how a new career could be more fun than the stale problems of dealing with managed care and cranky patients. But then she also fumed that the attractions of computer work were not *all*-enticing. She complained that the detractions of podiatry were not stupendous. "Why SHOULD they be?" I asked. Later, Ariana saw her answer as classically preposterous. At the time, however, she took it very, very seriously: "Because if I hated podiatry and if I knew for sure that computer work was going to be the right choice, it would be easier to decide!"

I also showed Ariana the humorous irony of her choice to continue working as a podiatrist to get ego-inflation. Ariana saw that she could live without the approval of others, but also saw—ironically—that these others didn't even approve of *her*. They liked her for her *profession*, rather than liking and accepting her as a person. I particularly got Ariana to laugh at doing what she really didn't want to do any more, podiatry, mainly to get the acceptance of her patients and her friends, who really weren't interested in her. Instead, they were interested in the "noble" medical profession that she was part of.

I used with Ariana some of the rational humorous songs I give to many clients. When you sing these songs to yourself, it helps you powerfully dispute Irrational Beliefs. For example, you can select, or even compose, rational humorous songs to help you when you are overserious about making money, being approved by others, or going through some of the inevitable discomforts of life. Rational Emotive Behavior Therapy uses rational humorous songs to help people see how they foolishly and needlessly upset themselves. The songs can work because they disrupt your routine way of thinking about yourself, others, and life conditions. Since it takes physical effort to sing, using the songs practically forces you to put some energy into your efforts to change your thinking patterns. You can sing some of these songs to yourself or with other people to help overcome your Irrational Beliefs. These songs work very well at public gatherings, such as workshops. Many of them, set to popular tunes, are available from the Albert Ellis Institute for Rational Emotive Behavior Therapy on cassette and in a book of sheet music. You say you can't sing? That's even better! It will give you a great opportunity to attack any Irrational Beliefs you have that you MUST perform well and receive the applause and admiration of others. As Oscar Wilde once said, "Anything worth doing is worth doing badly."

To combat her low frustration tolerance, Ariana sang to herself these two rational humorous songs:

OH, HOW I HATE TO GET UP AND GET GOING
("Oh, How I Hate To Get Up in the Morning" by Irving Berlin)

Oh, how I hate to get up and get going!
Oh, how I live to procrastinate!
For the hardest thing I know
Is to hear the whistle blow,
"You gotta get up, you gotta get up,
You gotta get up and stop slowing!"
Someday, I promise that I will get going,
Someday, but never of course today!
I think I'll still procrastinate
And always get my ass in late,
And piss the rest of my life away!

WHINE, WHINE, WHINE!
("Yale Whiffenpoof Song" by Guy Scull [a Harvard man])

I cannot have all of my wishes filled,
Whine, whine, whine!
I cannot have every frustration stilled,
Whine, whine, whine!
Life really owes me the things that I miss,
Fate has to grant me eternal bliss,
And since I must settle for less than this,
Whine, whine, whine!

Then, to counteract her "need" for status and approval, Ariana used this rational humorous song:

I ADORE THE WAY YOU WORSHIP ME
("Toreador Song" from *Carmen* by Georges Bizet)

I just adore the way you worship me!
Happy that you are so true blue!
Your approbation stations me on high,
Fills me with thrilling elation!
My own approval swells, and in a trice,
My shithood smells so nice!

Just in case Ariana went overboard in her efforts to dispute her Irrational Beliefs and build up her Rational Beliefs in their stead, I assigned her the following song. It nicely illustrates that rationality is a desirable standard. However, if you MUSTurbate about becoming perfectly rational, you will end up disturbing yourself. Rationality is a good goal, but don't demand that you reach it in some absolute sense, because you won't.

PERFECT RATIONALITY
("Funiculi Funicula" by Luigi Denza)

Some think the world must have a right direction,
And so do I! And so do I!
Some think that with the slightest imperfection,
They can't get by—and so do I!
For I, I have to prove I'm superhuman,
And better far, than people are!
To show I have miraculous acumen—
And always rate, among the Great!
Perfect, perfect rationality!
Is, of course, the only thing for me!
How can I ever think of being if I must live fallibly?
Rationality must be a perfect thing for me!

As she kept using these rational humorous songs, Ariana also kept looking humorously at how she was demanding that life be easy—and thereby making it much harder than it need be. Because she kept making status-seeking the be-all and end-all of her existence, she was not focusing on what she really wanted to do in life. When she did focus on that, she started thinking she shouldn't have to put out the effort to go back to school and change careers. Besides, it was *too hard* a challenge. Ariana saw the irony of this and went a long way toward conquering her low frustration tolerance and her dire need for status. She started studying to become a computer consultant, and found that she enjoyed doing it much more than she had ever enjoyed podiatry. She also started doing several other things in life because she really wanted to do them, rather than because she wanted people to look up to her for doing them. She laughed some of her former Irrational Beliefs out of existence.

Ariana also changed her implicit idea that at the ripe old age of 52, it was too late to change careers because there wasn't enough time left. Early in her therapy we very briefly talked about how it's self-defeating to think that *because* there is less time left, therefore it's useless or impossible to make changes in your life or to try new things. However, we did not specifically work on this issue. Ariana changed in this respect as part of the other changes she was making in therapy.

Time does have special relevance for us as we get a bit older, because we have less of it. Your age, however—how many or how few years you have left—has no direct connection to how happy you are about anything, including your age. Unhappiness and despair about your age and how few years you have left stems from your Irrational Beliefs, not from the fact that your existence is finite and will end someday. The future does not exist, so in itself it cannot "make" you feel or do anything. Your Belief System, your B.S., does that. Typically, the relevant Irrational Beliefs in this kind of problem are along these lines: "I MUST not die and MUST be able to do everything I want to do before dying." Fat chance, as you well know—rationally. But irrationally, you think you MUST. This MUSTurbation will focus you on your dwindling years, lead you to awfulize about their dwindling, and will only detract from your enjoyment of those years. It you MUSTurbate about how much time you have left and how *awful* it is that you won't have saved the world, it detracts from the enjoyment you *could* be having now. If you want satisfaction in life, your best bet is to commit to and involve yourself in activities and projects meaningful to you. And to devote yourself to doing them, now.

Retirement is not what it used to be. Nevertheless, you may feel its pull. That may happen no matter how vitally interested you are in your work, your career, your ideas, your family, your health, your hobbies, or your recreation. You may get the urge to move away from where you've roosted. Now let's look at a subset of concerns and questions related to retirement. Namely, is it good to *go* somewhere to retire or to start a new career? And if so, where? Now let's consider these timely issues. But first let's look at the question: Florida? Arizona? California? Nevada? or Texas?

A Place in the Sun?

One common problem in free societies where many people have the means for mobility has a special urgency for older people. Where do you live? It could literally be a place in the sun—a mobile home in Sun City or some other age-segregated community, or a beachfront condo in Florida. It could be a little place near the kids, a loft downtown, or forty acres in the country. You could just stay put where you are—there are many possible choices. Moving costs money and usually requires a great deal of strength, work, and stamina just to bring it off. Let's face it, moving can be a royal pain in the behind.

Most commonly, when people think about retiring and relocating, they think of moving to Florida, California, Arizona, Nevada, or Texas. Of those who relocate, an increasing number move to places they've visited or enjoyed on vacations—places not in the sunbelt—like the Ozarks, the Jersey Shore, the Rockies, the coast of Maine. Beauty and comfort, whether for climatic or other reasons, guide people's decisions.

Younger people can face such moving decisions, too. With older people, the decision can have a different flavor to it. What's different? For one thing, there's an implicit time factor for older people. Retirement, a fixed income, plus a shorter life expectancy can be part of the picture. They can help push you toward a decision. Countless people think, too, "This is my last move." A sobering consideration that might or might not be true. (I [Emmett Velten] have already had my "last" move three times and have begun to fantasize about another, so it's not *really* over till it's over.)

Relocating, though often exhausting and expensive, can revitalize you. If you stay put, but retire, you may find it useful to renew your purposes, make new friends, take on new challenges. Stimulation and change can help keep your mind, body, and spirit in shape.

Practical and Psychological Considerations of Relocating

If you think you might want to relocate someday, whether it is to retire or start again, you'd better consider as many of your preferences and other factors as you can. How much income will you have to live on? How much income do you need to maintain a realistic lifestyle? That had better be a prime consideration, and it may limit many of your choices. If you very much want to live near particular family members, that of course limits your choices. Sometimes you think it would be better to live near your children. Could be. Not that *they* will stay put, of course. Your family members, you think, will be more likely to take care of you than others will. But what if you have no family members? Or, what if they're counting on *you* to take care of *them*?

List some of the qualities you think you would like in the new place. In bookstores and libraries and over the Internet, you can do some research. There are a number of easily-available books that analyze communities across the United States and rate them by various standards. A good, up-to-date one covering communities in the 15,000–50,000 population range is *The New Rating Guide to Life in America's Small Cities* (1997), by Kevin Heubusch. That kind of information might help stimulate your thinking about new possibilities. It might help you resolve difficult decisions.

Climate and the beauty of their environment are key factors in most people's thoughts about relocating—not that those are necessarily permanent. El Niño makes sunny and dry places cloudy and wet; overdevelopment can ruin natural beauty. Nevertheless, very few people want to go to where it's ugly and the weather is lousy—unless there are other, overriding factors in their minds. Such as jobs. Such as family. Such as cultural activities. Such as accessible public transportation. Such as access to other services. If you have a heart condition that requires frequent monitoring, then it might be better not to live in a trailer out in the middle of nowhere.

More often than not, people of any age, particularly older age, seek warmer, sunnier climates. The migration of Americans to the Sunbelt stems from several factors, but climate is a prime one. In colder, snowier climates, you have more chance to be housebound due to weather than in, say, Florida. Of course, in Florida you have more chance to be blown away in a hurricane than you do in most locales. Think about what, on balance, seems as if it would be your cup of tea. Study the almanac; send off for information from Chambers of Commerce; visit the finalists.

Some people want to go back to their roots when they retire. Back to where they came from decades ago. Those places, of course, do not exist any more as you remember them. Visit before moving. You may be a stranger to the people there and feel disappointed that it isn't the way you remember it. Some people want to relocate to smaller towns. If you haven't lived in one, the change from a large city will be dramatic and you may find that you long for the din of traffic and the rush of crowds. Try it and see. If you do relocate to a small town, that's fine, but keep in mind that if you want to go there, other people do, too. Your small town may not remain small. In co-ops and some shared living situations, you *can* choose your new neighbors. However, for the most part in America it really isn't possible to shut the door after yourself to keep others out. Except, of course, in gated communities. The crime rate in gated communities and in age-segregated communities is wonderfully low— if the communities are separate, geographically or otherwise, from the rest of the world. Sun City, Arizona, for instance, has an extremely low crime rate. Arizona as a whole, however, claims the dubious distinction of having the highest crime rate of any state. Second place? Florida. If you want the highest degree of personal safety, and if you want to live in the general community rather than an age-segregated one, do some research about specific cities, neighborhoods, and living arrangements.

You can apply the ABC model to reducing needless emotional upsets triggered by considerations about moving or staying put. Given that most of us would like to make good decisions that help us realize our objectives, what stops us? What do people specifically tell themselves that makes it difficult or impossible for them to make up their minds? What do they tell themselves that leads, later, to their second-guessing their decisions? What are some self-defeating Beliefs that could detract from your ability to make decisions, in this case about where to live, or to deal productively with the results of decisions, come what may?

Accepting Lack of Guarantees

The first way you can drive yourself up the wall about a decision is to hold the Irrational Belief that you MUST not make a mistake. And, if you do make a mistake, it's *awful* and *intolerable* and you'd be *a jerk of the first order* for having done what you SHOULDN'T have done, namely make a mistake. To combat that "must," first you'd better accept the idea that even the best decision, given the information you have available at the time, may turn out to be unfortunate. Therefore, it is useless to drive yourself crazy *ahead of time* with demands for a perfect or mistake-free outcome.

If you believe you MUST not make a mistake, you may obsess endlessly. You may plague your friends by asking them what *they* would do. Then, usually, if they are foolish enough to make a firm recommendation, you do not follow their advice. Still later, when you wish you had followed their advice, you may even complain to them that they did not insist strongly enough on their point of view. Of course, if you do follow their advice, and it does not work out well for you, then you can complain to them that their advice was no good. The possibilities are almost endless! You may make yourself anxious and panicky and feel dread about the impending doom of a possible "wrong" decision. You may waffle between two (or more) choices, each with its own positives and negatives. As you draw yourself closer to your "final" decision, fairly confident about all its advantages, what can happen then? Its *negatives* begin to well up in your mind. You then reel back toward the other choice, whose positives now seem so great and so obvious and whose negatives seem, for the moment, rather acceptable. As you then move in that direction, its negatives start to loom larger! And so on, interminably back and forth. These "double approach/ avoidance conflicts," as we call them in psychology, can be hell. They stem partly from perfectionism: I MUST not make a mistake!

Even when some choice really is perfect, you believe, perfectionism can do you in. You will put yourself down when you later notice bad features in your choice you had not noticed before. Or when bad features emerge that weren't there when you made your "perfect" choice. Most complex choices cannot be perfect. Further, in the important choices you make (relocation, job, partner, and so forth), perfectionism can lead you to see unfortunate, but normal features as *awful*. The "reasoning" is, "If it's not perfect (as it MUST be), then it's *awful*."

Refusal To Whine

OK, let's say you have overcome your perfectionism to a good degree and you have made your choice. You relocated to the Jersey Shore rather than to Florida. You have accepted the reality that every complex choice has its negatives, and even has negatives that you did not or could not have foreseen. You are a fallible human being. Your lack of a crystal ball does not make you a bum, a failure, an idiot. You accept yourself even if your decision later turns out bad. So far, so good. It remains a good idea, however, to hold onto your list of possible negatives about living on the Jersey Shore. You may need that list, depending on how much you hold the awfulizing, I-can't-stand-it philosophy. The MUST underlying that philosophy is "People and things (in this case, the Jersey Shore, which is A, the Activating Event) MUST act and turn out the way I want them to. Otherwise, it's *awful* and I *can't stand* it, and life sucks!" Then, your MUSTurbation and awfulizing at B lead you to the emotional Consequences at C of whining. There are higher-class ways to describe it, but complaining, moaning, griping, and self-pity do boil down largely to whining. Not very attractive. Not at all productive. But quite common. If you whine about the bad aspects (Adversities) of living at the Jersey Shore, you detract immensely from your enjoyment of its good aspects. The bad aspects of what you have chosen—say, to live at the Jersey Shore—may even include the fact that the Jersey Shore is not Florida! If you notice yourself awfulizing about a decision that you have made, dispute the relevant Irrational Beliefs and build up more rational ones.

Here is another way to counteract the self-defeating tendency to obsess ahead of time about a decision, and to whine about its bad aspects after you've made it. Develop a list of rational rebuttals to Irrational Beliefs related to *bad* outcomes. Yes, don't merely hope that the bad outcome does not come about. It *could*. If it truly *could not* happen, then you would not be giving it a second thought. Have you worried lately about whether gravity will fail and you'll float off into space? Unlikely. So, face the possibility head on, by thinking about, in detail, how you would plan and what you could do, if each of the possible *bad* outcomes really did happen. That way, if they do happen, you will be much more prepared to deal with them productively. Again, if you are prone to obsess, keep a written record for later consultation.

How Green Was Their Valley?

When I (Emmett Velten) first met Bev and Warren, a retired couple, they had spent most of their lives in suburban Philadelphia. Their son and his family had lived where many people like to retire—Tucson, Arizona. Bev and Warren wanted to live near them, so, after much thought and advice from family about their decision, they moved to a retirement town south of Tucson, Green Valley. Things were fine for a few months. Then the bank their son worked for merged, made him an offer he couldn't refuse, and transferred him to Delaware—less than 40 miles from Bev and Warren's former home! Bev and Warren went through a long period of depression, kicking themselves for their "stupid" decision, moving to Green Valley. They felt lost without their old friends *and* without their son, daughter-in-law, and granddaughter. Should they move back to the Philadelphia area? They'd sold their house there and had bought one in Green Valley. If they *did* move, should they sell their place in Green Valley (due to overbuilding, the market there was crummy) or rent it (with the possible attendant long-distance rental hassles)? Disown their son? Tempting.

Over a few counseling sessions, Bev and Warren first challenged the awfulness of being "stuck" in Green Valley. They also challenged the idea that suburban Philadelphia had been the one true heaven on earth and that they were unbelievable fools for moving away from it. They also accepted, this time really accepted, their son's decision to move from

Tucson. At first they definitely had not, even though they had repeatedly
told him they didn't mind one bit and felt overjoyed by his promotion.
They finally decided that it would be feasible and fun for them to spend
the summer in one of the beach communities in Delaware near the kids.
Bev and Warren began to make friends in Green Valley. Warren became
a volunteer at the Titan Missile Museum and Bev took some training as
a docent at the Arizona-Sonora Desert Museum. The last I heard, they
were becoming a bit happier, though not ecstatic, in their new locale.

   To make any decision, especially an important one, puts you
dangerously close to two common emotional problems that plague the
human race: perfectionism and awfulizing. Moving when you are older
and deciding on a "final" home often involve both these difficulties.

   First, what about perfectionism? You, of course, can be— and you
may well earlier have been— perfectionistic about practically everything. As were May and Abe most of their lives. Maybe that's why they
married each other when they were in their late 20s, and stayed
together 35 years. They both had to do things perfectly— never be late
to work; do their jobs remarkably well; prepare meals superbly; shop for
the best bargains; and so on. If one of them had been a nonperfectionist,
the other would have been "driven" crazy. Luckily, they both demanded
perfection, so they nicely understood and tolerated each other.

   When it came to retiring to a "final" home they were stumped. They
had little surplus money and expensive tastes. May doted on a warm,
moist climate and very little traveling. She was a homebody and wanted
to get somewhere and stay. Besides, she had mild arthritis and walking,
much less skiing, was not as easy for her. Abe was still a ski fan and in
love with the great outdoors. They both wanted to be close to their
children and grandchildren, who lived in New York City, but they and
the children had little travel money. Neither Abe nor May wanted to
remain in New York. How could they perfectly resolve these problems
and differences as they had been able to do when they were younger?
They perfectly couldn't!

   Perfectionists also tend to have the other common emotional
problem—awfulizing and low frustration tolerance (LFT). May and Abe
had managed fairly well for most of their working lives, since they had
good jobs (he was an accountant, she a nurse) and two relatively
inexpensive children to support. So they often ate out, saw expensive
shows, and gave (perfect) dinner parties. Now with pension and Social
Security incomes that were secure, but far from large, they had to live
abstemiously and to find living quarters that didn't cost too much. Not

easy! In fact, most depriving. So, no matter how they sliced it, comfortable homes at reasonable rentals were not easy to come by. They managed to get by without going into debt, but it was quite a strain.

So for the first major time in their long years of marriage, May and Abe were at loggerheads. I (Albert Ellis) first got them to work on their perfectionism. I helped them ask themselves why they HAD TO have a perfect final home. It would be nice if they could find one, but considering their different tastes and "needs," why MUST they? Answer: They could have an *imperfect* home, one that would *partly* satisfy both of them. Question: Why MUST the home they chose be final, for all time? Answer: It didn't have to be. They could experiment—rent one apartment for, say, six months or a year, try it out, and if it wasn't suitable, try another for a year or so. In fact, why couldn't they try a different apartment every year or two, and never have a final one? They could.

Why again, did they HAVE TO get *one* final home? Maybe they could have two apartments—say, one for summer and one for winter. They could sublet the summer one when winter came, and the winter one when summer came. Or in winter, for two or three months, Abe could be something of a ski bum, while May stayed in their regular summer place and they could enjoy an uncommon vacation from each other.

I proposed—and helped them propose—several alternative *imperfect* solutions. Once they disputed their demands for a perfect solution and accepted that several imperfect solutions were possible, they put their minds to making some of them feasible.

This meant working on their low frustration tolerance (LFT). No living arrangement, I showed them, would be absolutely nonfrustrating to either of them. If Abe skied regularly, for example, it would cost money and either May would be deprived of his presence or she would suffer, with him, in a cold climate. Also, he might see little of their children, who didn't like skiing and lived in New York. If May lived most of the time in a warm, moist climate like Florida, she, too, would rarely see the children and grandchildren. She would also have to put up with a potentially cranky Abe who would rarely be able to ski. So, one way or the other, they both would often be deprived if they got their "ideal" living quarters—and also had to put up with *its* restrictions. Too bad— but some distinct degree of frustration was going to be their lot.

A *hassle*, I told May and Abe, was not a *horror*— except by definition, by viewing it as such. Abe would never like it if he skied minimally— but he could stand it. May would prefer a warm, moist climate plus seeing her children and grandchildren regularly—but she didn't have to have both and could live happily without either of them.

Once I helped May and Abe see that they didn't NEED what they wanted, including perfect solutions, they relaxed, took their "final" moving decision with some amount of humor, and started working things out—imperfectly. They spent two years experimenting with three living quarters, and they were fully satisfied with none of them. Nevertheless, they didn't feel "horribly deprived." They finally settled in Las Vegas, which was warm enough for May, though very dry, and which had nearby mountains where Abe could ski fairly frequently. Cheap airfare to New York was often available. Neither was perfectly happy with their living conditions, especially with the expenses they incurred and their only occasionally seeing the children and grandchildren. But their increased frustration tolerance, which they kept working on, enabled them to get by satisfactorily.

Age-Segregated Communities

What about age-segregated communities? What are their pros and cons? An advantage is that you may not face as much age-based discrimination. May not? Never underestimate some people's ability to figure out ways to try to feel superior to their fellows. More reliable advantages of age-segregated communities include amenities designed with older people in mind. There can also be safety in having numbers of retired people live in the neighborhood. In actual retirement towns or communities, such as Sun City, the crime rate is usually extremely low. In Sun City, for instance, there are active Neighborhood Watches. Residents easily spot people who don't live in the area and ask them their business. Older people are much less likely to commit crimes than are younger people. In some categories such as violent crime, older people's crime rate is dramatically low compared to the general population. Some retirement communities are gated, which affords greater security, and the same is true of multi-story retirement buildings with security guards.

Communities popular with retirees benefit greatly from having a large older population. If you are an older person with time on your hands, you can bring large supplies of usable skills and wisdom into your community. When you relocate, you can frequently involve yourself in new careers, hobbies, and active leisure. The more you do so, usually the better—if you want to keep what you have (physically and mentally) and perhaps regain some of what you lost in your non-retired, more sedentary days. A common problem in Florida, now, is the strain involved in communities' adapting their medical specialties and social services to their older population. On the other hand, the medical specialists and other service providers in such communities get more practice working with older people, and you may get better service from them.

There are several disadvantages to living in an age-segregated community. One of the most important to many people is that living in an age-segregated town or apartment building gives you much less access to a wide age-range of friends and associates in the larger world. Why is this important? Several studies indicate that your happiness and health are greater if, as an older person, you hobnob with people of many ages and types. Many older people themselves consider it impor-tant to their health and mental vitality to have some young friends. Some older people prefer only to interact with people like themselves. In research studies, such people appear less active, lonelier, less confident, less satisfied, and even less healthy than older people who prefer to socialize with people of all ages. If you are an older person and isolate yourself from the rest of the world, this may play into ageist perceptions, such as that the aged are very different from other people. So if you live in an age-segregated community, you may experiment with keeping as wide a social circle as you can.

Another important disadvantage is much more common for those who live in an age-segregated community than for those who live in the wider community. Age segregationists will probably experience more frequent death of friends and neighbors. This can be quite tough to cope with. Then again, you could live in the outside world, and if you only or mainly associated with old people, you could have the very same experience. In either of these cases, you had better consider extending your circle of friends to people of all ages. That way, you may have less death to cope with during any period of time. To feel sad at losses, and to deeply regret them, is rational. It reflects the importance of people in your life. What REBT can offer you, if you experience many deaths of friends and neighbors, is ways to dispute Irrational Beliefs. Is it truly *awful*, meaning 100 or 101 percent bad, that a friend died? And are sadness and grief 100 percent *unbearable*? Does loss mean your own life is over? Remember, your rational efforts to deal with death fully acknowledge that loss is very bad. After you lose someone important, your life will never be the same. But what can it be?

Some old people, who live in age-segregated environments and thus experience a greater concentration of death than do most people, choose another option. That is to withdraw from social activities, from human contact, as much as possible. Tempting though it may be to withdraw from getting to know people because they will die someday, presumably ahead of you, that's not a great solution to your uncomfortable feelings about death and loss. In chapter 15, we discuss death and dying issues more completely. For now, we will point out that withdrawal frequently promotes depression. It can promote physical and mental decline. Withdrawal from severely ailing friends is not a *horrible* and *awful* thing to do, and of course there is no reason that you MUST not do it. Nevertheless, when you withdraw, you do unto others as you may not want yourself or your loved ones done to. It builds a strange, cold world, where you disappear from friends and neighbors who are ill and who may die, just because you *can't stand* your possible feelings, such as grief and sadness. As well, people may be able to sense your withdrawal from them, and their intuition may tell them why it's happening. Why not talk about your thoughts and fears and listen to theirs? Facing these feelings takes some courage and maturity, but you can develop it. It's a skill that can be especially handy if you live in an age-segregated community.

11

Stand Up for Yourself

In a surplus labor market, the squeaking wheel does not get the grease; it gets replaced.

Miller's Maxim

There are things you would like to ask for or do. But you are afraid that your request—or you—will be rejected. So you don't ask. You hold back. There are ideas or feelings you'd like to express, but again, you stifle yourself. Or there are times when you would really like to say no, but you find yourself saying yes. Later you kick yourself for not sticking up for yourself. For not asserting yourself. What exactly is assertiveness?

Assertiveness is distinct from nonassertiveness, of which there are three kinds: Passivity, aggressiveness, and passive-aggressiveness. Let's look first at passivity. Passivity means not asking for what you want, or not declining what you do not want. It means letting things slide or going along with them when you very much don't want to. When you behave passively, you refrain from expressing your preferences, your wishes, your desires, whether they are for something that you want or against something that you do not want. If you are passive and you don't want to be, you may resent the people who "take advantage" of you. Still you do little about it.

A second nonassertive pattern is aggressiveness, which is quite distinct from assertiveness. Aggressiveness, as we use the term here, means being offensive and rude. It means being insensitive to, even riding roughshod over, the wishes and feelings of others. Aggressiveness means that you forcefully demand your "rights," often with anger, pushiness, and a mean attitude. You act inconsiderately. You may go ballistic. With aggressiveness, you may make a request or decline one, but you do so offensively, putting people down, stepping not just on their toes but sometimes (purely metaphorically, we hope) their faces! By "aggressiveness," as we use the term here, we do not mean physical aggression. Actual resort to physical pushing and shoving is not part of the "nonassertion" category.

You may have heard the term "passive-aggressive." It refers to a pervasive pattern of expressing anger and desire for independence in a way that combines elements of both passivity and aggressiveness. The worst of both worlds! While inwardly resentful and angry, the person behaving passive-aggressively usually does not become openly aggressive. If you have this pattern, you indirectly resist and obstruct the reasonable requests of others, such as your boss and spouse. You may try to get back at people, but in underhanded ways. You put off doing things you are asked to do. You claim to have forgotten your instructions. You may lose things, dawdle, sulk, do an intentionally slow or bad job, or otherwise sabotage. Not exactly self-helpful, rational behavior!

There is a fourth strategy, and it's far more effective than these three. In fact, it's usually the optimal strategy. Assertiveness, of course. In assertiveness, you make a request, or decline one, but you do so without stepping on the rights of others. If you are assertive, you calmly, coolly, and consistently express your wishes, without displaying (or feeling) anger or provoking resentment. For many of us, assertiveness does not come naturally. We have to make an effort to acquire the skill.

Roger and Gloria started with passivity. They almost, but not quite, detoured into aggressiveness, and they ended with assertiveness. They loaned their eldest son, Sean, $10,000 as part of the down payment for his first house. It was clearly understood as a loan, and in fact Roger and Gloria and Sean had signed a formal repayment note, including a schedule of payments. But there were no payments. And there were no mentions of the loan, certainly not by Sean, nor at first by Roger and Gloria. When they did "mention" it, they did so indirectly and Sean steadfastly didn't get the message. Gloria, for instance, mentioned that their back fence needed replacement. Get the hint? Sean didn't. Roger mentioned he only wished they could afford some plush carpeting he had seen on sale at Macy's. Sean missed that hint, too. After Sean got a big raise at work, Roger and Gloria thought for sure he'd start making the payments, probably even doubling up on them. Guess again! Many months passed, many similar incidents piled up. What really burned Roger and Gloria up and brought them perilously close to angry rebukes was Sean's announcement that he and his wife were going on a long trip to Jordan to visit her parents. By way of Paris, Rome, Cairo, and Jerusalem! (Roger and Gloria had managed a week's vacation at a campground in Yosemite.) Sean's wife mentioned that she was afraid their gorgeous new luggage would get battered in transit and asked if they could borrow Roger and Gloria's beat-up suitcases.

Briefly, Roger and Gloria wanted Sean's head on a stake—his wife's, too—but just briefly. Instead, they happened to notice an ad for my (Emmett Velten's) two-day assertiveness training workshop. The other workshop participants really got into helping Roger and Gloria detect their Irrational Beliefs that kept them from discussing the loan situation with Sean. What do you think their IBs were? Generally along these lines: "We SHOULDN'T have to mention it to him, that *dirty rat!*" "If he loved us, he'd repay us the money without our having to ask him." "We'd be *too uncomfortable* having to bring up the topic—can you imagine having to do that?!" In addition to disputing their Irrational Beliefs and practicing more helpful Rational Beliefs, Gloria and Roger rehearsed reasonable, assertive conversational ploys. They rehearsed with the other members of the workshop, who played Sean's role.

Day two of the workshop came one week later, and Roger and Gloria reported back on their homework. To their complete shock, Sean seemed astonished and embarrassed and said he'd just assumed that the loan was actually a gift. On the spot he wrote out a check for half the amount owed and said he would stick to the payment plan. He also asked his parents why they didn't bring the subject up earlier! Good question.

What Irrational Beliefs lead *you* to say yes when you want to say no? Or to feel guilty if you do manage to say no? Or to stew in your juices because you haven't asked for or declined a request and the other person didn't read your mind to find out your wishes? What Irrational Beliefs stop you from setting limits? If you do (or have) willingly made *genuine* loans—that is, you truly expect repayment—what Irrational

Beliefs could undermine your pushing your children (or other people) to stick with a repayment schedule? You *can* learn to refuse to feel guilty. You *can* set limits, when that is your desire, on their borrowing from you.

Not only can assertion skills be helpful to your psychological health and sometimes to your pocketbook, but possibly to your physical health. Studies of immune function have suggested that depression, helplessness, hopelessness, and despair—which can relate to lack of assertiveness—have strong correlations with decline in immune function. Increases in immune function, on the other hand, seem to correlate with a sense of control and with the ability to express yourself assertively.

The Three Patterns of Nonassertiveness

The ABC model helps you analyze situations where it seems sensible to assert yourself. Instead of asserting yourself, though, you act with passivity or with aggressiveness. Or with both. The passive-aggressive pattern combines elements of both passivity and aggressiveness. It is a passive way of expressing aggressiveness.

Passivity

Let's first look at some of the Irrational Beliefs and automatic negative thoughts that underlie passivity. Your Adversity (A) may be some situation where you would *like* to assert yourself or *wish* you had done so. However, at C, you didn't or "can't." Perhaps you stuffed your feelings and pretended you didn't even care when you *did* care very much.

What stopped you from asserting yourself the way you probably already knew would have been preferable? What did you tell yourself at B that defeated you? Some of the possibilities are:

- It SHOULD be easier to assert myself.
- I don't feel like asserting myself.
- It takes too much energy.
- It's too much trouble.
- I don't really have the right to stand up for myself.
- I'm nobody. Nobody is going to listen to me.

- What's the use in asking?
- At my age, what difference does it make? I'll be dead in a few decades anyway.
- Maybe I'm just being selfish and stingy.
- It's better not to make waves.
- I'm too old to change. When I was young, I could have learned to stand up for myself better, but it's too late now. You can't teach an old dog new tricks.
- People won't like me if I stand up for myself. They'll think I'm just an old grouch.
- Maybe I'll hurt their feelings.
- Maybe they will stop loving me if I speak my mind.

Aggressiveness

Let's now look at some of the Irrational Beliefs and automatic negative thoughts that underlie aggressiveness. Your Adversity (A) is the same as above. It is some situation where you'd *like* to assert yourself or *wish* you had done so. This time, however, at C, you overreacted with anger or vindictiveness. You may have rudely told the other person off. What did you tell yourself at B that made you aggressive and defeated you? Some of the possibilities are:

- Those dirty so-and-so's! How dare they infringe on my rights?
- People who don't do what I want are bastards.
- I deserve to have my way.
- People owe something to me.
- I have more rights to this than they do.
- If I want it, I deserve it and have GOT TO have it.
- Other people's feelings don't count—screw 'em!

One of the rational humorous songs I (Emmett Velten) often recommend to people with aggressive inclinations at work and else-where is this:

GO TO HELL!
("Jingle Bells")

If you would get release,
And let your anger out,

Disrupt the blasted peace,
And scream and yell and shout!
Just go to any length,
To show you can't be stilled,
And you will prove enormous strength
Up till the time you're killed!

Pow! pow! pow!
Pow! pow! pow!
Pound your enemies!
Oh what fun it is to stun
Anyone who dares not please you.
Sock! sock! sock!
Knock! knock! knock!
Howl and whine and cry.
And everyone from you will run,
And hate you till you die!

Pout! pout! pout!
Shout! shout! shout!
When things are a mess.
Rip! rip! rip!
Slip! slip! slip!
Into a profound depression.
Drink! drink! drink!
Think! think! think!
Only of cruel fate.
Keep your mind preoccupied
With everything you hate!

Passive-Aggressive

Now let's look at some of the Irrational Beliefs and automatic negative thoughts that underlie nonassertiveness of the passive-aggressive variety. Again, your Adversity (A) may be some situation where you would *like* to assert yourself or *wish* you had done so. However, at C, you didn't. You *appeared* to agree with what was asked of you, but inside you bitterly resented it. You worked slowly, phoned in sick on the most crucial day in completing the big project, and you complained a lot about working conditions. What did you tell yourself at B that defeated you? Some of the possibilities are:

- Little do they know, but they can't make me do this. How dare they try?
- I SHOULDN'T have to deal with this nonsense. If they cared about me, they wouldn't make me do this.
- I'll get back at them.
- The boss has no right to ask me to do this, but I'm too afraid to speak to her about it.
- I bitterly resent how little they pay me. After all the time I've worked here!

One of the rational humorous songs I (Emmett Velten) often recommend to people with passive-aggressive inclinations at work is this:

BUMMERTIME ("Summertime" from *Porgy and Bess* by George Gershwin)

Bummertime, all the pissin an' moanin',
Piss 'n' moan, all the work day through.
Your boss is a bitch,
And your foreman gives you work to do,
So, whine, little baby, all the work day through.
One of these mornin's,
You're gonna wake up smilin',
Saturday mornin', you're gonna feel real fine.
But until that mornin',
Ain't nothin' gonna pacify you,
So, whine, little baby,
All the work day through!

It probably can go without saying, but if you are a therapist, do *not* use this song with a client until you have established a very good working relationship! And make sure the client well understands the rationale of singing his or her blues away.

Stand Up For Yourself No Matter How Much Shorter You've Gotten

Assertion has special importance with increasing age. Let's consider several of the special reasons that can make it easier for older people to act unassertively. These include:

- Social status and assertiveness are linked, and older people have lower status.
- As you get older, you tend to get smaller, shorter, lighter, and have a less commanding voice.
- Older people often have less money than younger people.

Any or all of these factors, or others you may think of, can add to assertiveness problems older people may experience.

One of our friends, Ella, said that she had noticed that as she got into her later sixties, people paid less attention to her. "I became less visible." The farther she got beyond middle age, the more invisible Ella said she became. Specifically, she was referring to shopping situations. While standing at a counter, she said, salespeople were more likely to attend first to younger people, no matter who was there first. That kind of thing had happened to her more and more as she got older. Whatever the causes, if it looked as if she was getting bumped to the end of the line, Ella said in a strong voice, "Excuse me, I believe I was next." She explained to me that since no one else was there to stand up for her, she had taught herself to do so.

There are a number of emotional hang-ups that prevent people from asserting themselves. Most of them fall under three main headings, and Harriet had several of them. At the age of 56, she hadn't done too badly in life. She was head of her English department at a good high school. She had a solid, 30-year marriage with a substantial, loving husband, and a son and daughter who were finishing up their studies for good careers of their own. She had many years of practice as the head of her department. However, she experienced a great deal of difficulty in asserting herself with her principal and with practically all the teachers who were under her and who respected her. Her spouse and her children were hardly dictatorial or dominating individuals, but Harriet rarely asserted herself effectively with them. She often gave in to them on important matters rather than speak her mind and negotiate with them.

I Won't Do It Well

First, as is true in so many cases of a lack of assertiveness, Harriet was afraid that she would assert herself badly. She never had been a fluent and fast speaker, as her younger sister had been. She was always afraid that she would get stuck in the middle of a sentence and wouldn't finish well what she had started. She felt mortified by the idea that she wouldn't be understood and someone would ask her to repeat herself. Or, she worried, "What if I bother people and they look at me critically?" So she often said nothing when others would speak volubly. She had a lot to say but was afraid of saying it badly.

I'll Get Rejected

Second, Harriet felt terrified of rejection if she *did* ask for something and she was refused. She took all refusals personally, and never considered that people often said no just because they said no, and that it didn't matter who was requesting something of them. In a situation where she'd like to ask for something, Harriet would enter the situation already thinking that she was probably wrong to ask for favors. Then she asked in such a hesitant manner that she made it easy for people to refuse to give her what she asked for. Once they had refused her request, Harriet was more certain than ever that they were refusing because she, in particular, had asked, and they, like herself, really felt that she was unworthy.

I'm Not Deserving

Finally, because Harriet put herself down so much and found flaws in herself that others didn't see, she concluded that she was a weak, worthless individual. She concluded she didn't truly deserve most of the things she might have asked for. She thought that only more accomplished and nicer people were deserving, and that she never made it in either respect. She wasn't good *enough*, and she wasn't nice *enough*. Harriet felt convinced of this, and she was sure that others could see it, too. Therefore, she *was* undeserving. To buttress this view, she knew that she was afraid to be assertive, and she put herself down for that, too. So all in all, she did fairly well by others, though definitely not in her eyes. She considered herself inept, useless, and unworthy of reciprocation, let alone any gifts from others.

USA

I (Albert Ellis) first had difficulty in getting over to Harriet the idea of USA—unconditional self-acceptance. She saw human deservingness as a profit and loss statement. You give much of yourself to other people and to worthy causes, and then you get back a little of what you want—but not much. If you received too many goods and services for the work and help that you gave, you were selfish, and really had no interest in helping others. You, or at least Harriet, then felt guilty and more worthless than ever.

REBT has nothing against being kind and devoted to other people and espouses the principle of UOA—unconditional other-acceptance. According to that philosophy, you fully accept people and try to be kind and considerate to them, even when they act badly toward you or others. You accept the sinner, but not the sin, and you try to make the world a better place to live in. Why? Because you like being a responsible member of the human race, and not because you gain personal worth and some degree of beatitude for being good to others. This brings us to the Sixteenth Rule for Optimal Living:

Rule #16: Be Interested in Yourself and in Others

To remain emotionally healthy, have interest not just in your own welfare but in that of others. Sensible and emotionally healthy people do tend to put their own interests at least a little above the interests of others. They sacrifice themselves to some degree for those for whom they care, but not overwhelmingly or completely. Social interest is usually rational and self-helping because most people choose to live and enjoy themselves in a social group or community. If you do not act morally, protect the rights of others, and promote social survival, it is unlikely you will create the kind of world in which you yourself can live comfortably and happily.

Harriet enjoyed serving others, both at home and at work, but she still thought that she did not help them *enough*. She thought she was not bright and charming *enough* to make people eager to be in her presence. Because of her good deeds (in combination with her perfectionism), however, Harriet did not consider herself a wicked or evil person—just an inadequate person! She couldn't at first understand, much less apply, the notion of USA—that you always, regardless of your lack of proficiency and virtues, accept and honor yourself. You seek to lead a good life, just because you are human. Harriet thought, instead, that you had to buy approval, and consequent worthiness, by your good deeds.

I was able to show Harriet that this plan of *conditional* self-acceptance just would not work. Even when she had a good reputation, because of her productivity and her consideration of others, she could still say that it was not good *enough*—since it SHOULD be outstanding. Even when she temporarily felt good about herself for her apt functioning and her kindness to others, how would she know that this good level of efficiency would continue? She might later do poorly and be disapproved! Because adequate functioning and approval of others were sacred to her—not merely important but sacred—she was always anxious that she might not maintain these goals.

The proof was her unassertiveness. People liked her because she did not ask too much of them—but they also thought her weak and unprepossessing. They saw that she did good enough work as a teacher and as the head of her department. They also saw her lack of confidence in herself, and therefore kept taking advantage of her. The teachers she supervised were repeatedly lax about handing in their reports and they had more lateness and absences than the teachers in the other departments. When she didn't get after them sufficiently, her principal held *her* responsible for the lack of discipline in her department. Finally he threatened to demote her.

Harriet's lack of assertiveness was "nice" but it didn't work. The less she asserted herself, the more the teachers under her and even her family members asked things of her. They didn't follow the principle of live and let live, but the principle of take and take more.

As Harriet's problems increased, and as her anxiety and feelings of worthlessness also mounted, I showed her that her attitudes and her resulting actions—or inactions—were quite ineffective. Though she had a hard time seeing it, she finally realized that unconditional self-acceptance was the only realistic way out of her difficulties. With unconditional self-acceptance, she could continue to work hard and be considerate to other people. Instead of letting her good work and kindness "make" her worthy to herself, however, she could achieve acceptance as a human merely by deciding to have it. She could *define* herself as a worthy individual just because she, as a human, chose to do so. She could accept herself just because she was alive and a unique person. Then, with her decision and choice to be an okay person because she existed, Harriet gave herself unconditional acceptance. USA allowed Harriet to keep up her accomplishments and to get along with others just because she enjoyed doing so and got good practical results.

Harriet, in other words, began to see that she could obtain good things in her life, as a teacher and as a parent, because she behaved well. In this sense, she earned those good things. She could see that she did not have to derive her *personal worth* from anything but her being alive and human, from her humanity. She deserved to live and enjoy just because she decided to do so.

Harriet finally seemed to get this concept of USA, but she still had trouble applying it to being assertive. She had behind her a whole lifetime of acting passively, and she found it awkward and at times embarrassing to ask for something she wanted or to refuse something she didn't want to do. So at first, we used one of the behavioral methods of REBT, role-playing. This gave Harriet practice in asserting herself. I played her principal, the teachers she headed, or her family members, with all of whom she was passive. I gave her practice in asking them for things that she normally would never ask for. Then, when we had done a number of role-plays, and she was becoming more adept at being assertive in them, we graduated to her doing real-life homework along similar lines.

This was still difficult for Harriet to do, even though she wanted to accomplish assertiveness in several areas. We would develop homework assignments for her to speak up to people—and then she copped out of doing them. So we used another of the behavioral techniques of REBT to help her do so—that of reinforcing or rewarding her, with something she really wanted, only *after* she had forced herself to assert herself. She was not to allow herself to do this distinctly pleasurable thing *until* she had been assertive.

This is the most valuable aspect of self-help. To do things you are afraid to do or would feel uncomfortable to do is indeed hard. To be assertive even in simple ways when you have practiced passivity (or aggressiveness) for many years can be most difficult. In Harriet's case it was. So she picked a few pleasures or reinforcers that she really loved— such as talking to her children about their daily activities, and relaxing with her husband while they listened to the nightly news. She only allowed herself to do these things after she had done something to assert herself with various people that day. If she copped out on being assertive, no talks with the children and no news-watching with her husband. Only if she was properly assertive as she wanted to be, could she enjoy these pleasures.

That worked fine. Harriet kept showing herself that there was nothing wrong in doing what she wanted, even though she risked the disapproval of others. She saw that if she did not accomplish certain tasks or if others did not thoroughly approve of her, she was still an acceptable, worthwhile person. Why? Because she chose to be, because she was determined to accept herself with no strings attached. When she really reached this stage of thinking, and used assertiveness and risk of others' potential disapproval to back up her philosophy of USA, she became much less anxious and more enjoying. If anything, she accomplished her activity of teaching and parenting more efficiently.

Do Your Detective Work

If you, like Harriet, are passive, and you fail to ask people for what you want and hesitate to refuse them when they ask you for too much, do your detective work. Look first for what you are telling yourself. Irrational Beliefs most probably are creating your passivity. Usually, though not necessarily always, you have a fear of rejection. Usually you would not only think that it's disappointing to fail to get what you want when you assert yourself, but that it also means something about you as a person. Usually you would think that the individual who refuses you, looks down on you, and that she or he is right in putting you down. Then, again, like Harriet, you may think that you are a moron for *not* asserting yourself as others do, and you berate yourself, your being, for having that weakness. So you are doubly self-downing. Then you may go beyond that and think that if you *do* assert yourself, you will do it very badly. Or you may think that you really don't deserve to get what you want. You may have other self-downing thoughts, but lack of self-acceptance is often the prime reason for your passivity when you would like to act assertively.

In regard to low frustration tolerance, you may feel that it's *awful* to ask for what you want and be refused. You may declare that you *can't stand* not getting what you desire. You may call it *too damned hard* to keep asking for what you want and to often get refused. So you whine and scream about the hassles of being rejected, and this keeps you from continuing to assert yourself until you at least partially get what you desire.

Sometimes, when you first get refused after being assertive, you make yourself feel very aggressive toward the refusers. You may insist that they SHOULD NOT be the rotten way they are. This, of course, often encourages them to be angry in return and deliberately not give you what you want. It may even encourage them to vindictively give you what you *don't* want! Then you make yourself feel aggressive toward them again, and 'round and 'round you go. Finally you may stop asserting yourself and get in the habit of "keeping peace" by falling back into passivity.

Look, therefore, at your Irrational Beliefs leading to nonassertiveness. The Irrational Beliefs (IBs) we have outlined above, or variations on them, most likely will underlie your particular brand of nonassertion—whether passivity, aggressiveness, or passive-aggressiveness. Then vigorously dispute those IBs in various ways that we have been describing in this book.

Along with this disputing, however, you had best make yourself distinctly uncomfortable by forcing yourself to be assertive when you are reluctant to do so, until you finally become comfortable and even enjoy asserting yourself. You may do this first by role-playing with a friend of yours. Rehearse brief assertive scenes repeatedly. Not once or twice, but more like 15 or 20 times in each practice session with your friend. In these role-plays, your role is that of the would-be assertive you. Your friend plays the person toward whom you would like to act assertively. First, prepare your friend by showing him or her how to behave as your "assertive target." Record your role-playing on an audio or videotape, and then you and your friend can critique it. Or you can ask other friends to watch your rehearsals and critique your assertive efforts. Do this until you improve your assertive behavior and are able to feel comfortable and effective while doing it.

Finally, however, there is nothing like exposure—real-life exposure and practice—to make yourself comfortably assertive. Try it in action, with friends and relatives who may well refuse you but will not actually penalize you if you ask for something that they do not want to give. Be very careful in being assertive with bosses, supervisors, traffic cops, judges, muggers, or other people who have power over you. They may penalize you for your assertiveness. Watch it! In these cases, compliance, without anger or footdragging, is often the best policy. Try asserting yourself with people and under conditions where you will not be shot down—literally or figuratively—and get used to doing it in those relatively safe circumstances.

If you still have trouble, you can do what Harriet did. You can reinforce yourself with some pleasurable activity only after you have bothered to assert yourself with some people with whom you are usually passive and acquiescing. If necessary, you can also penalize yourself by doing some chore or task that you hate doing—such as talking to a boring acquaintance or eating distasteful food—each time you do *not* assert yourself. Choosing penalties can be quite amusing. Implementing them may prove less amusing. Remember, they are *supposed* to be penalties. The more undesirable they are, the stronger your motivation will be to avoid them. There's a very easy way to avoid penalties entirely: do your assertive homework! By using these thinking and behavioral methods you can become much more assertive than you usually are. You can overcome some lifelong bad habits of nonassertion. It's about time that you did—no matter how old you may be.

Break the Chains

Now it's your turn to think about what someone, in this case Abdul, might be telling himself to make himself nonassertive. You can take the role of the therapist, which will considerably help you learn how to help yourself. Abdul's example has more zigs and zags in it than some we have used earlier. This time we will show you a chain of ABC's. As you read this example, think how it might help you target some of your own assertion problems. How would you detect your own self-defeating Beliefs that create nonassertion, whether the passive, the aggressive, or the passive-aggressive type? Can you effectively dispute those Irrational Beliefs? Are you willing to put into practice, in real-life, what you have learned?

First, break your targeted assertion problem into the A, B, and C. A, the Activating Event, is your desire for assertion. C, the Consequence, is your not fulfilling that desire by asserting yourself. Instead, you behave with nonassertion, which, again, has three general possibilities: (1) passivity, (2) aggressiveness, and (3) the worst of both worlds—passive-aggressiveness. As you study Abdul's case, consider how the elements in *your* targeted nonassertion correspond to the elements in his.

Here is the apparent—at least the first—Activating Event that Abdul presented. He lived in a high-rise apartment complex whose parking garage had just been repainted. Some of the parking spaces, including his, were renumbered. His new space was in an area of the garage where it was quite easy for guests "just stopping for a minute" to block one's car. Abdul wanted to assert himself, but instead—at C, his Consequences—he seethed and didn't go to management to protest. Why didn't he? What stopped him? What do you think were his core

Irrational Beliefs at B? I MUST be successful, or else? I MUST have approval, or else? I NEED fairness and comfort, or else? If Abdul had one or more of those "musts," what other negative automatic thoughts might he have derived from them? What is *your* "must"? What additional automatic negative thoughts stem from your "must"?

If you suspected that Abdul thought his request to get back his old parking space MUST NOT be turned down—a fear of rejection or fear of failure—as I (Emmett Velten) first did, you'd be wrong. "What are you telling yourself at B that prevents you from asserting yourself?" I asked Abdul.

"I might be nervous" was Abdul's answer. You will notice that there is no "must" there. By itself, just being nervous wouldn't stop you from asserting yourself. So, I looked farther for a "must."

"And if you were nervous? What would that mean to you that would keep you from going to the manager to request your old parking space back?"

"At my age," Abdul replied, "I'd look foolish if I were nervous about something like that." Again, there is no direct statement of a "must" there, though "foolish" might mean "worthless" to Abdul.

At this point, I offered a hypothesis about the "must." First, though, I transferred "could be nervous" and "look foolish" to the Activating Event category. That is, Abdul's Activating Event is not just the parking space situation and his wish to speak up about it. His Activating Event also could include that he might well feel nervous and look foolish when he went to the manager to protest.

"I suppose that's very possible," I replied, "that you'd feel nervous and *look like* a fool. I've looked like a fool before and have been nervous. But that still doesn't stop you, all by itself, from asserting yourself. What might you have told yourself, that would stop you from asserting yourself? What might you have told yourself *about* the possible facts that you'd feel nervous and look foolish?"

Abdul then came right out with a "must": "At my age, I SHOULDN'T be nervous. I'd be a fool if I were nervous," Abdul said, stating a "must."

First we worked through the idea that one MUST NOT be nervous and would be *a fool* if one were nervous at Abdul's age. Or at any age. Abdul concluded, after a good bit of discussion, that it would be *preferable* not to feel nervous, but hardly *awful* and *intolerable*. He also concluded that nervousness did not make one a fool, but merely someone who was nervous.

"And what do you think you might be telling yourself about going to the manager to get yourself nervous in the first place?" I asked, expecting that Abdul would then say that he feared rejection or failure.

"If the manager turned me down, then I'd have to move, and I don't want to move."

"Why would you have to move?"

Abdul replied, "Because I'd be too ashamed that the manager would know I wanted my old parking space back and didn't get it back."

Underlying Abdul's feelings of shame was the Irrational Belief, "I MUST NOT be *known* to have failed." While Abdul didn't like failing, he was not putting himself down as a person for failing. But he would put himself down if someone *knew* he failed! Abdul and I then worked through the Irrational Belief that it would be *horrible* and *unbearable* for someone to know that he, Abdul, suffered an emotional disappointment. He came to see, and believe, and feel, that if someone knew you had a disappointment, this would not be such a big deal.

Abdul and I also examined the seething feelings he had described as associated with his nonassertiveness. We soon detected the "must": "The manager SHOULDN'T put me in this position of having to go to him and be nervous and have him maybe turn me down." Abdul worked this one out by seeing that the manager had free will; the owner of the apartment building had free will; and the painting contractor had free will. Even the universe had free will, or at least, did not have to do what Abdul wanted. Therefore, they could do whatever they chose to do, whether or not it was beneficial to Abdul. As he thought more about it and let go of his anger at the manager, Abdul recalled having heard some interesting gossip poolside. Namely, the manager's wife had been complaining about *their* parking space having been shifted!

Did Abdul ever get his old parking space back? No. He took his plea to the owner of the building, but the latter turned down his request. Abdul felt irritated and annoyed, but not off the wall. In addition, as a shame-attacking exercise, he told a number of his neighbors about having been turned down.

What are some situations where you would like to speak up or say no, yet you don't? List them. These are the Activating Events. Your *not* speaking up or saying no is the C, the Consequences. What are your IBs, your Irrational Beliefs that prevent you from speaking up or saying no when you would like to? Can you find underlying "musts"? Once you do, you can use the form on pages 198–99, *The ABC's and the Three Key Questions of Rational Emotive Behavior Therapy*, to dispute your Irrational Beliefs and to develop Rational Beliefs.

Let's now look at an example where a woman learned assertiveness skills to apply in one situation, and later applied them successfully in another frustrating situation related to healthcare. Stephanie, age 48, first sought help with her two almost-teenage children who, she said, were "out of control." She admitted, "I am, too!" Stephanie was quite inconsistent in her way of managing the children. There were some "house rules," but after a few days of firmly enforcing them, she would taper off. Why? "It's too much trouble." Her children would soon see that they could do their chores haphazardly or not at all, and Stephanie would let it slide. And slide, and slide. Until some particular infraction would "set me off." She said she would "go ballistic" and "go off on the kids." She didn't hit them, but she yelled and raged and told them what brats they were. After one of these episodes, the kids would be good as gold for a couple of weeks in doing their chores. Then, the cycle would repeat.

Stephanie was highly motivated and bright and we quickly got to her core "musts." They were:

1. I SHOULDN'T have to tell them more than once.
2. They HAVE TO obey me.
3. It's too much trouble (as it SHOULDN'T be) to keep enforcing the rules.

The third "must" was the most important. After Stephanie disputed it, her Effective New Belief was "It's really not *too* hard to enforce the rules. It's just a real bother. And it's a hell of a lot *harder* if I don't enforce the rules!" How would you dispute Stephanie's first two "musts"?

Well over a year after working with Stephanie, she called me (Emmett Velten) to bring me up to date. Things were generally OK with the children's behavior, but she had really called to tell me how well she'd handled an exceptionally frustrating Activating Event. It seems that Stephanie routinely did breast self-examinations for lumps. When she found a lump, she called her managed care "gatekeeper" primary provider doctor for an appointment. After a long rigmarole by voice mail, she finally succeeded in leaving a message. He did not return her call. She called again in a day or two. Same story, but she did get a call back—on her message machine at home (she had left her work number)—from his physician's assistant. The latter told her to make an appointment to come in for an examination. Stephanie called, selected

The ABC's and the Three Key Questions of Rational Emotive Behavior Therapy (REBT)

A   B   C

Activating Events   **Beliefs**   **Consequences**
Things: past,   Thoughts,   **(actions and**
present, predicted   assumptions   **emotions)**
Adversities
Aggravations

Epictetus   "People are disturbed not by things, but by the
                          views they take of them."

Shakespeare/ Hamlet   "There is nothing either good or bad, but thinking
                          makes it so."

John Milton   "The mind is its own place, and in itself can make
                          a Heav'n of Hell, a Hell of Heav'n."

Basic Self-Helping Beliefs	**Basic Self-Defeating Beliefs**
I'd PREFER success and approval; I'd PREFER that you behave correctly; and I'd PREFER comfort and fairness in life. BUT these things are NOT ABSOLUTELY NECESSARY.	I ABSOLUTELY MUST get success and approval; you ABSOLUTELY MUST behave correctly; life ABSOLUTELY MUST give me comfort and fairness. It would be the end of the world if I don't get these things!

The Three Key Questions To Ask About Your Beliefs

1. Does my Belief help me or hinder me over the long run?
   Rational thinking is defined as tending to be helpful to you over the long run. Irrational thinking is defined as tending to hinder you over the long run.
   Follow-up question to #1: If my Belief hinders me, that is, it's irrational, what Rational Belief (RB) would help me reach my goals better and feel better?

2. Is my Belief consistent with known facts and reality?
   Rational thinking is defined as consistent with known facts. Irrational thinking is inconsistent with or unsupported by known facts.
   Follow-up question to #2: If my Belief is inconsistent with reality, that is, it's irrational, what Rational Belief (RB) would be more consistent with reality?

3. Is my Belief logical?
   "Logical" can be illustrated with examples. Let's say you very much preferred to succeed at something; would it logically follow that *therefore* you MUST succeed? No, the *necessity* for success does not follow logically from the fact that success would be beneficial.

	Logical	Illogical
Major premise	All people are mortal.	Success is good.
Minor premise	Elvis is a person.	I would like to succeed.
Conclusion	Elvis is mortal.	Therefore, I MUST succeed.

Follow-up question to #3: OK, if my Belief is illogical, what Rational Belief (RB) would make more sense logically?

HOMEWORK: Analyze these four statements in terms of each of the Three Key Questions, and change the statements to rational statements from irrational ones. (1) Everything I do is wrong. (2) Because I had such a tough childhood, I deserve things to be easier now. (3) I've been addicted to cigarettes too long to change. (4) People who fail are complete failures as human beings.

Do the same for four of YOUR Irrational Beliefs (IB's). HINT: Look for Beliefs that express these three MUSTs: I MUST succeed and get approval; you MUST behave correctly; circumstances MUST be comfortable and fair.

the "make an appointment" option, and endured a long voice mail message that asked this question, "Is this an emergency?" After some hesitation, Stephanie pressed 2, for non-emergency. The voice mail system then gave her options about which doctor to see, or which physician's assistant to see, and offered options about the date and time of day. Stephanie did not have her appointment book at hand, and by the time she got back to the phone, all she heard was music. After a minute or two, she hung up, called again, and underwent the whole touch-tone routine again. She took the earliest appointment available, which was three weeks away.

Stephanie worried for a while, then called back. This time she pressed 1 for emergency, to see how much sooner she would be able to get in for an appointment. The voice mail system told her to dial 911 or to go to the nearest hospital emergency room. Stephanie found this quite annoying, especially since the voice mail system did not then give her any other options, such as pressing 0 to reach a live human being. Instead, it hung up on her. She called back, this time selecting 2 for non-emergency, which *had* offered the option of pressing 0 to reach "an attendant." Having dialed 0, she did not get through to a human being, only to the "message center." It gave her the same string of choices about what doctor and what physician's assistant she wanted to see, and when. Stephanie suffered through all the menu of choices again before being allowed to leave a voice message. A firm one.

Stephanie was smart enough to instruct her secretary that he was to put through any calls from her doctor's office, and to track her down if she wasn't in her office. Sure enough, within the hour, Stephanie's secretary put a call through to her from the same physician's assistant. After some discussion of the appointment three weeks away, Stephanie said, "That's not acceptable." After being told to go to an emergency room, she firmly held her ground: "It's not that kind of emergency. I really don't think that the administrators at (naming the managed care outfit) will like it if I have a very expensive emergency room visit. Dr. O'Neill could save them a great deal of money and save himself a whole lot of explaining. I want an appointment this week. It is not acceptable to wait three weeks."

Stephanie repeated two or three times more the basic theme that she was going to make really big waves with the managed care office. She also added, unangrily, that her friends thought that having to wait three weeks when you had detected a lump was malpractice. Stephanie got an appointment two days away. She felt regret that her medical care was in the hands of managed care, and she regretted the inconvenience. She wished she hadn't had to persist and be a "hard-ass" to obtain the service she wanted. But, reality was reality. It would be desirable if medical care were as good as it had been only ten years ago, but it wasn't. And it didn't HAVE TO be. Stephanie explained, "When you deal with these managed-care people, you have to be persistent. *Very* persistent and firm." So, Stephanie had acted assertively. Not passively, not aggressively, not passive-aggressively—but calmly, firmly, and assertively.

12

Romance, Love, and Sex Never Get Old

You can know something has gone wrong only when you make an odd number of mistakes.

Murphy's Uncertainty Principle

Zack had just about all the trouble you could have in the love, sex, and family area. He fell in love with Zelda when he was 70 and she was 48. Many of his friends didn't think it seemly for him to be head over heels in love, like a teenager, when he was entering his eighth decade. His three children, who were then in their forties, particularly did not think it was proper for him to be romantically gaga over a women who was not much older than they were. They were sure she was after his money. They thought she was penniless after having taken care of her husband who had died following a five-year bout with cancer. Zack had plenty of money, about half of which his wife had left him, and left him outright, not in trust for the children. His children were quite afraid that if Zack married Zelda and she outlived him—which she most probably would—he would leave most of his estate, including his wife's money, to her. Not to them. So they were doubly or triply unenthusiastic about this romantic ardor for Zelda.

To make matters worse, Zack's friends and close relatives, most of whom he had known for many years, also tended to think that his passion for Zelda was foolish. They thought that it would hardly survive a year or two if he married her. There's no fool like an old fool was their motto, and they held pretty closely to it.

To make matters still worse, Zack was very anxious about satisfying Zelda sexually. His wife had been someone who loved intercourse and who rarely climaxed in any other form of sex. He had often been anxious about satisfying her. She died in her early sixties (they were the same age) and at that time Zack was still fairly arousable sexually. He had barely managed to keep up with the once or twice a week that she wanted intercourse. Now, almost ten years after her death, he was distinctly less able to get and maintain an erection. He had ended several affairs with women on that account. Not that they felt dissatisfied with sex—for most of them had much less interest in it than Mary, Zack's previous wife. But he either failed to get an erection or came too quickly for his own satisfaction with them, and he would break off the affair after a few sex "mishaps." Zelda seemed to be just about as sexy as Mary—and don't forget that she was only 48. Zack was afraid that her love for him, which was just as tempestuous in most ways as his was for her, would definitely go to pot once they had sex regularly. So he only occasionally, when he felt particularly horny, had intercourse with her, and more often than not was exceptionally romantic but not very sexy.

Zelda, who was truly in love with Zack, was tired of living alone for the last several years, and was eager to marry. Not, as many people (and especially Zack's children) thought, for monetary reasons. She still worked as a teacher and fairly comfortably supported herself. Zelda wanted to marry because she had found few suitable men in any age bracket. She thought Zack was quite a find. Yes, he was 70, but still vigorous and athletic, bright and cultured, and an excellent companion. He came from a long-lived family, which she did not, and he might well outlive her. As for sex, she enjoyed it a good deal—but could also live well, as she had for several years, with a minimum of sex with another person. Also, she knew she could easily come to orgasm without intercourse, and tried to convince Zack that that would be fine for her.

When I saw Zack for several sessions of REBT, we soon arrived at a number of his Irrational Beliefs:

- It's great to be so passionately in love with Zelda, and even more so than I was with Mary for a number of years. But maybe at my age it's merely a flash in the pan and won't last very long. It would be *awful* if we married and I then fell out of love.

- My children and many of my friends think that I'm much too old for Zelda, and that I'll be a *real* old person long before she becomes one. Suppose we marry and I can't keep up with her youthful energy? What an *old fool* I'd be then!

- It was hard enough for me to satisfy Mary sexually and I barely made it at times. She was exactly my age. Zelda's 22 years younger and even if I now once in a while have great sex with her, what's going to happen in that respect five or ten years from now? If I don't satisfy her sexually, she'll grow to despise me and regret that she ever married me. I NEED a guarantee that our sex life will work out, and at most I have a slight chance that it will. Older age has robbed me of some of the manliness of my youth, and it is certain to make more gruesome inroads on it, especially sexually, a few years from now.

- My children will never accept Zelda if I marry her and that would be *horrible!* I can see that they're worried about my estate, and I'll make sure that they are well taken care of when I die. But how will they know that for sure? I could change my will at any time and leave everything to Zelda. They'll rightly have great fear that I might do this. They'll hate Zelda if I marry her, and they may end up hating me, too. I *couldn't bear* that if it occurred!

I (Albert Ellis) first helped Zack see that if he kept these Irrational Beliefs he would do himself—not to mention Zelda and possibly his children—much more harm than good. I had him do what REBT calls a hedonic calculus, invented in the early 19th century by the English philosopher, Jeremy Bentham. To perform this calculus, you make a list of all the advantages you can think of if you make a certain decision and of all the disadvantages that will probably follow if you make it. Then you rate all these advantages and disadvantages from one to ten (or one to a hundred), depending on how important they are to you.

Zack first rated the advantages of marrying Zelda. He gave a ten to his romantic passion for her. He gave a seven for the fact that Zelda was younger than he, would probably outlive him, and might take good care of him in case he became somewhat incapacitated. Zack also rated the disadvantages. He put down a rating of nine for the fact that his children would disapprove of his marrying Zelda. He gave an eight to the possibility he might not be able to satisfy her in intercourse as much as he wanted.

Zack made a fairly long list of the advantages and disadvantages of marrying, or not marrying, Zelda. After he rated each item on the list from one to ten, he discovered that in his eyes and by his ratings, the advantages of marriage far outweighed the disadvantages. Therefore, he would be unwise to let the disadvantages—which definitely did exist—rule out his marrying her. Looking back at his Beliefs listed above, Zack could see that each was indeed irrational. They were self-defeating since they would prevent him from choosing the advantages of marriage even though these outweighed its disadvantages.

Zack also went over his Irrational Beliefs about the possible *disadvantages* of getting together in marriage with Zelda. He concluded, in reviewing them that:

- It would not be *awful,* but only highly inconvenient, if he married Zelda and later fell out of love with her.
- If he could not keep up with her energy as the years went by that would also be highly inconvenient, but he could still live and be happy with her.
- He and Zelda could live happily even if they did not have a great sex life—though possibly happi*er* with a great sex life.
- It would not be *horrible,* but only quite sad, if his children never accepted Zelda.

So, by redefining these possible disadvantages as annoyances and inconveniences, rather than as horrors, Zack again concluded that marrying Zelda might well have its drawbacks. However, he and Zelda could live with a reasonable degree of happiness even with these drawbacks. He also saw that some of the drawbacks that he imagined might well never occur at all if he and Zelda married and lived together.

Zack also did a reality check to dispute his Irrational Beliefs about marrying Zelda. In doing so, he was able to conclude that the sorrowful fact—if he married and fell out of love with Zelda—would not be *awful* or disastrous. At worst, it would only be highly inconvenient. It would also be unfortunate if he failed to keep up with her energy after marriage, but hardly the end of the world. There was no guarantee that he could have good sex with Zelda after marriage, but a reasonably good chance that they would somehow work it out. There also was no reason that his children MUST NOT hate Zelda and keep estranged from him and her forever if they married.

Finally, Zack disputed his Irrational Beliefs logically and saw that they had little logic to them. Thus, it didn't follow that his love for Zelda would *necessarily* be a flash in the pan, because it might last forever. It did not follow that if their love *were* a flash in the pan that it would be *awful*, or 100 percent bad. Similarly, it did not follow that his marriage to her couldn't survive their possibly falling out of love. It also didn't necessarily follow that, because he was older than Zelda, that he would become a "real" old person before she did and be unable to keep up with her youthful energy. Even if that did occur, it would not cause disaster for both of them. It was illogical to assume that because his former spouse, Mary, had not been too satisfied sexually that the same thing would prove true with Zelda. It was certainly illogical to assume that even if he could not satisfy Zelda sexually, he no longer would be a man. Manliness and the ability to give sexual satisfaction were merely connected in his head, not in real life—unless he invented a connection. It wasn't logical to assume that his children had to hate Zelda because of their fear of inheriting less of his estate. Even if they did hate her forever, it didn't logically follow that he and she couldn't bear their opposition and would have to be utterly miserable because of it.

Zack really went to work with REBT; he kept showing himself that his Beliefs about the awfulness of his marrying Zelda:

- were exaggerated and unrealistic
- were also illogical
- were self-defeating in that he would probably have much greater advantages in marrying her than he would suffer disadvantages.

Therefore, his awfulizing about the presumed disadvantages led to much more harm than good. They impeded his making the best kind of decision that he could make about marrying Zelda.

After Zack had kept disputing his Irrational Beliefs for two months, and had thereby seen that they did not hold water, he got formally engaged to Zelda and planned to marry her within a year. However, the two of them saw no reason to wait that long, and were married five weeks after they announced their engagement. To the best of my knowledge, very few of the dismal possibilities that he dreamed up about his marrying Zelda ever occurred. Zack overcame his anxiety about satisfying Zelda sexually, by giving up the Irrational Belief that he absolutely MUST satisfy her in intercourse *or else* he was not really a man. Once he reduced his anxiety, he had a great sex life with her. He got quite comfortable bringing her to orgasm with his fingers or his mouth when his penis wasn't fully erect. To his surprise, she found that her sex life with him was better than it had ever been with anyone else.

Zack's children did feel displeased by his marriage but got over their qualms about it and became quite accepting of Zelda. His friends forgot their fears about his being too old to marry a younger woman and acknowledged that he and she seemed remarkably compatible and happy. Zack lost most of his other anxieties about marriage soon after he and Zelda announced their engagement. He began to refer a number of his friends to REBT whenever he learned that they were anxious about relationships, work, or anything else.

Old Flames

Romance, love, and sex—important to people of all ages—can have special significance for older people. In the ABC model, age-related love, romance, and sex issues, events (and *non*-events), are Activating Events (A's), often Adversities. *About* these A's, older people may harbor a variety of self-defeating Beliefs that disturb them and cause self-defeating reactions at C, their Consequences.

Older people may have all the *regular* love, sex, and romance traumas met with by people of any age—which is bad enough—but may also have some extra ones, among them:

- There are traditional assumptions that older people SHOULDN'T seek love, romance, and certainly not sex, because it's icky and unseemly when they do and they would then be "dirty" old men (or women).
- Children often aren't thrilled at dad or mom dating or remarrying, to say nothing of "living in sin" or getting into a lesbian or gay relationship.
- Many men tend to throw in the towel, sexually, when they meet with performance problems.
- Older males are scarcer than older females and often prefer younger women.

Most older and younger people are alike in definitely wanting love, romance, and sex. The biggest difference between these two age groups is ageist prejudice. Older people, but not younger people, often face embarrassed tittering as they go after what they want. For example, a woman might assume, self-defeatingly, as Sarah did when she was only 50, that she could never date a younger man. When opportunity knocked in the person of Tim, 24 years her junior, what did she do? She copped out and spoiled her chances by subjecting him to nonstop "witty" (sarcastic) remarks. Her relevant Irrational Beliefs were "It would be *awful* if people thought I was robbing the cradle!" Plus "I *couldn't bear it* if a younger man rejected me after first going with me for a while." Sarah held, to some extent, the traditional foolish viewpoint that the man must be older than the woman. Why foolish? Perhaps that custom had great relevance back when survival of the human race was unsure. Then, matches between younger, fertile women, and older, successful men, were the most likely to keep the gene pool going—and expanding. That's now irrelevant. It is largely a convention that older women shouldn't date younger men. Why not? Does it harm anyone?

As you read this chapter you can note some of your own possible self-defeating Beliefs related to romance, love, and sex. How have or might such Beliefs change with your aging? Can you challenge and dispute self-defeating assumptions that could interfere with your dating, mating, and sex life?

If you are a widow or widower, do you need your children's blessings, for example, to date, live with, or marry another person of your choice? Perhaps you, or they, think it unseemly for older people to feel romantic or sexy? The reminder to "act your age" *is* ageist, and it's directed at least as much at elders as at children. To create a great life for yourself in the years to come, act the way you want to act, act in your own best interests, no matter what your age.

How Long Do You Wait?

Kevin was widowed at 50 after Willa had died of cervical cancer. Their children, ages 10 and 12, felt quite upset when he started dating only five months after Willa's death. So, guilt-ridden, he stopped dating. What self-defeating Beliefs might he have held to lead to his stopping? How could he have changed his Beliefs to get better results? What might Kevin's children have been telling themselves to upset themselves?

Kevin harbored several Irrational Beliefs. They included these:

- It's completely wrong to do something my children dislike when their mother died only five months ago.

- If I date now, they definitely will feel very upset, and I will have caused their upsetness, and I would therefore be a very bad father.

- Other people, too, will think that it is much too soon for me to date, and I couldn't live with myself if they had bad opinions of me.

Kevin also understood that according to conventional views, a widower or widow should wait at least a year, maybe two or three years, before starting to date. True enough, those are the conventional views. However, Kevin also believed, "These are proper views and I am a selfish *and improper person* if I go against them."

Kevin, and others in the same boat, can keep these conventional standards if they want to. It may mean, however, that they will feel lonely and lack sex and love satisfaction by holding off dating for a year or more. You can question these standards and risk disapproval if you want to begin dating others only five months after the death of your partner. Or five weeks. Thus, in Kevin's case, he thought about the problems involved in his dating and came up with these conclusions for optimal living:

- Perhaps my children will not feel extremely upset if I start dating. I can talk to them about this and see. If they are upset, I can explain my reasons for trying for a good love relationship with another woman. Perhaps I can convince them that these are legitimate reasons.

- If my children do get quite upset, I will have contributed to their disturbed feelings but will not have directly caused them. They have a choice of feeling sorry and disappointed about my dating other women so soon or else feeling depressed and angry. I will try to help them mainly have the healthful feelings of sorrow and disappointment rather than the unhealthful feelings of depression and anger. I will show them that they indeed do have a choice in this respect. If they still choose to feel very upset, that doesn't make me a rotten father and a bad person. I will just be a father who thought of himself first and his children second in this respect.

- Other people may also feel that it is too soon for me to date, although probably not all of them will feel that way. But if many do and therefore have a bad opinion of me, I can live with their view of me and not put myself down. After all, it is more important what I think than what they think. I do not have to agree with them that I am a louse for dating so soon. They may be somewhat right in thinking that my behavior is not the most conventional or the best in the world. They are wrong, however, to put me down as a person for behaving in that "bad" way. I can think about, and partially agree with, their negative attitudes, but still not beat myself up.

- Yes, it is the conventional thing for me not to date for a year or two after my wife's death, but I do not have to agree with this convention and follow it closely. I can follow my own opinion in this respect and conventional people can follow theirs. I am somewhat unconventional if I date other women so soon, but I am not wholly a selfish and an improper person. I can stick to my guns and take the consequences of not pleasing a number of other people.

If Kevin's children disturbed themselves about their father's dating only five months after their mother's death, what might they have been telling themselves? They could have been telling themselves both Rational and Irrational Beliefs. Rationally, they could have said to themselves:

- It is far too soon, in our eyes, for Dad to be dating. We would prefer him to be with us more of the time and help us accept the death of our mother, but he doesn't HAVE TO. Her death is a painful blow to him, too, and he is very lonely without her.
- The universe doesn't prevent him from dating this soon, even though it is a little shocking for us to see him do it. Perhaps he is somewhat selfish about doing this at this time, but he has the right to be wrong. He is largely a good father and he might be much worse off if he did not do any dating.

Irrationally, Kevin's children might be telling themselves, *along with the above Rational Beliefs:*

- It's *terrible* that Dad is dating so soon! How can he do this, when Mom died just a short while ago!
- He's callous and selfish! He doesn't think at all of us and how we might feel about this (as he SHOULD).

- He's a rotten *person!*
- We *can't stand* his behaving this way!

Kevin, some friend or relative, or perhaps a cognitive-behavioral therapist, could then help his children see that Kevin's "unnatural" behavior as an Activating Event at A did not cause their great upsetness. Their Irrational Beliefs at B *about* his behavior caused their disturbed feelings as a Consequence at C. They might then more easily conclude as follows:

- It is not *terrible* that Dad is dating so soon, though we wish he wouldn't.
- He can easily act the way he does, and it doesn't prove he didn't love Mom.
- Dad is not a rude and selfish individual, though there are some things about him we don't like at all.
- He can still think of us and understand that we're upset. But he has the right to decide what's best for him, such as dating.
- Though we don't at all like dad going out on dates, we can definitely stand it and still be fairly happy kids.
- At worst, Dad sometimes acts badly or rottenly, but he's not a terrible person and is actually a pretty good father.

This situation, with Kevin and his children, certainly might create problems for him and them—and for the women he might date—and for his friends and relatives. If, however, Kevin and his children look at their ideas rationally, and if they vigorously dispute their Irrational Beliefs, the difficult situation may well turn out to be just that—quite difficult and troublesome. But not exceptionally disturbing for Kevin or for his children.

Get Over It

We recommend that younger people begin to become used to the idea that older people have romantic lives and sex lives. Not that all your relationships and all the parts of your body work as well as they did when you were a teenager. Sometimes they work better! Love, sex, and affection are some of the nicer things in life for most people, including most older people. Aging does not mean good-bye to all that. What Irrational Beliefs lead to your feelings of shame, keep you from bringing up your sex pleasure when you talk with your mates, friends, or doctors? Or could even keep you from buying books with "that kind" of title? Or keep you from mortifying the nice young librarian by asking for a sexy book?

Again, we'd better replace the notion in our culture that there is a "right" time for education, romance, marriage, child-rearing, careers, and retirement. Yes, there are laws and regulations about ages for school attendance, marriage (but not child-bearing and divorce), full-time employment, IRAs, pensions, Social Security, and capital gains. Our own personal and societal prejudices—"I'm too old for . . . ," "If only I could do it again, I'd . . . ," and the like— cause unnecessary trouble. They are ideas *about* social reality, not immutable laws or facts of nature. People live much longer now than in the good old days. There is no need to cram all the major "duties" of life—education, marriage, family rearing, working, and a few years of retirement—into a short space. You can do things in different, unheard-of orders. You can go back to some of your favorites. You can skip some. You can invent new ones. You may have a couple of families, careers, retirements, and other involvements. You can have none.

So, MUST we carry out traditionally important life activities according to old timetables? MUST we carry them all out at all? Of course not. You can help develop a new culture in which people responsibly do what feels right for them. Why can't you go back for more education several times, have a number of primary relationships, have different careers interspersed with retirements? The old traditions sprang from times when life was much shorter, work and family options much more limited. Those times are gone and you don't have to carry on the old traditions if doing things your way seems worth it to you. This is an age for invention of new ways of life, for breakthroughs, for casting off the shackles of the old ways that hamper. These are times for experimentation and adventure. You may create changes and challenges you never even dreamed of a few decades ago. This brings us to the Seventeenth Rule for Optimal Living:

Rule #17: Remain Flexible

Healthy and mature people tend to be flexible in their thinking, open to change, and unbigoted in their view of other people. They do not make rigid rules for themselves and others.

A Rainbow of Lifestyles

Well, Zack's and Kevin's cases, while tough, could have been tougher. Some older people have it worse than others. Can you imagine what it would be like if it were *against the law* for you to pursue and enjoy the love, romance, and sex life you desire?

Recent years have brought progress, but the world is still much tougher, more dangerous, and less fair for gays, lesbians, and bisexuals than for comparable "straight" people. Older people may be able to learn a thing or two from the experience of gay, lesbian, and bisexual people. How so? Because the latter often had to create good lives with few or no guidelines. They had to do it over practically *everybody's* dead bodies, including most parents, relatives, teachers, neighbors, religious leaders, and the legal and mental health authorities. What if *you* did not have the conventional roles of marriage, parenting, and child rearing to support you in youth or in age? If a good life is going to happen for gays, lesbians, and bisexuals, they have to make it happen. They have to fashion their ways of life. From this handicapping Adversity, they may derive some advantage over more conventional people—though, of course, it would be preferable not to have had those Adversities. Some of those skills may serve them very well in facing the additional challenges of ageism and older age.

Sexual minorities may face several special issues with aging or the prospect of aging. For one, they face ageism *and* homophobia. Older gay men can confront extra helpings of Adversity—from younger gay men. Why? Men—no matter their sexual orientation—tend to feel more attracted to youth and looks than is true of women. Thus, older gay men and older straight women both may run into the same Adversity— men's nature! Women, including lesbians, tend to give greater importance to companionship, love, and shared values than men do initially. There is a saying in marriage counseling and sex therapy that "Women give sex for love, and men give love for sex." The saying is a "Venus versus Mars" type of overgeneralization, of course, but it does capture some aspects of problems in courtship and marriage. When the people courting and partnering are of the same sex, it can make for variations on age-old themes.

Love Is Not Necessary for a Happy Life

Jed was 52 and had had a fifteen-year relationship with Rod, who died of AIDS at the age of 48, having been very healthy, though with a low T-cell count, until he developed lymphoma. He quickly succumbed. Jed had mourned for over a year about the loss of this fine relationship but now was ready to move on to a new one—as he knew Rod would have wanted him to do. But how? He was short, bald, overweight and out of shape, never had been attractive physically, and had no fashion sense at all. He was so different from the stereotype of gay men, Jed said, that many gay people thought he was straight! Jed also said there were plenty of others—not that he was interested in *them*—in the same boat. He'd been extremely happy with Rod, who admired him for his intelligence and character, and not for his beauty, and found him to be such a satisfactory partner. Now, at 52, he was balder than ever, older and paunchier than ever, and still dressed like a nerd. No great adornment for a gay bar! So where and how was he to find another partner who would be as kind, as suitable, and as nondemanding of physical attractiveness as Rod? Nowhere, as far as he could see.

I (Albert Ellis) had to admit that when he came to see me for REBT, that Jed's plight was realistically bad. What he truly wanted for the rest of his life, and what he luckily had had with Rod, was not easily or quickly available. He might well be exaggerating its *complete* impossibility, but there was some likelihood his older age and lesser looks might indeed be a problem. We developed several therapy homeworks to improve his odds.

Jed really tried. For months he went to gay meetings, to bars, and even to museums and libraries, hoping to meet someone. He read my books for both men and women on how to meet people. He used the services of two highly-touted matchmakers: "If I can't do it, nobody can" was the motto of one of them. She couldn't do it. This did very little to improve Jed's hopes. He tried personal ads in gay publications. For the most part, no luck. The ads he answered all seemed to be run by handsome, studly young men. They were looking for someone who looked like them (if not better)—whether for the possibility of LTR (long-term relationship) or for brief encounters. Occasionally an ad would say its writer was looking for an older, "daddy" type—Jed's hopes would rise—until he reached the end of the sentence, "28-35 years old." That was older? Jed was aghast. If the ad did not state the age the writer was looking for in a man, Jed would answer it. Some—the few who returned his calls—seemed frankly shocked that Jed answered their ads, but he plowed ahead, doing his therapy homework. Occasionally, given that Jed was bright, a good conversationalist, and interested in others, he did form nonsexual friendships with those he called. No one like Rod. At times, Jed thought seriously about suicide and rejected it partly for religious reasons. At times he even thought fleetingly that it was too bad he wasn't HIV positive, because then his misery might not be as long as it probably was going to be.

As for his own ads, Jed's first effort yielded no responses. He had thought the honesty of his ad—"older, average looks, overweight and out of shape, but with a heart of gold"—would melt the hardest of hearts. Zero response. We worked a lot on his second ad, which highlighted his assets and interests and which mentioned qualities he was looking for in a partner. Not zero response this time—just close.

Discouraged and depressed, Jed irrationally concluded, "I'll *never* find a loving, long-term partner like Rod! Like I truly NEED! I'm too old, too ugly, too fat for anyone to accept me! If I go on for the next twenty or thirty years alone, missing what I had with Rod, I'll be completely miserable. Growing older will only be grimmer and grimmer. I won't be able to bear it. I hate life. Nobody loves you when you're old and gay!"

To help Jed dispute these Irrational Beliefs, I deliberately considered one of his basic ones—that he absolutely NEEDED a loving, long-term relationship like the one he had with Rod and could not be *at all* happy without it. I showed him that he almost certainly would be *happier* if he had another mate like Rod, but that the "fact" that he couldn't be happy *at all* was a fiction. He was making that fiction into a "feeling" by devoutly believing it. Only his rigid conviction that he would be completely devoid of satisfaction in life without a loving relationship would ensure his achieving this gloomy state.

Why was I so sure that Jed's Belief in his aging doom would be the only reason for his *feeling* doomed? Because, primarily, I think that almost any reasonably healthy individual, as Jed was, has many possibilities of pleasure in his life. Even if an important pleasure, like participating in a long partnership, never happens again—which was not a proven fact in Jed's case—a good many solid opportunities for enjoyment remain.

Jed had a number of potential assets and interests. He worked as an attorney for an environmental protection agency, and he greatly enjoyed prosecuting polluters and other degraders of the environment.

He had three sisters with whom he was close, as well as being close with their children. He was a writer who had published some stories, and was still hopeful of writing the Great American Novel. He excelled at bridge and had won or come close to winning a few tournaments. He also had various other interests and aspirations.

"Could anyone with such a range of possible pleasures," I directly asked Jed, "possibly not enjoy *anything?* Even if your main life goal—to have a long relationship like the one you had with Rod—were completely nullified, could you not, fairly easily, have other enjoyments and fulfillments? You *could*—if you let yourself have them. Damned right you could!"

At first, Jed was adamant. "No," he said. He stuck with his conviction that now that he had lost his partner, everything had to be bleak and glum. No, he used to enjoy his work, his family, and several other things, but now they were all insignificant compared to the great loss that he could never replace. "No," he would say, "how can I enjoy anything else?"

"That's just the point!" I answered. "You preoccupy yourself so much with how *awful* it is not to have Rod, or at least a suitable replacement for him, that you're driving all possible other enjoyments into oblivion. You're saying that they don't really exist. But they do—if you let them exist. You're choosing to focus—and I mean strongly and persistently focus—only on the negative. That will naturally drive the potential positives, practically all of them, out of mind and seemingly out of existence."

Well, Jed gave me a rough time, but I, together with his capacity for optimal thinking, finally won out. "Yes," he agreed in time, "my loss was great and I'll always, maybe for the rest of my life, feel it, think about it, sorrow over it. But you're right, of course. At 52 I'm still as worthwhile a human as ever—even though parts of the gay world may not think so. My family is long-lived, and I may have another 30, even 40, years to go. I *can* enjoy several things, many things, in that time. If I only stop obsessing about Rod and my great loss. And what I don't have. So, it was a loss. It's surely possible that I won't ever again meet a man like Rod who likes me. But I didn't lose *me* and I'd better not act as if I did. I'm alive and potentially can enjoy life. I'd better act on that."

Once he resolved that he *could* get back to his other life enjoyments, Jed did so—particularly with visits to his sisters and their children and to working on his novel. His years became older, but not grimmer. His searching for a long-term partner was no longer desperate. He still knew it would be rough finding one, but he no longer thought it impossible. He almost found a suitable partner, but 2,500 miles kept them from living together, and they only saw each other infrequently. He kept hopefully looking.

When the Pickings Are Slim

You, like Jed, may be gay and older. Therefore you may be limited in the number of partners who will find you desirable and that you also find desirable. Keep in mind that difficult does not equal impossible. Keep in mind that great looks may attract many potential partners, but do not ensure great relationships and happiness. It's even possible that less good-looking people make better partners! They may have to cultivate their personalities and skills more than the good-looking people do. Or, you may be heterosexual—especially if female—and somewhat limited in mate selection by your years. Certainly many older straight women find it much more difficult to find a mate than when they were ten, twenty, or thirty years younger. Don't forget that a great freedom can come from not "having to" attract a mate. You can live more of your life the way you want—though mateless. You do not have to have a partner, of any gender, to be happy. You can have friends. You can have pets. You can have roommates. You can have neighbors. You can live in shared housing. If possible, and it's your cup of tea, you can even share a man with someone else.

Men, in our culture, may suffer from less age discrimination by women based on their looks than the amount of age discrimination women—again, because of looks—face from men. Yet, an older man with infirmities and disabilities can easily find his selection of suitable women quite limited. For example, I (Albert Ellis) recently saw a 60-year-old widower who had met three different women he was very interested in. However, they rejected him because of his insulin-dependent diabetes, which none of them wanted to cope with in a mate.

Jed's Adversities, therefore, were perhaps more serious because he was gay. No matter what your sexual orientation or gender, the loss of a partner is difficult. If you are beyond middle age, the loss can be even more difficult—and inconvenient—because of the practical problems of replacement. Millions of widowed individuals have to face the predicament of greatly desiring to remarry, but being limited in opportunities to do so. If you are in this predicament, don't irrationally give up all hope and endlessly depress yourself. First, if you are in this predicament, thoroughly convince yourself that you want—maybe greatly want—another mate, but that you can be, assuredly can be, happy in many ways without one. Like Jed, you can!

Believing this, you can make a list of several things—projects you really enjoy doing, goals you would enjoy reaching. It is nice, of course, if you do them well, but that is not *necessary*. The main thing is enjoyment—your enjoyment. What you want to do is very important—and not what other people, including relatives and friends, think you should do, that you properly ought to do. Let them think what they think! List your own possible enjoyments and then figure out what you can do to involve yourself with them and really find pleasure in them. Yes, what can *you* do to make these chosen pursuits enjoyable?

Even though you have lost a spouse or partner, a relative or friend, you can find that you can to some degree still enjoy yourself. Once you have made that determination, you will tend to obsess and focus on your "terrible" loss much less. This is not to minimize loss. For loss is real and it may be a great loss. If you focus strongly and prolongedly on loss and convince yourself repeatedly how *awful* it is, you will mainly depress yourself. You will make yourself "know" that you will be in agony forever. You will make yourself "feel" that there is nothing else in life, absolutely nothing else, that you can enjoy.

Give yourself time to heal yourself. No matter how tremendous your loss, if you let the months or years go by—and they will—you will forget some of it and remember other things. You have to give yourself time. If you insist on concentrating on the loss of a loved one, or on almost any other kind of loss, you can easily magnify and prolong it. You can even make it much worse than it is. However, you can let yourself see the wide possibilities of other enjoyments—yes, even when you are older and grayer, or older and grayer and gayer. If you do so, you will still feel strongly the loss of your loved people (and objects). However, you will not irrationally contend that loss MUST NOT have occurred and that it is *devastating* that it did.

Again, look at your potential goals, projects, and enjoyments! More than likely there are quite a few of them. Find them. Involve yourself in them. Make up your mind that you'll enjoy life if it kills you! If you do, you may find, as Jed eventually did, that you do begin to encounter a romantic possibility here and there.

13

Must We Go the Way of the Roman Empire?

If anything is used to its full potential, it will break.

Poulsen's Prophecy

There are some people, like Dave, who frankly expect to decline and fall. Not long after retirement, he took to saying, "I'm old." His wife, Maribel, told him "You're only as old as you feel," and he replied "Then I'm *really* old!" Dave developed more aches and pains and indulged them by "resting." The less he did, the less he felt like doing, and then the less he could do. Then the less he felt like doing! Eventually Maribel talked Dave into taking a jazzercize class with her. He slowly became a little less averse to exercise, began to feel better, and then became still more active.

Disuse, like the downward cycle Dave got himself into, contributes to much of the decline in mobility and vigor many older people suffer. If we don't use it, we *do* lose it—much, much faster than we otherwise would. People who remain interested and active have good chances for continued mobility and vigor. If we don't use it, we may also get sick more often. Exercise seems to improve resistance to some germ-caused diseases. Exercise may release natural brain chemicals, called endorphins, that appear to increase both the number and activity of helpful

219

immune system cells. This effect seems more marked in older than in younger people.

So here's our Eighteenth Rule for Optimal Living:

Rule #18: Use It Or Lose It

Use your mind, your body, your talents, your human potential, or you will lose opportunity for optimal living, and for optimal aging.

"Use it or lose it" is one of those common sayings with much truth to it. Why *don't* you and other people follow it more often? What stops you? One of the major reasons you don't use it (and *do* lose it) is that you may not have goals that keep you active. If you do have such goals, you may nevertheless block yourself from taking action.

Decline To Decline

A most important, disliked, and dreaded aspect of getting older is physical decline. It may include decline in strength, visual acuity, sexual prowess, agility, and beauty. Assuming you will decline at least a little bit someday, do you ever wonder how far you'll go? Will you decline only mildly, as seems to be true of some people? Or will you be more like the Roman Empire? Well, your genes play some part in these future scenarios. As yet, nothing much can be done to change them. But, your lifestyle plays a large part in how you will fare physically over the years. Eat right, exercise daily, don't smoke, don't overdo it on alcohol, develop vital absorbing interests, have a good social network, and accept new challenges. You already know these things. It would be hard not to! But do you do them? Maybe that's where your attitude comes in.

In this chapter, we will look briefly at some research that contradicts the popular image of older people as fated for decrepitude. This chapter will not give you an exercise and diet program—that information is available abundantly. We will give you some important information that contradicts many of the myths about aging. This information shows you what to do to keep what you have, and in some cases regain some of what you may have lost. It also shows how decline is considerably helped along by your not using what you have.

How you age, and how fast you age, then, are partly dependent on your behavior and attitudes, rather than being purely biologically programmed. There is strong evidence from research by Alvar Svanborg and Jim Birren that most older people do not decline mentally or even much physically before their eighties *if they remain active in their communities.*

We, therefore, will show you how to combat the internal *psychological blocks* that can prevent your doing what you probably already know would help—if you did it! These blocks keep you in the same boat with people who fail to stop smoking, or to watch their fat intake and weight. In the same boat with people who don't consume enough dietary fiber, who don't wear seat belts or condoms, who don't get pap smears, who don't do breast or testicle self-exams.

That much said, we hope you do not feel petrified that your fate may be to follow rapidly in the footsteps of the Roman Empire. Now, what are some of the things you can do to decline and fall more slowly— much, *much* more slowly? What are some of the things you can do to reverse, though not forever, some of the slippage fate tends to send your way?

Buns of Steel and Amazing Abs

When you reach a certain age, comedian Bette Midler remarked, your body has a mind of its own. Yes, that seems true, but let's face it. Your body's "mind of its own" after that certain age has some little helpers. Not just gravity either, but your own sedentary lifestyle and poor diet. Fortunately, there's now a strong trend toward people getting regular exercise. Only about half of the adults in America report that they get some form of regular exercise. It's *easy* to be sedentary; we would never claim otherwise. As we age, it gets *easier* to slip into less and less activity. Some people don't slip into a sedentary lifestyle as they get older. Why not? What's to slip? They were sedentary all along, but they don't get bad results until middle age or later. Even if you were active when younger, you may rest on your laurels (if you want to call them that) as you put on the years and the pounds. The "trend" toward exercise in our culture may fail to carry you along. What to do?

Let's start with the plain point that there are some advantages to getting into shape and staying in shape. There is some research, for instance, on the prevention or reversal of loss of bone and muscle mass. In one study at Tufts University, people aged 58 to 72 followed an exercise regimen, and their muscle mass and bone mass increased markedly.

Most people have seen news articles about that sort of thing—it's widely known and accepted. You've also possibly seen late-night infomercials that sometimes show *really* old people who have buns of steel and amazing abdominal muscles. So, we all know it's possible. But does this knowledge lead most of us to adopt and stick with an exercise program? No. Why not? The "why nots" are the ones that keep people from stopping smoking, from reducing fat intake, and from exercising *when they are younger!*

What are the self-defeating Beliefs that slow you, stop you, or keep you from starting? Let's address the twin roots of procrastination: (1) perfectionism and (2) low frustration tolerance (LFT). Together they contribute to your unrealistic goals, unproductive or impulsive efforts, and giving up.

Fat Chance With Perfectionism

Nicole thought she must be perfectly skinny and perfectly toned, and must look far better than Jane Fonda did in her deservedly famous workout videos. But without Fonda's hard work and discipline! So, did Nicole work toward her goal? No, she felt very depressed and ashamed, thought at times of killing herself, and sometimes starved herself for a few days. Mostly she sat on her duff, ate Danish and potato chips to console herself, while she flipped through magazines and watched soap operas. Fortunately, in one of the magazines, she saw my (Emmett Velten's) ad for personal coaching and phoned me long distance for a consultation. I persuaded her first to use Richard Simmons as a role model. Though far from perfectly slim himself, Nicole saw that he not only exercises but radiates cheerful energy and compassion toward the same overweight people Nicole hated—people like herself! I persuaded Nicole to accept herself, even as Richard Simmons would undoubtedly accept her, but to work her butt off (figuratively and literally), if she so chose, to achieve her fitness and weight goals.

There's GOT TO Be An Easier Way!

While demands for perfect slimness and perfect fitness foul up quite a few people and keep them from ever looking like Richard Simmons, much less Jane Fonda, low frustration tolerance (LFT) fouls up many more. What is LFT? It's a self-defeating view about frustration, about difficulties, about hard work. The LFT philosophy says that difficulty

SHOULDN'T be difficult! Hard things SHOULDN'T be hard. That, at the very least, difficulties shouldn't be *this* difficult! The most common self-defeating philosophy that stops most of us from exercising and dieting is low frustration tolerance: "It *should* be and *needs* to be easier than it is! I *can't* (and of course won't) do it till it's easier!"

The very worst and most common LFT Belief is "It's *too* hard!" Not hard, which is true, but *too* hard! Such Irrational Beliefs accelerate your slowing down. They can keep you from returning to your normal activity pattern after, say, you've been sick or on vacation. Yes, we admit that when you get older you may have to work harder than young people do to get into shape and stay in shape. Tough! The young, lucky souls that they are, even if inactive, don't seem to go downhill the second they stop exercising. But we do!

I (Emmett Velten) never exercised even 15 seconds willingly in my whole life until age 51. Unlike James Thurber, who once remarked that whenever he got the urge to exercise, he would lie down until it went away, I had no such urges. At 51 I decided to start exercising, to keep my weight down and to lower my very high resting heart rate (100 beats per minute, when relaxed). Well, exercising wasn't *awful*. And you know why not? Because, at least according to the noble theory of REBT, *nothing* in the universe is *awful*, that is, 100 percent bad or more than 100 percent bad. I will say that exercising was very close to awful. I hated it and it took major effort to get myself to go even twice a week to the YMCA. Soon, I got the bright idea of using REBT methods on myself! I went through the more gentle REBT methods rapidly with no progress. I decided to use penalties, pledging to friends that I would, say, exercise three times a week. If I didn't? I would send in a check for $50 to a hated cause. This worked. I went three times a week and stayed for about 15 minutes each time. You see, I was a difficult customer. A progression of "contracts" ensued, each one designed, by me, to force myself to exercise more often and more vigorously. My progress was slow.

Finally I scheduled myself for a weight-machine orientation, again with the help of a self-devised contract. The instructor did not show up precisely at the appointed time. I took off, having kept the appointment, which was what the letter of the contract specified. The next contract was more specific, I was there, the instructor was there. At about the fourth of twelve machines in the orientation, I remember thinking, "I *knew* this would be fun!" Part of the orientation involved keeping a record of my efforts on each of the machines, which had lights, sound effects, and read-outs. Somehow all this struck me as fun. Thereupon, I went to the Y and exercised something like 40 days in a row, with no contracts and with the beginnings of enjoyment. Those habits, and that enjoyment, remain with me, and it is a rare day that I do not exercise. My resting heart rate? Sixty-three beats per minute. You may not take to exercise as I did—under duress. You may take to it more easily. Who knows? The human enjoyment of exercise is common enough that you will have a good chance of enjoying it—if you do it long enough.

A friend at the Y, Jesse, began his exercise program after he retired at 65, at the urging of his wife and his doctor. He lost about 30 pounds and toned himself up quite well. However, even then he could see that his stomach was far flabbier than the *before* pictures of *much* older men he saw on late-night Amazing Abs Exercise Machine infomercials. He told me he'd gone through a stage where he *couldn't stand* the way his stomach looked. For a while, he got so focused on how his mid-section looked, that he partly demoralized himself and began to skip a number of his workouts. How did he re-moralize himself? He said, "I just decided to mellow out and not make a big deal about it."

With one of those unlucky throws of the genetic dice, I was diagnosed about eight months ago with a hereditary, progressive neurological disorder. My peripheral nerves slowly die, and then the muscles die that they operate. I modified my workout, learning how to use free weights, to concentrate more on the most affected peripheral muscles. I will try to keep as many of them as strong and flexible as possible for as long as possible, even though my nerves and muscles will continue to fade.

I (Albert Ellis) have a good many physical problems, partly due to my 84 years and additionally due to my last 45 years of dealing with diabetes. For example, I have somewhat wobbly legs, and am no longer the champion walker that I used to be before I got diabetes. Up to my fortieth year, I was one of the best and fastest walkers in New York City. I could easily walk several miles, and often did so in record time. Walking was one of my greatest pleasures and I would forgo taking the bus for ten blocks or more, walk instead, and would get to my destination before the bus got there. I enjoyed pacing myself and beating the bus!

Then came my diabetic condition. Almost immediately my great walking ended. I could still walk quite fast—but not for long. Within a few blocks, my legs got tired and I felt dragged out. My long walks all stopped and even at the airports I sometimes used the electric carts rather than go for long distances on foot. Too bad! However, I put up with it and stopped my whining and screaming about not having my former, no longer existent, walking prowess.

Instead, I do my exercises and compensate as best I can. I spend some time exercising every day—though, like Thurber, I hardly enjoy it, and I particularly rue the time that it takes. Because I live in the same building as the Institute where I work, I don't get much exercise commuting. Nonetheless, just about every day I deliberately get in some walking up and down our stairways, when I could easily take the elevator. When I do take the elevator up and down several floors, I do knee-bend exercises while I am on it—to save time exercising and to keep my feet and legs in shape. Easily, easily, easily, I could live without doing any exercise whatsoever. But I don't. Like it or not, I consistently do it—and thereby keep myself and my legs in much better shape than we would otherwise be.

For many years I followed Thurber's famous saying about exercise. It wasn't that I hated exercise—for example, I have always loved playing tennis and table tennis, and spent a good deal of time doing both when I was in my teens and twenties.

Not later on, however. Even tennis and ping-pong take time—which I rarely have available. Yes, they are pleasant and healthful, but my usually busy life leaves no time for them. From 8:30 in the morning until 12 midnight, I run a psychotherapy institute, see clients, supervise and train therapists, give talks and workshops in New York and throughout the country and the world, write one article after another, complete a book or two every year, and continue a 32-year relationship with Janet. Never a dull—or unbusy—moment!

So for many years exercise went by the board. Dieting and taking care of my health—oh, that's fine. Having been an insulin-dependent diabetic since age 40, I watch my food carefully, never overeat, keep clear of salt and fatty foods, see my many doctors regularly, and keep myself trim and fit. Nonetheless, as I approached my eighties, older age crept up. I am now often afflicted with unsteady legs, slower walking, a back that easily goes out of kilter, tender feet, mild high blood pressure, troublesome eyes, osteoarthritis, and several other physical ailments. Nothing too serious, considering diabetics' proneness to physical ills, but often painful and restricting.

So, dammit, I now exercise! Every day, usually just before bedtime, I do my bending, stretching, flexing, massaging, and other exercises. Nothing stops me: my constant out-of-town trips, my impossibly busy schedule, my occasional lack of sleep (mainly from getting in late due to airline delays), nothing stops me. Do I like exercise? No, not really. Do I dislike it? Unlike Emmett, quite often. Do I make up excuses for letting it slide? Often, *but I don't give in to my excuses.* Unless I am physically sick—and rarely even then—I exercise. Result: My legs are less wobbly; my back rarely goes out of whack; my internist is delighted with my 95 percent low-fat ratio; and I am rarely ill. No, I still don't like exercise. But I uncomplainingly do it.

"Well, OK," you may think, "If I exercise and stay fit, I have the best chance to minimize age-related slippage (so to speak), even if I never do have buns of steel and amazing abs. My looks and physique are one thing, but what about mental decline? What if my *mind* goes? Now that would truly be unbearable!"

Sharper Image

Let's now tackle the dread that many people feel when they think about possible loss of mental sharpness someday. Most people probably assume that such losses *automatically* come with increasing age. Jokes about "early Alzheimer's," for instance, are unpleasantly common and show how prevalent such fears are. The expectation that you lose it mentally as you age is common. References to older people as "spry," "alert," or "sharp as a tack" are considered compliments, rather than possibly offensive ageist remarks.

The first hopeful point in this respect is that the scientific evidence does not support the conclusion that we all get dumber and dumber as we age. Just like physical decline, mental decline considerably stems from non-use. Numerous studies have shown that people who stay physically and intellectually active maintain their mental alertness, live longer, and stay healthier than those who simply retreat from engaging in social activities and keeping active. Researcher Daniel Ogilvie found that the chance to spend time in meaningful activities predicted people's happiness levels three or four times better than did their health. Sometimes someone may say, "If you've got your health, you've got everything," or words to that effect. It would be good to add, "Staying active, mentally and physically, *promotes* health and happiness."

The everyday environment of many old people provides little intellectual stimulation or challenge. It lacks novelty and complexity and does—of course—lead to atrophy of the little gray cells, to say nothing of the human spirit. Nevertheless, much of the "evidence" of the dire mental effects of old age, such as the supposed loss of 100,000 brain cells per day, came from poorly-done research that people accept as gospel, possibly because it fits with ageist stereotypes. These "everybody knows" examples are not true of normal aging.

Vital new brain connections can continue to develop at any age. It depends on whether you use your brain. Decline is possible, but so is growth. There are many reasons why you may let yourself slip into decline as you age. Many of them stem from stereotypes about older people. Do you for instance, as a younger person, seek out older friends? Think that one over. If not, why not? Negative stereotypes about older people can lead to younger people avoiding them. If *you* feel avoided, you, too, might begin to withdraw socially. You might feel less control over your life and start to feel helpless. Then you *do* begin to feel and act dull. It is important to understand the connection between Activating Events, such as being shunned, and your Beliefs in contributing to dullness at C. Rather than attributing dullness to inevitable results of aging, you can see that it stems considerably from "use it or lose it." You can challenge through your actions the Belief that there's nothing you can do about people's avoidance. Seek them out. Reach out to them. Take steps to cultivate friends. If you persist at it, you have a very good chance to succeed.

Mia, age 78, assumed that she was way over the hill and was far too old for any young person to want to be around. I (Emmett Velten) persuaded her to try a homework experiment. Mia had lived in the Southwest for about 30 years. Also for about 30 years, she had wanted to learn Spanish. She had always thought that she would someday move back to Minnesota where she was unlikely to get any practice with Spanish, so why bother? She had no plans to move. As a therapy homework assignment and for the fun of it, she agreed to register for a Spanish class at the local junior college.

Mia found that everyone in the class was younger than she. Somewhat to her surprise, many of her fellow students seemed eager to join her in forming a study group. Joining young people in a study group was another homework Mia had discussed as possibly helpful for her. In this case, the homework assignment did itself! So far, so good, but right away another kind of "aging" problem came up for Mia. She reported to me that the previous week she had forgotten something she had just heard a minute earlier in her Spanish class. This worried her greatly with the usual "I must be getting senile" kind of thought.

I asked Mia to keep track of whether any of the young people in the study group ever seemed to forget anything they had just heard. Of course, they did. She even noted that Valerie and Chuck, the two "kids" (each about one-fourth of her age) in her study group, said the same thing of themselves when they forgot something—namely that they must be senile! Mia felt reassured, but unfortunately, still later, she went back to worrying that *she* was going senile. She agreed to look for her "musts" and challenge them. Mia had the demanding thought, "I MUST function perfectly." She was able to dispute this Irrational Belief and replace it effectively with "I'd like to function perfectly, but I don't HAVE TO." Instead of giving herself a panic attack, she resolved to pay better attention to what she told herself—and to what she heard in class.

There are some encouraging studies that show how older people can profit very well from exercises to improve short-term memory. Much decline in short-term memory probably stems from its non-use. With older age, *developmental* tasks are different. Children and young people need to memorize and learn large numbers of *new* facts. Their short-term memories get a super work-out. Not so with older people. Most of what we learn as adults, and more so as older adults, is not truly new—it attaches to what we already know. IQ-type tests, however, tap the ability to learn new material, which is something young people have a great deal of need for and practice in. So, IQ-type tests are unfair to older people. Though that may be so, the fact is that you will do better at keeping your brain in shape if you learn new material. Learning a new language, as Mia did, is one of the best ways to do so. Another is learning how to use a computer and surf the Net. The supposed mental decline programmed with age does not occur if you continue to use your brain to learn and to carry out your purposes.

Depression, drug interactions, and lack of proper nutrition and exercise are additional factors that lead to loss of mental capacity readily interpreted as due to aging. Senility is a social disease. If you isolate people, young or old, they become less social and less active mentally. Their "loss" of intelligence is due to their isolation, not to age-related biological programming.

Most of the losses in mental capacity happen to the very old, not to people in their sixties, seventies, and early eighties. Such losses are due not to age itself but to depression, drug interactions, lack of exercise, or some other reversible condition. As we attack these problems with greater public awareness and proper care, the percentage of people who lose mental faculties as they age should decline greatly. If you or someone you love is older and has seemingly lost mental capacity, ask yourself: Is it depression? Is it lack of stimulation, lack of exercise, or even poor diet? What about drug interactions? Many healthcare providers are poorly informed about drug interactions in older people. It's not uncommon for us, as we age, to have more prescriptions. Are all those drugs necessary? Are they from the same doctor? Has the doctor done a review lately of all the medications she or he has prescribed for the older patient? Talk with your doctor. Conduct an on-line search about interactions among medications you may be taking. Make yourself into an informed consumer.

The basic REBT teachings show you how to face the possible Adversity of losing mental sharpness, reduce your dread about it, and then refocus on retaining and increasing your vitality. What are some of the specific Irrational Beliefs we can hold that *promote* unhealthful or self-defeating Consequences at the prospect of losing mental sharpness? One is LFT—low frustration tolerance. Another self-defeating Belief that can contribute to inertia relates to some older people's perceptions of time. "It's no use doing [whatever it is] since I'll kick the bucket before long anyway." Guess what *young* people with *similar* low frustration tolerance (LFT) attitudes tell *themselves*? "I'll grow out of [my inertia] someday." Good luck.

Have I (Albert Ellis) been afflicted with some memory loss at the age of 84? Frankly, I have. My clients, some of whom I have seen for several months or even a year, don't seem to think so, and often compliment me on my "perfect" memory. For, when they have forgotten that they hated somebody, say, a half year ago and now perhaps love that same person today, I remind them of what they told me months ago. Then they remember it quite well. They feel amazed that they have forgotten that important aspect of their life, while I nicely remember it.

Nonetheless, I sometimes tell myself that I will eat, or make a phone call, or read an article in five minutes. Then, fifteen minutes later, I remember that I have not done this thing yet. So my short-term memory is a little shaky—as it was not ten years ago. That's a nuisance—but hardly a catastrophe. I am less in control of my memory than I used to be—but I never put myself down for this. I do not HAVE TO have an almost perfect memory—as I once had. There is no reason that I MUST be as sharp and alert as I previously was. It's not good—in fact, it's bad—that my acuity is somewhat limited. But it's not *awful* and *horrible,* and it never makes me an *inadequate person.* No, merely a person *with* some inadequacies that I did not have several years ago. Loss of acuity is also not a *horrible, intolerable* fact. It's a fact, an inconvenient one, but not *awful.*

So I do my best to compensate for my memory lapses. Instead of waiting five minutes to make that phone call or read that paper, I do it now, immediately, pronto. Then I cannot forget to do it. Or I get someone to remind me that I'm going to do something. I may ask people to call me, instead of waiting for me to call them. I put my peanut butter sandwich in full view on my desk, to remind me to eat it soon. Or I use some other memory-instigating device.

I also take more notes. In the old days when my memory was almost phenomenal, I took minimal notes on my clients' problems and referred to them rarely. For I naturally kept their doings in mind and had no difficulty recalling them. Now I take much more detailed notes and refer to them more readily. If anything, my therapy therefore depends on more accurate recollections than ever.

The same thing is true of my talks and workshops. Formerly, I knew them practically by heart and used few notes. Now I outline them beforehand and use a few notes. I have these ready in case I somehow do neglect to mention an important point that I have made perhaps hundreds of times before but that this time just slipped my mind. My notes prevent me from slipping, or when I do forget something, they inspire my quickly putting it into my presentation.

So, if you are somewhat more forgetful or neglectful than you once were, first do not be ashamed. Accept yourself *with* your limitations. Second, acknowledge your frustrations, but don't dwell on them or magnify them. So your older age has some slip-ups that your younger years didn't have. Too bad—but you can live with them—if, again, you don't beat yourself up for having them. And *if* you don't moan and whine about the inconveniences of having them. Keep in mind that your *younger* age had many slip-ups that your older age does not! There are many *improvements* with age. We discussed some of them earlier in this book, and by now you may have thought of others to add to the list.

Third, once you refuse to put yourself down for your infirmities and once you stop whining about how *horrible* they are, you can find many ways to compensate for and reduce them. Once you stop upsetting yourself about them, you can make up for them in various ways, and even enjoy how well you can do in spite of them. Then, you will be able to minimize them and do just about as well as you did in your earlier years. Maybe better!

"Well, OK. So, losing my mind is not inevitable, thank goodness!"

"As Mae West said, 'Goodness has nothing to do with it.'"

"*Especially* if I use it, stay active, and involved in life, and keep learning. It's comforting to know that one thing I don't have to worry about is losing my mind."

"That's right. But unfortunately, there are plenty of other losses that are all but certain."

14

Seven Ways to Leave Your Losses

The best parts of anything are always impossible to remove from the worst parts.

The Pineapple Principle

Back when I (Emmett Velten) still lived in San Francisco full time, a 62-year-old client, Tony, told me something surprising when he first sat down in my office. I asked him what problem he wanted to work on, to which he replied "I don't ever want to fall in love again." He didn't want to, Tony explained, because it had hurt so much when he and Marie had broken up. His goal was never to go through *that* again. His only chance, he figured, was not to fall in love.

After some discussion, I could see that Tony had very little chance of *not* falling in love again. Why not? For one thing, it was very much against his nature. He was someone who fell in love early and hard. He wasn't *opposed to* love—he liked love, as most people do. He just did not want to go through another breakup. In theory of course, Tony could isolate himself from all social contact with women and that might keep him safe. Possible, but very contrary to his open, loving nature. Maybe get put into quarantine? Impractical. Just be friends with nice women he meets? Tony said he might fall for them if they were quite nice and in the available category. And sometimes even if they were not in the available category!

I pointed out to Tony that it seemed to be his nature to fall in love—he'd had several relationships in the seven years since his divorce that had ended some 25 years of marriage. But, I went on sagely, Tony could never be completely safe from a relationship break-up. This was true even though he and his wife had been together for a very long time. Any future relationship might last that long or longer, even forever. Or it could be brief. He could never get a guarantee.

Tony said he knew that, and that was why he was seeking therapy, so he wouldn't fall in love again!

I asked Tony what ideas he had considered that would improve his situation. He said he had tried to convince himself that he was hopeless in relationships. What for? Because then he wouldn't even feel tempted to date.

"And how did that work?" I asked, knowing it hadn't worked too well or else he and I would not even be having our conversation.

"Terrible." Tony had checked his idea against his experience. "For one thing, it's not even true. I'm *not* hopeless *in* relationships," Tony said. "Just *after*!" He said he had also thought about making up his mind that women just can't be trusted. And? "They aren't any worse, on the average, than anyone else." Marie, for instance, had been as trustworthy as the day was long. The same was true of his ex-wife. His and Marie's problem with each other came once their infatuation wore off. Which took quite a while—they maintained separate homes and both traveled a lot in business. Eventually, though, they noticed they had little in common. And lots in uncommon. Like values and interests and personality traits!

After some discussion with me, Tony restated his objectives in therapy, which I wrote down on a whiteboard:

1. To get over being sad about breaking up with Marie; also stop feelings of impending doom when thinking about dating.
2. To learn how "to pick 'em better."
3. To not be sad in case he "failed" and *did* fall in love again, and it didn't work out.

"Well, two out of three's not bad," I said, adding, "Number 3 would take a miracle—a change not just in *your* basic nature, but in basic human nature. Because, how do you think you're *supposed* to feel after you lose something important to you, like a relationship? Deliriously happy? Completely neutral and serene? Totally uncaring?"

After a pause, Tony said, "Sad, I suppose. That does makes sense. I loved Marie—until we found out we had lots of differences and grew apart."

At that point I explained to Tony the difference REBT sees between healthful (rational) negative emotions, on the one hand, and unhealthful (irrational) negative emotions, on the other hand.

Tony's painful negative emotions—about the break-up—were, in fact, optimal and healthful. That is, he felt sadness, regret, and disappointment. Not depression, not guilt, not shame, not horror. Nor did Tony hold any "musts" about himself or Marie. He did not, for instance, believe that he MUST have a wonderful, permanent relationship, or else he would be a *failure in life*. Though he didn't like some of her actions, Tony did not at all damn Marie. Tony's negative feelings were rational, that is, healthful.

Did Tony solidly hold a "must"? Very definitely. It was a "must" *about* his feelings of sadness, regret, even grief, after loss of his relationship with Marie.

A. His Activating Event was his *healthful* negative feelings of sadness and loss.

B. The Irrational Belief (IB) Tony and I identified and worked on was "I *can't stand* those feelings."

C. Tony's IB produced unhealthful feelings and actions of anguish, depression, and avoidance. In addition, his Irrational Beliefs *about* rational sadness vastly prolonged his healthful feelings of sadness. How so? Because of his attempts to avoid having the sad feelings, Tony denied himself the chance to work them through and let go of them. This Irrational Belief at B about sadness also produced his sense of impending doom at the prospect of ever falling in love again.

So Tony had a series of ABC's. First, at A, he and Marie sensibly—because they had little in common other than infatuation—broke up. At B he rationally evaluated the loss of the relationship as very unfortunate. At C, he felt healthful sadness. Then Tony made his sadness *itself* into another Activating Event at A. Then, at B, he evaluated the sadness as *awful* and *horrible* and *unbearable*. At C, as a result, he *produced* unhealthful feelings of anguish and depression, as well as avoidance.

Tony's "I-can't-stand-it-itis" Beliefs *about* healthful negative emotions prolonged and increased his suffering in a second way. Since he *could not stand*, he told himself, the uncomfortable feelings, he did everything he could to avoid having them. Such as trying to avoid all relationships. Such as overwork and occasional overdrinking.

Taking my advice, Tony learned to dispute his I-can't-stand-its about his deep feelings of loss and sadness. He wrote out lengthy proofs that he *could* stand uncomfortable sadness and feelings of loss. He described ways he would go about standing them. He shortened some of his favorite disputes and used them as optimal coping statements. They included: "I don't like sadness, but it *can go with the territory* of caring. Caring about anything!" "Dealing with loss is hard, but *not horrible!*" And: "Unless I risk losses, I'll miss out on much caring and other real pleasures."

Tony overcame his depression, which had arisen from his intense demand not to feel healthful sadness. He learned to accept feelings of loss and sadness as part of having attachments. "It's the price you pay," he said. "Because it *is* better to have loved and lost, than never to have loved at all."

The first of the seven ways to leave your losses, then, pertains to negative, but healthful, emotions that you might feel in connection to losses.

1. Accept negative healthful feelings related to losses.

In Tony's case, this meant *accepting* the sad, the regretful feelings following the loss of the relationship with Marie. Such feelings *are* the risk you take for caring about or for having anything. Give your feelings time to mellow out as you adapt, possibly make replacements, and then move on. Don't glory in negative feelings, even healthful ones. Don't wallow in them, don't prolong them forever and a day. But accept them, so that you can move on and see what else you want to do in life and decide whether you want to replace the loss.

As for unhealthful feelings of depression and despair, first accept that you have them, if that is true. Then, get to their irrational roots and dispute them, so that you feel appropriate, healthful sadness or grief. For remember, with no feelings of attachment, most of us would not recognize ourselves. Feeling attached to people, possessions, and even to abstract notions, is part of being human. Since just about everything is impermanent, suffering loss is inevitable. Sadness, loneliness, even grief, and other healthful negative feelings are the minimum price we pay for caring.

Healthful negative feelings can spur us to cope with loss by finding new friends or interests. If you, as Tony did, feel afraid of additional future losses, you may at times try to avoid attachments. You may sabotage some attachments, for fear of getting hurt. After losses, you have a choice of feeling *healthful* sadness or *unhealthful* depression and misery. In either case, you may think you *can't stand* your negative feelings. You *can stand* them, of course, painful though they may be. Feelings of depression, however, you can change and would do well to change.

Once Tony had ceased trying to avoid his feelings of sadness, and once he had fully accepted the discomfort of the sadness and worked it through, he considered whether he wanted to return to dating. He did. In Tony's case, he opted for replacement, which is a practical solution rather than a psychological one. Tony and I worked on how he could go about meeting women with whom he would have more in common, such as values and interests, personality and intelligence. If he could obtain a better sample of candidates, then his tendency to fall head over heels in love very early in the game might not be as potentially detrimental. He'd fall fast, yes, but maybe with candidates with whom he had much more in common!

We spent several sessions designing personal ads Tony could run in weekly newspapers and on the Internet, and working out details about methods for assessing possible candidates. This seemed to work very well. By the time he concluded therapy, Tony was dating but had not found a new partner. Several years after our last session I saw him at the Museum of Modern Art. He introduced me to his girlfriend and said they had been going together for a year and had been living together for about six months.

The second of the seven ways to leave your losses pertains to unhealthful negative emotions about losses.

2. De-awfulize losses by accepting the facts of life as just facts. Not *horrible*, *unbearable* facts that absolutely MUST NOT be. Through acceptance, you can see loss—even by death—as part of the flow of ever-changing life. You can see that losses are the price you pay for caring about, or having, anything.

Losses are an unavoidable part of life. The longer you live, the more losses you will accumulate over the years. You may suffer more losses over shorter periods of time, and you have less time to recover from those losses. If you make it to, say, your 50th high school reunion, the number of your surviving fellow graduates will be somewhat less than at your 40th. At your 60th reunion, the drop-off rate—unfortunately due to reasons other than boredom with high school reunions—will have been steeper. Among all major demographic groups in the developed nations, old people have more exposure to the death of their peers than do people in any other group, except gay men.

Loss Goes With the Territory of Life

Losses almost unavoidably go with growing old, but the same is not true of loneliness and despair. You can increase your skills at adapting to losses. You can learn to remedy losses, reduce loneliness, and then move on in life. Everyone's heard the saying, "Time heals all things." Well, it's false. This fact is fortunate, since older people have more things—losses—to heal, and less time left for the healing. The old saying is false because it is not time itself that does the healing. The healer is *you*. You heal yourself. You do so, of course, over some period of time. You can learn to improve your self-healing skills in several specific ways.

Gayle said that it had all seemed to start around the time of her 40th high school reunion almost a year ago, which had not been fun. The person she'd most been looking forward to seeing, Norma, was not there. Gayle saw Norma and got together with her for dinner every few years when Gayle visited Washington, D.C., where Norma and her boyfriend lived. Though their contacts were infrequent, their 44 years of friendship were treasured. When she got a moment at the reunion, Gayle looked through the printout of the database to see whether she could get updates about several people who weren't there. She was stunned to see next to Norma's name "deceased." There were blanks for a number of other entries. Moved on? Gayle had wondered. Or six feet under.

During the next few weeks, as Gayle recounted it, she had started thinking repetitively about "the old days" when she was in high school. The music was gone—except for golden oldies radio. Their neighborhood, completely changed. The high school had a new name. And

Norma dead! She couldn't believe it. The good times and the bad times she and Norma shared years ago. With Norma gone, it seemed to Gayle that the history of her own life was gone. The continuity, the connection to the past was gone. Now there was no one who knew about, or would care at all about, those old times she and Norma had shared. Gayle felt desperately alone, and she became more and more depressed. I'm old, she thought. No children. No one will remember me. The image of herself that was most frightening was of a child's balloon, floating into space.

Everything Must Go!

Losses can include just about anything that was ever important to you. People, of course—your partner, family members, relatives, neighbors, and friends. They may move, grow apart from you, die. Aspects of *you* and things you are familiar with—youth, health, job, mobility, eyesight, hearing, hair, your neighborhood, possessions, the popular music you favor, heroes, et cetera! Pet owners lose pets; plant owners lose plants. Owners of anything can lose what they own, what they've built, what they love. If you move, as I (Emmett Velten) am prone to do, you could have The Move From Hell—as I recently did. At best, moving will hardly do your treasures any favor. The same is often true of *not* moving. Favored possessions fade in the sun, decay, crumble, get lost in the shuffle, are stolen, or fall off the mantel and break in a quake. If you retire or become unable to work, you lose your job. Even if you exercise around the clock and eat all the right foods, you'll lose some mobility. What you can lose can be very important, and your life won't remain what it was. So what *can* it be? A favorable answer to that question is a key to adapting to loss and compensating and continuing to enjoy life.

After such losses or others you can imagine, you *could* feel emotional Consequences of despair, painful despondency, depression, or even terror. Unhealthful responses, of course. But what's the *healthful* response to loss? The healthful responses, alas, as we described in chapter 3 and alluded to earlier in this chapter, are also negative. They include sadness, grief, disappointment, frustration, and concern.

Depression Can Look Like Something Physical

Though it is psychological, depression is often mistaken for, or presented by older people as, vague physical complaints. The same is true of other emotional troubles. After hearing symptoms of their older patients, doctors do what? They prescribe pills. The depression gets no better, the patient may feel worse. Medication side effects, if sedating, can then combine with already-existing low feelings of depression. Time and money get wasted looking for physical causes when the cause is depression. Are we "against" antidepressant medications, such as Prozac? Not at all. They can make a big difference. They can help you get yourself moving. If you phase out a medication that helps you, and if you have not made changes in your depressive thinking and in your habits, and if your original, "depressing" Activating Event is still in effect, then back to depression you may sink. The best way to avoid depression, and depression-masking physical complaints, is to develop a meaningful, involved life and teach yourself how to detect Irrational Beliefs, dispute them, and build Rational Beliefs.

The RAND Corporation did a thorough study of older patients suffering from eight conditions common to elderly people. One of them, depression, was equal to a serious heart condition in negative effects. Depression was more disabling than the other conditions for many routine activities. These activities include bathing, dressing, walking, working, climbing stairs, and socializing with friends. The only ailment people rated as more painful than depression was arthritis. The only condition that resulted in more days in bed than depression was serious heart disease. What were the other conditions? Chronic angina, back problems, coronary artery disease, diabetes, high blood pressure, gastrointestinal and lung problems. Not exactly the common cold!

Let's look at how Gayle broke out the ABC's, as well as the DEF's, of her depression.

A. *Activating Event, or Adversity:* Her great friend from high school, Norma, died. No one remained alive who remembered the good old days as Gayle had lived them and remembered them. Her neighborhood had changed, the high school had a new name, and other reminders of the old days were gone. This loss of the past rekindled issues in Gayle's mind about never having had children.

B. *Self-defeating Beliefs:* Now I'm completely alone. These losses are *too painful* to stand. I NEED a family and children like everyone else. It's *unbearable* to think that no one will remember me after I die. I'm not important to anyone.

C. *Consequences, unhealthful negative reactions:* Depression, terror, feelings of alienation.

D. *Disputing:* Do I NEED the world to remain unchanged? Is there any evidence that losses MUST not occur? Do I HAVE TO be surrounded by a family to have a meaningful life? What proof is there that I MUST be remembered after I'm gone?

E. *Effective New Thinking:* I *miss* Norma and I miss the old days, but there is no reason that life MUST not change as it goes on. I can accept sadness when I have it. I make my life meaningful and do not NEED to have a big, loving family in order to enjoy life. Maybe it would be nice to know I'll be remembered until the end of time, but I don't NEED that kind of guarantee. I'd also better work hard at accepting and enjoying *myself* even though I'll probably not be remembered after death.

F. *New Feelings:* Sadness, mourning the loss of Norma and what Norma symbolized. Enjoyment when remembering the old days.

3. Do the practical things that help you adapt to or postpone unavoidable losses. Do what you can to prevent avoidable losses.

An Adversity that often goes with older age is health problems, ailments, and diseases. With longer life, we have more opportunity to catch or develop *some* malady. At any age, health problems may trigger a swarm of self-defeating B's (Beliefs). Such Irrational Beliefs hinder your efforts to take care of yourself and maintain your health. They obstruct your efforts to tackle problems sensibly if it's too late to avoid them. Such Beliefs create and maintain anxiety, dread, or depression. Often they lead you to make no effort, unproductive effort, or even counterproductive effort in the face of Adversity.

We are learning more about aging all the time. Much of that information—such as why we age—is beyond the scope of this book. The same is true of how to extend potential life span—or the maximum in years a member of our species *could* live. It's a little too late for us to do the one best thing any of us could do to live longer—pick our parents and grandparents wisely! However, almost everyone knows the basics about how you can probably live longer and better. To do so, you head off the diseases and ailments common to older age that knock you off before your time. You can do that—of course—by changing some habits and some attitudes to reduce your risks of cardiovascular disease and certain cancers. You can also increase your chances of living longer by preventive medicine and early detection. Some diseases, like diabetes, you can often partly control by sticking to diet and other guidelines.

Pearls of wisdom like "just exercise, watch your diet, stop smoking" are easier said than done. Much easier. Fortunately, you can uproot attitudes and habits that interfere with your carrying out these life-saving and life-extending actions. The main such interfering attitudes include these: "Things SHOULD be easier than they are! It's *terrible* and *intolerable* that they are so hard!"

Aging is Not a Disease

In present-day society, people often act as if aging is a disease requiring "care." Aging is not a disease. It is not an illness. Many people mistake diseases such as arthritis or Alzheimer's for the aging process itself. When you go to the doctor because of a pain in your shoulder, don't be too quick to accept the suggestion that it's expectable for someone *your age*. For one thing, your other shoulder may not have the same pain. Your health, your vitality, your life, your happiness are just as important as anyone else's. It's important *not* to think that every ache and pain you get as an older person results from "old age" and that each one is inevitable. Alzheimer's Disease is a scary example of a *disease* often thought of as simply part of old age. Aging is not a disease.

Some aches and pains *seem* to stem from age, but they don't. They stem from self-defeating Beliefs, from inactivity, and from other lifestyle factors. These include your diet and smoking, overweight, underactivity, poor nutrition, not enough rest, not enough stimulation, too much routine. You may slow down and feel worse for many reasons as you age. But not *because* you age as much as because you are human and you *let* those factors influence you as you age. The more years of overeating and inactivity, the more ill effects you may accumulate. These effects are not due to aging. They are due to your behavior.

Much of the deterioration many of us will undergo in our later years is not a natural result of aging. Rather, it's the result of our own present behavior—our lifestyles. Cigarettes, too much fat, too many calories, too little exercise, too much stress. These are all things you can do something about. The same is true of the fading of mental alertness we've all seen in some older people and may fear in our futures. Such fading frequently stems from lack of stimulation, from isolation, from having unknowingly bought into stereotypes about aging. Depression does slow the mental processes, but depression is not an intrinsic part of old age. Some fading stems from overmedication and drug interactions that do not happen with younger people. Again, all these are things you can do something about. They are not "natural" results of aging, but result from *how* aging is viewed in our culture, *how* older people are treated, and how *you* think and act.

Nevertheless, it's true that most of us do become more susceptible to diseases as we age. If you already suffer aging ailments, be they nagging or worse, you can teach yourself optimal ways to make the most of your situation. You can learn to enjoy what you can enjoy for as long as possible. Then you can stubbornly refuse to make yourself depressed, anxious, hostile, or otherwise miserable over just about anything—yes, anything!—that life doles out without your permission. And does it ever!

The ills that become more likely with older age are many. Some of them—such as cardiovascular disease, cancer, osteoporosis, Alzheimer's—can be quite grim and unfortunate. We had all better face those uncomfortable possibilities squarely. It is important to know what you can do to head diseases off, how to recognize them, and how to combat them medically. What you don't know about these important topics you could learn by consulting resources in your library, over the Internet, or from your doctor. While some ailments do become more commonplace as you age, they affect fewer old people than popularly supposed.

New Year's Resolutions

Books and programs to improve your health (and maybe live longer) are legion. It's almost impossible to avoid them. They show you how to modify your diet, what vitamins and other supplements to take and in what doses, and what exercises to adopt to benefit your health and perhaps add to your years. This information is abundant, but the ability to get yourself to *act* on the information can be scarce. Goofing off is part of human nature. *Also* part of your human nature is the ability to stick to a plan and work hard in your behalf. You can detect, dispute, and overcome attitudes that may lead you to stop—too soon—carrying out your New Year's resolutions about diet, exercise, time management, completion of a project, and other improvements.

At A, as an Activating Event, is your New Year's resolution to go to the gym three times a week. However, at C, your emotional and behavioral Consequences, you do not go to the gym at all. Or you go a few times and then drop off. What's B? What were you telling yourself to stop yourself from fulfilling your New Year's resolution? Typically, it is some variation of the low frustration tolerance (LFT) Irrational Belief. Attitudes along the lines of "It's *too hard!*" and "I *don't feel like it* today (and I MUST feel like it if I'm to do it), so I'll wait till Kingdom Come or a big wave of spontaneous eagerness for exercise—whichever comes first." Your low frustration tolerance attitude can defeat you in your resolutions to make improvements in your health-promoting habits. Such resolutions may have little chance unless you effectively dispute the low frustration tolerance attitude and replace it with a high frustration tolerance attitude. The latter would usually be phrased along these lines: "Yes, carrying out my resolution is hard, but it's far *harder* for me if I don't! I *can stand* frustrations, and I'd better do so—*if* I want to have a less frustrating and more comfortable life over the long run."

You can use several ways to de-awfulize health problems and diseases, to suffer less emotionally from them, and to have more energy to prevent them, reverse them, cope with them, and fight them. I (Albert Ellis) have been an insulin-dependent diabetic for over 45 years. While I would give plenty to never have had diabetes, it did help me learn to discipline myself. I rigorously monitor my blood sugar level, watch my diet, and do the things doctors tell me to do. At 84, I'm still alive and kicking and maintain a very busy schedule.

In fact, as a result of my diabetes and my 84 years, I have to spend what I consider an inordinate amount of time routinely taking care of my health. About once a week or so, for example, I visit one of my doctors—my regular internist and diabetologist, my orthopedist, my urologist, my ophthalmologist, my dentist, my audiologist, my ear, nose and throat specialist. Et cetera! Nothing too serious—but that is because I make these regular visits, and keep practicing what my doctors preach. I don't mind all these medical visits themselves for I have been regularly seeing my physicians and dentists since the age of five. But I hate like hell to take all the time it takes to see them, to wait while they see other patients, to have special tests taken, and to arrange for other medical routines. I could well live without all that crap! However, I make myself view it as an ounce, or many ounces, of prevention, which is worth pounds and pounds of cure. Prevention is worth it because it *saves* me time, discomfort and inconvenience, and keeps me going strong. Therefore, I uncomplainingly go through with it. A hell of a lot of time consumed—but not exactly wasted, since I am relatively vigorous in my ninth decade.

Janine's Double Bind

Janine had two almost opposite forms of anxiety—and suffered anguish from both. On the one hand, she felt petrified about having a serious disease, such as cancer or cardiac arrest. At 67, she was relatively healthy and only had sinus trouble. She had survived her spouse and her two brothers, all of whom were 40 pounds or more overweight and had serious heart problems. But suppose she became *really* ill? And couldn't take care of her self? No close relative was available, as her only son lived in Japan. Who would take care of her? Not a horrible, uncaring nursing home! Oh, no! So, depending on the site of her aches and pains, Janine worried one day about heart disease, and another about cancer, another about kidney trouble—her list of possible major ailments seemed endless.

At the same time, Janine did little to ward off serious disease. She still smoked a pack of cigarettes each day, indulged in the high cholesterol foods that tasted good, had brandy in her coffee at meal-time, and was so sedentary she drove to the grocery store, although it was only two blocks away. As soon as she started thinking about doing things to improve her health, she thought, "Why bother? I'll die regardless." Was she depressed? Partly. But also under her "why bother?" attitude was "It's too hard (as it SHOULD NOT be)," a low frustration tolerance attitude.

So Janine had two forms of discomfort anxiety—first, she worried incessantly over the discomforts that might occur if she had a serious illness. Second, she avoided the discomforts that she would have to undertake to reduce her health risks and keep them at a minimum.

I (Albert Ellis) kept showing Janine the futility of these two forms of low frustration tolerance (LFT). It was easy for her to keep worrying about her health—as it is for millions of older (and younger) people—and hard for her to stop worrying. So she did the easier short-range thing, endlessly worry, and she refused to do the *harder* long-range process, train herself to feel rational concern. I showed her how to worry less by disputing her Irrational Beliefs. The ABC's and DEF's for Janine's panic about ending up in a nursing home went something like this:

A. *Activating Event, or Adversity:* Janine thought, "A serious illness would be very bad and could leave me at the mercy of people who don't care much about me."

B. *Irrational Beliefs:* That would be *awful!* My whole life would be destroyed forever! It MUST not happen!

C. *Consequences, unhealthful negative reactions:* Incessant worry, depression; overeating, smoking, drinking to avoid her worrisome thoughts; starting to think that the chances of a prolonged, disabled existence in a nursing home were nearly 100 percent.

D. *Disputing:* MUST I have a guarantee that bad things won't happen? Where is the evidence that I truly *could not stand* the discomforts of being in a nursing home?

E. *Effective New Thinking:* I *hope* I never end up in a nursing home, particularly one where they don't care much about the patients, but I don't have to have a guarantee that it won't happen. If it does happen, it may be very unpleasant, but bearable. I haven't been taking very good care of my health, and that's something I'd better work on, so I can cut down the chances I'll end up disabled. I'd also better start figuring out a better arrangement than a nursing home.

F. *New Feelings:* Calm, amusement, occasional qualms about her future, but not depression and panic.

In disputing her Irrational Beliefs, Janine realized that she *probably* would not suffer a disabling illness. If she did, however, she saw that she could somehow handle it, even without "caring" help. It would not automatically end her whole life. Moreover, as I rationally showed her, constant worry would probably *increase* her chances of getting seriously ill and would definitely not, magically, ward off illness.

At the same time, I showed Janine that healthful concern about being ill could *reduce* her chances of being afflicted. *If*, that is, she used her healthful concern to motivate herself to do the things that would make illness less likely. But healthful concern could only be achieved by tackling her second form of discomfort anxiety, in which she focused on the "horror" of being uncomfortable when she stopped smoking, when she ate low-fat foods, and when she cut down on her brandy-filled coffee. By disputing her LFT philosophy, Janine made herself able to face these deprivations with much less discomfort. Like most people, once Janine got rid of her "horror" of depriving herself of cigarettes, fatty food, and brandy, she was able to discipline herself in those areas. In time, she became comfortable with self-discipline. Meanwhile, her health improved and the specter of becoming seriously ill and incapacitated waned.

Like Janine, if you constantly worry about your health waning, let yourself see that your anxiety may well help your health wane, rather than stop it from waning. Anxiety, like anger, can lead to psychosomatic illness. If you stop making yourself panicked, and if you start making yourself rationally concerned and careful about your health, then you may well live longer, be fitter, and feel happier. Several research projects have suggested an enhancement of one's immune resistance to disease through psychological treatment, biofeedback, yoga, or meditation exercises. These psychological methods move you from the state of passive victim (of disease, of aging) to having optimal control over the quality of life. Using these disciplines, you are likely to feel a sense of self-control that will help your confidence that you *can* take care of yourself. Despite some of the hazards of aging!

4. Continue to look to the future. If you do, you will have more interests and involvements and less time to wallow in losses and worry yourself to death.

When you have fewer, even very few, years left to live, you can fall into a "why bother?" attitude. The reasoning goes like this: "Because I'm not going to be around that much longer, what difference does anything make?" The answer, of course, is that it makes exactly as much difference as it ever did.

It's an odd idea that there is no "use" in doing something if (1) you won't be around later to see it or (2) it will only be temporary. Yes, earth—which itself is temporary—is a speck in the Milky Way, and the Milky Way is one galaxy out of billions. Our lives are brief flickers in time. So what? Your life does not have to possess cosmic, eternal importance. Maybe it does have such importance. Maybe it doesn't. You will get more out of life if *you deem* your life important and *if* you focus on how you can give your life meaning. You are likely to feel happier— no matter what your age, no matter how short your life may be—if you focus on doing things that you enjoy. It is quite good enough for you to simply see that *defining* your life as valuable gives it value, whether or not the universe agrees. Whether or not the universe takes any notice. Whether or not anyone or anything remembers you at all after you are gone. You can define your life as valuable no matter how long or short it is, no matter how much you achieve or how much you fail. Your life is valuable because you call it valuable, because you are alive. You can continue to work for what you prefer even though you won't be around to see how it will all turn out. Even though, probably, you won't be around to see how the world will turn out. (It will end someday.) It has been said, "Live each day as if it is your last, but also live each day as if you will live forever." A combination of the two serves you well at, say, age 40. It serves you just as well in most respects at age 90.

The "what difference does it make?" attitude of some older people can have these roots:

- It SHOULD make a big difference!
- It SHOULD make a permanent difference.
- "Why bother to take care of my health that much? Sooner or later I'm going to die anyhow" (as I SHOULDN'T).
- "Nobody cares anyhow" (as they SHOULD, because I NEED someone to care).

Society may not think you deserve its precious healthcare dollars as much as younger people do, but you do not have to agree. Many people in our society, including older people, are in big trouble if they pay much attention to society's opinions of them. You'd better put your opinion first, society's second—maybe a distant second. Research, for example, contradicts the general opinion that old people are over the hill so far as health care is concerned. Older people respond to most medical treatments just as well as younger people do. It's fine to want to stay alive and kicking and to enjoy life as long as you can. You can make that decision and not feel apologetic about using every available resource for that purpose.

5. Use distractions to deal with losses. Stay busy, stay active, help others, do enjoyable things, *especially* if you feel depressed and do not think you will enjoy them.

A few weeks after Chris and Sally's golden wedding anniversary, Sally died, and Chris seemed to become more depleted than depressed. A couple of years passed, and Chris became more isolated and visibly depressed. His kids and several friends tried to involve him in activities. No dice. *Until* plans were announced for a commercial building that would block his view. It wasn't long until Chris had organized neighbors to oppose the planned building. Much more important, he became the kingpin of the opponents to the development and made many new friends in the process. His feelings of depletion, his depression, lifted—though that was not his purpose in getting involved. He continued to miss Sally keenly, but his depression had lifted and did not return. He kept up, and increased, his contacts with his neighbors and new friends.

Chris's solution to his loneliness problem brings us to an important technique of REBT, the method technically known as cognitive distraction. When you are anxious or depressed about almost anything, one quick way to get over your feelings of disturbance is to use distractions. You distract yourself, *really* distract yourself, by thinking about and doing something else.

Cognitive distraction is utterly different from trying *not* to think about a problem, an approach which won't work and may make matters worse. The more you try not to think about your serious problem of loneliness, failing at some project, or even how frustrated you are with unpleasant things, what happens? You tend to think more about how *terrible* and how *awful* these problems are! You'd think that focusing on a serious problem would help you come up with several possible solutions for it and that you could then work on one of these solutions. But this focusing strategy has its own problems. It's the same thing as being told that you can save your life *only if* you don't think—even for a split second—about pink elephants for the next minute. It's a near certainty that you will then think about pink elephants. Sometimes, if you have been obsessing about a problem, you may resolve to think sanely about it. So, you begin to do so. Before you know it, your focus shifts from solutions back to how gruesome the difficulty is. And then your focus slides into how you absolutely MUST quickly solve it or be destroyed. This will lead to awfulizing, to figuring out only poor solutions, or even failing to figure out any solution that seems workable. Focusing on practical problems is good. *Over*focusing on the "horror" of having such practical problems interferes with solving them.

Distractions of various kinds can help you deal with losses. Many useful distraction methods are "thinking distractions" in which you deliberately focus your thoughts on something. Even when you engage in a physical activity, such as a sport, or do body exercises such as yoga, you can't help concentrating on what you're doing. Hence your mind as well as your body is attending to problem-solving. Your anxiety and depression and sense of loss will tend to take a less important place in your life.

Cindy became deeply depressed after she retired and her best friend, Pat, died about one month later. They had planned to travel and take classes together. Neighbors in the mobile home park became concerned when Cindy began to leave the food, mostly uneaten, that they brought to her. They called the local health department in alarm when Cindy began to casually offer them items like her collection of house plants and her television, saying she really didn't need them any more.

The public health nurse visited Cindy regularly and provided some anti-depressant medication. It would take several weeks before the medication worked, if it did work. In the interim, the nurse provided basic anti-depressant counseling. She insisted that Cindy carry out every day several brief activities that she had found pleasant in the past. Cindy didn't want to, saying there was no way she could ever enjoy anything again. The nurse challenged Cindy to experiment and see whether she would enjoy each activity, even a little. Cindy began to increase her level of activity, because she did see that she enjoyed some of the activities to some degree. The more the nurse pushed her, and the more Cindy pushed herself, to do the pleasant activities even if she didn't feel like it, and even if she predicted she wouldn't enjoy them at all, she began to feel better. By the end of the first week, Cindy felt substantially better. The method Cindy was persuaded to use, namely increasing her pleasant activities even though it seemed futile to do so, is a simple method you can use to tackle the blues.

An activity many people enjoy, including many older and retired people, is volunteer work. A friend, Carlene Sampson, who read an early draft of this book, pointed out that we had omitted to mention volunteerism. She wrote, "I have found this type of activity to be valuable, and I am sure that other older people do, too. In my case I found an opportunity to use acquired skills in organizing a project at the museum, following through on development of the department, and then training others to help with the work. There are five or six hundred volunteers in just this one county, all older people."

The possibilities for volunteer work are plentiful and can give you something useful to do. Don't limit yourself to volunteering to do some job you are already familiar with. In Carlene's case, she volunteered at the Frontier Historical Society and Museum in Glenwood Springs, Colorado. And got the job of classifying and organizing thousands of old photographs people left to the museum. Organizing them how? By year? By township? By family? By type of activity depicted—

agriculture, mining, the railroad, tourism? In creating a system to organize the photographs, Carlene became engrossed in the project and expert on the history of her county.

6. Cultivate as wide a circle of friends and companions as you can, including young friends. Develop your social network and support system.

Most people are healthier and happier if they have social connections. With a social safety net, most of us can cope with and recover from losses. Particularly for men, social connections benefit both health and longevity. Yet the average man seems to have less talent than the average woman for re-establishing social support after losses.

When a man's wife dies, he is much more likely than other men his age to become sick and die himself within the next few years, from any number of ailments. If you are a man, and you make it alone for five years, or if you remarry or repartner, your chances for dying are the same as for other men your age. Is that something you might be interested in? Your chances will be better if you get yourself involved with people.

In heterosexual couples, often the woman is the "social" one. My (Emmett Velten's) dad was a case in point. My mother was friendly, poised, and intuitive. She had a knack for sizing up social situations and for noticing and remembering details about others. People gravitated to her. When she was leaving the hospital after her second surgery for the cancer that was fatal six months later, the nurses had a going-away party for her. My dad, on the other hand, was reserved and a little shy—he liked people all right, but preferably at a distance. After mother died, within a year or two he blossomed socially. She wasn't there to organize his social life, so he had to learn to do it himself.

What can you do, if you need to, to reorganize or rebuild your social life? First, if you are older and so are your friends, you are in a riskier position in terms of maintaining companionship and friendship. They could die or become disabled or move to live near their children, leaving you high and dry. So it's important for you to cultivate friends of all ages. Below, we discuss ways an old person can make friends, including younger friends.

Second, of course stay in contact with your family. Through phone calls, by email, by letter, and by visits. If you are typical, your children or other relatives—if any—live all over the continent, even the world. It may take some effort to keep in contact, but make the effort. Don't assume that their not calling shows they don't care. Often they are simply busy and involved in their everyday lives. When you talk with them, be careful not to scold them for not calling you more often. It's also not a good idea—however tempting it may be—to dwell on your aches and pains or other "negative" topics. That's a sure way to receive fewer calls. Instead, make yourself interested in their doings, and think of what interesting things you can do to relate to them.

A third and very important way to develop and maintain your social network is to get a pet. You have probably read articles about how it's been shown that people with dogs and cats suffer less depression, fewer illnesses, and live longer. That's right. Because they have something to live for and care for and love and that gives love in return. Corny? Fine. Then be miserable and lonely if that makes you happy.

Pets do, of course, have their requirements and expenses. Like people. They get sick. They have to be walked. They have their own ways of doing things. They die. Just as is true in relationships with humans, you'd better accept that relationships with animals are two-way streets. Nevertheless, the rewards you may gain from having an animal companion may eclipse those you feel from most, if not all, humans! If you live where pets aren't allowed, you may still be able to have an illicit hamster, parakeet, or goldfish. You may also be able to do volunteer work at the Humane Society. If animals are not your thing or truly impossible in your circumstances, don't ignore plants. Yes, you can talk to them. They are attractive. But, like animals, even the lowest-maintenance plants have their requirements. Caring for them, as is true of caring for any other living thing, is not just a distraction, but it adds meaning to existence.

You probably have neighbors you've not gotten to know at all. You've said hello to them, but that's it. You can create a social network of neighbors even if it's limited to visiting over the backyard fence. Neighborhoods are not what they once were, and it does seem much harder to get to know neighbors than it did, say, 40 years ago. When was the last time you went next door to borrow a cup of sugar or flour? These were common practices once upon a time. You can check on your neighbors, gather their mail or newspapers when they are away. If you live in an condo or co-op, attend homeowners association meetings. You will begin to get to know people that way. Volunteer for one of the committees. If you attend many meetings and make yourself reasonably active at them, you may find yourself nominated and elected to office. The same is true of almost any smaller organization or group in which you involve yourself.

Making Friends

Older people frequently complain to us that the time for making friends is past. They easily made them in grade school, high school, or college. They also made them in business. Now schooling is past, and business and professional life may also largely be a thing of the past. What to do? Where shall you go to meet new people, especially if people who are around your own age are not available in public places as much as they once were?

The answer is—everywhere there are people. Even if you live in a small town or on a farm, rather than in the city like most people these days. You don't have to live in New York, San Francisco, or Tucson. You can live in Eldon, Missouri; Putney, Vermont; Muleshoe, Texas, or Nome, Alaska. Anywhere! People, including older people, do go out. They are in public places such as stores, libraries, museums, recovery meetings, and eating establishments. They just don't, all of them, hole up in their own homes and never go out. They go out for air, for walks, for sitting in the park, for shopping, doing volunteer work, holding a job, and a hundred other things. Many of them are certainly just as lonely and shy as you are. Talk with them, meet them, say hello to them, comment on their pets, speak to them on the bus or train.

Can you really greet people, strangers even, on the street, in the supermarket, in bookstores, in libraries and museums, and at the health club? At church, temple, mosque, or skeptics' meeting? Yes, you can. It's not against the law! Perhaps it would be unwise to try it in a dark alley. Maybe not when they are walking briskly in the opposite direction, nor when they are busily engaged in talking with someone else. Otherwise, however, they are often fair game. Especially when they are seated, alone, in the park or on a bus, or standing in a checkout line. Especially when they are eating alone at a restaurant. Especially when they are looking at the presentations in a museum or art gallery. Or at the gym or health club as they do an exercise routine similar to or more (or less) advanced than yours. Talk to them. Make a comment on the book they are reading. Talk about what a beautiful—or lousy—day it is. Make a comment on some unusual ring or hat they are wearing.

When you start conversations, consider some of these guidelines:

- Look friendly and approachable. Smile, say hello to people. The best way to have a friend is to be friendly. Ask them how it's going.

- Use open-ended questions, meaning questions that cannot be easily answered with yes or no. For example, if you say, "It's a lovely day today, isn't it?" The other person may only answer "Yes." Which then makes it your turn again in the conversation. Instead, an open-ended question might be, "How do you like the weather today?" Open-ended questions pull for more comment, more detail from the person with whom you are trying to start a conversation.

- Listen for extra information in the other person's response. For instance, if the other person says of the weather, "It's great. It's sure not like this in winter back in South Dakota. I'm probably going out for a round of golf later." You would have at least two possible extra pieces of information with which to extend and deepen the conversation: South Dakota and golf.

- When you talk with someone, put in extra bits of information about yourself. For example, if the other person offers you an extra bit of information, pick up on it. Then, in your reply, offer some extra bits of information about yourself. For example: "I love golf and shot in the upper 70s last week. Where do you play?" "South Dakota! I went with my church group on a trip to the Black Hills last summer." "I play tennis, but I always wanted to get into playing golf, but never did because the town in Illinois I'm from didn't have a golf course. How long have you played?"

- Introduce yourself. How? As the conversation proceeds, say "My name is_____" and extend your hand to shake the other person's. It's as simple as that. Then use the other person's name several times in the remainder of the conversation. Use the person's name in greeting her or him later.

- If it looks good, you can say something like, "We should get together sometime and play a round (have coffee, play cards or chess, go garage-sailing, scuba-diving, walking, hiking, or antiquing)"

- You can also use the media to make friends. Run personal ads in the appropriate sections of your local weekly newspaper's personals section. Tell, briefly, your interests and what you are looking for in friends. Respond to ads, even if the people don't sound like your cup of tea. At the very least you can ask them how their ads have done and whether they have advice for you, since you are thinking of running an ad. You can do the same kind of thing easily over the Internet. If you search out locations on the Web for your interests, you will find email addresses of other people with the same interests. You can "talk" with them in chat rooms on-line. You can even set up or have someone else set up your own homepage. It can show your picture and state some of your interests and what you are looking for in possible friends.

What do you have to lose if you are lonely? My (Albert Ellis's) mother, for example, was a great talker. Whenever she sat down in the park or on a subway train or anywhere else, she immediately began talking to the man or woman or child sitting next to her. Many of them probably thought she was intrusive and soon turned away. Some quickly got up and left. A few told her they didn't want to speak to her. No matter, she kept talking to people all her life—and made more acquaintances and close friends than any other person I ever knew. Hundreds of them, and some of them were close. They were of all ages and other persuasions, which seemed to help her remain vital. One advantage of having a wide age-range of friends is that it's unlikely they will all kick off before you do!

Don't forget that even if you get formally introduced to people, most of them are not for you and will not know you very long. Their goals, values, educational levels, and tastes are different from yours. So they meet you today, are gone tomorrow, and mostly never see you again. It's a numbers game at all ages. Most of the people we like don't particularly thrill to us. Most of the people who like us, we can easily live without. Too bad. However, if you approach enough people, talk to them about their interests and problems, and persist for a while, out of many prospects you will find a few friends. The more people you approach, as I (Albert Ellis) pointed out in 1963 in my trailblazing book for women, *The Intelligent Woman's Guide to Man-hunting*, the more you will discover several who are suitable for you and who really want to continue the relationship. If you are lonely, what have you got to lose? Try talking to people, and see what you have to gain.

If you want to remain active in life, to reach out, to make friends, to act in your interest, to enjoy projects and purposes, you will probably deal constructively with the sadness of loss. It will be *harder* for losses to gang up on you. Successful living, and happy aging, require that you live in the present and for the future rather than dwell on losses.

7. Develop vital absorbing interests.

One of the best ways for you to be relatively free from emotional disturbance, and distinctly happier than you would otherwise be, is to acquire a vital absorbing interest. Robert Harper and I (Albert Ellis) found this in our study of ancient and modern history and pointed it out in the original edition (1961) of our popular book, *A Guide To Rational Living*. Interests are useful when you experience very significant losses, such as loss of your spouse, your child, your eyesight, or your job. Involvement is a way to cope with your losses. *If* you devote and commit yourself to a long-range goal, project, or involvement that you take a personal interest in and that you are willing to work very hard at achieving.

Why do you want to achieve this engrossing goal? Why do you work overtime to attain it? Well, because you *really* want to do it. Sometimes you are encouraged to do so by your parents or friends—as when your parents want you to be a doctor, lawyer, or teacher, and you quite agree with this goal. You easily make it your own because it already is yours. More often, though, you acquire a vital absorbing interest because you personally just want to devote yourself to doing that thing. You may never really be able to explain why you feel interested in that topic, but you do. Intensely. You *choose* to spend many years preparing to follow it and working at it. When you involve yourself in it, you frequently get "flow." You remain absorbed in it for hours at a time and thoroughly enjoy solving the problems connected with it. You consume a great deal of energy in keeping at it. Oddly enough, you do not consider your involvement "work." To many outsiders, it looks like work. Some of them will call it "workaholism." It is, if anything, one of the greatest pleasures of your life. It's fun. You often labor at it with great enjoyment, and you easily ignore what other people would consider the hardships of doing so.

What kinds of vital absorbing interests can you give yourself? Almost innumerable kinds. Some people get absorbed with other people— with building a family, helping other people, saving the environment, or devoting themselves to community projects. Some people get involved with collecting baseball cards, hunting, fishing, or model cars. Some involve themselves in research, book collecting, or literary criticism. Some get absorbed in money-making ventures—business, the stock market, organizing and building a chain of stores. Some people get involved in different kinds of causes—political, social, religious, or ecological. Others like to trace the history of their family or write their memoirs. The common thing about most of these interests is that you choose them yourself, because of your intrinsic interests, and you work quite hard and long at pursuing them. You motivate yourself so much, and get so eager to pursue them that you don't consider it unpleasant work (though many others would). You don't begrudge the large amount of time spent at this activity.

Well, by this time, you may well have guessed one of our main solutions to the problem of loneliness and for that of missing friends, children, or relatives who are no longer available for one reason or another. Yes, acquire if you possibly can, a vital absorbing interest. Pick some areas, whatever they are, to devote yourself to. Choose them because you personally like them, and not because other people, for whatever reasons, think that you should follow them. Don't, moreover, be too influenced by what others think of your involvement. *They* may deem stamp collecting, political activity, caring for orphans, or having eight cats a peculiar, and even bizarre, thing to do. If you like to do it, do it—and let them find their own interests.

The point is that vital absorbing interests vary widely, and they can be an interest in things and not merely people. When you were younger, for example, you may have had a good many friends, and even quite a few lovers, to devote yourself to. Now you are, perhaps, a little older, not to mention wiser, and more sedentary in your tastes. You may not want to travel very far from home. You may not have interest in most of the people who would like to befriend you. You may want a very intimate relationship that because of your age or physical limitations is not easily available. By all means keep looking for what you really want, and quite probably, if you make enough effort to get it, you will find it. Yes, even when you are over 60 or 70 or 80 or 90, as long as you are *alive* you may find an intimate companion who is suitable for you. If you want one, don't be desperate about it, but do some looking.

A vital absorbing interest need not be in people or in a group of people. It may be in books, in computer games, in antiques, in music, in raising African violets, in developing the perfect microbrew beer, in raising money for a worthy cause, in opposing some political or other development, in spreading the word for your religion—or in countless other things. It may involve research and study, which perhaps for the first time in your life you now really have time to do. It may require little study. It may help you to make friends with people whose interests are similar to yours. It may be done entirely in your own home or apartment and may so thoroughly occupy you that you hardly miss people.

If you do not already have such a vital absorbing interest, give it some real thought. Go to the library and read up on hobbies, interests, and crafts. Talk to people who have an absorbing interest, and see if they can help you come up with one. Consider something that you have given fleeting thought to but have never gotten around to doing. It may be something that you used to like to do. Work in a food bank, at a homeless shelter, in a political campaign, or teaching kids or adults to speak English. Go to museums, exhibits, art galleries, shows, bookstore signings, or discussion groups. *Modern Maturity*, AARP's monthly magazine, has many examples of people with vital interests. See what you can find, and you can be pretty sure you will find something. You, indeed, are an individual. There are many projects and interests in the world. Particularly if you live in a large city, there is a good chance that you can find one, two, or more that will vitally absorb you. It's well worth the thinking and the looking. At whatever age you are, and even if you have some serious disabilities, you can give it your best shot.

15

On the Whole, I'd Rather Be in Philadelphia
How To Deal With Death, Dying, and Nursing Homes

A crisis is when you can't say, "Let's forget the whole thing."

Ferguson's Precept

No matter how well you live and how long you live, there's no reason to think you will go on forever. You too will die. Every minute that passes brings us closer to that point. Older people in the developed countries have a higher death rate than do younger people. The opposite once was true. In the "good old days," if you took a random sample of 100 eighty-year-olds and 100 one-year-olds, what would you likely find a year later? More of the former 80-year-olds than of the former one-year-olds would still be alive. Modern medicine, at least in the developed countries, has changed the percentages by practically eliminating many formerly widespread and often fatal childhood diseases. The death rate for infants and small children is very low. The rate for adults has dropped, too—thanks to many miracles of modern medicine. Nevertheless, you stand a greater chance of dying with each year that passes. Sooner or later, of course, your chances reach 100 percent. Everybody dies.

Many people are afraid of death—not just of dying, but of death itself. We won't try to convince you as you grow older that you really are going to live forever after you die. Either you believe this already or you don't. If you don't have a problem with the prospect of death—your own—then that's good. Why? Because unlike taxes, it's a sure thing.

If you do have a problem with the prospect of your eventual dying that interferes with your current living, you can adopt a realistic attitude toward death. Not all the people who believe in everlasting life are brave when it's close to the time for the roll to be called up yonder. Most nonbelievers assume that when they die, they die, and will be dead as ducks. Some nonbelievers fear "being" dead because they think they'll "be" missing something. Not so! They will be missing *everything*. If death truly is the end, they won't be around to know any particulars of what they're missing. Because "knowing" means there's still a "you." At any event, if there is any "knowing" after death, each of us will find out soon enough. In the meantime, there's much to know about life.

You can learn to enjoy more thoroughly the one life you can be sure you'll have. It's never too late for you to cultivate attitudes and habits that can help you accept the harsh inevitabilities of life, up to and including death. It *is* possible to cultivate attitudes of equanimity and grace toward the inevitable, while continuing to distinctly enjoy life as long as you can. You can learn *not* to get that sinking feeling when you think of growing older and older. And dying. And "being" dead. So, here we examine optimal ways to live with, and overcome, fear of death. After death, we tackle a tougher topic. We look at what many people consider the single worst prospect: going to a nursing home.

The ABC's of Death

When you feel dread about death or dying, the Activating Event at A is an Adversity, a future one—namely the *prospect* of your death. Your emotional Consequences at C are your feelings of dread and panic. At B, you would hold Irrational Beliefs (IBs), probably along the lines of "It would be *horrible* to die! I MUST not die. I HAVE TO be sure I die comfortably and on my own time schedule." At B you would also hold Rational Beliefs that expressed your preferences in those regards. Being *against* death is fine and usually rational.

Usually? Recall that according to our definition, "rational" refers to those attitudes, feelings, and actions that help you meet your purposes and goals over the long run. Your long run may be short. And its prospect may be thoroughly unattractive. If you have terminal cancer, let's say, and you've reached a point where there's little to life but pain, and no prospect for anything else, thoughts about suicide—and suicide itself—could be rational.

Rational Suicide

One option some people think of to avoid a future of unending physical pain is "rational suicide." Does "rational suicide" exist? We define it as suicide that you think out, and carry out, in the face of unremitting pain or other deficits that thoroughly and permanently ruin your chances for future happiness. In our view, though we realize there are contrary points of view, your life is your business. We favor your having the option of rationally ending your life. You, in fact, always do have that option.

How can you know that you are rational in thinking about killing yourself? Well, mainly, you will have carefully assessed the facts of your case. You would have ascertained, with agreement by competent medical authorities, that there really is no hope for you over the longer or the shorter run for anything other than pain. You may feel sad, you may feel regretful, you may feel disappointed. You may feel relieved. You may feel happy. You will not, however, feel depressed and you will have done your assessment without depression. In concluding that death is the sensible option, you will think about whether you are overgeneralizing. Could you be unreasonably concluding that *much* pain, *now*, means *100 percent* pain *forever*? You will have read books on the topic of rational suicide. Because it is relatively easy for depressed or pessimistic people to convince themselves that their suicidal thoughts are entirely logical and obviously the most appropriate answer, you had better consult with others whose judgment you value. Talking with healthcare professionals is an option, but keep in mind they are legally obliged to try to keep people from committing suicide.

If you are depressed or habitually pessimistic, it can be easy for you to convince yourself that there is no hope, even though actual facts do not support that conclusion. Dr. David C. Clark studied all cases of suicide by people 65 and older in the first ten months of 1990 in Chicago. He found that only one in six had a terminal illness, and only one in four of them even had a chronic medical condition. In all but two of the 73 cases, the person who committed suicide was clinically depressed. The right to die with dignity? Yes, of course that choice is important. So books describing your options, and literature from the

Hemlock Society, can be worth reading. Such material may not be the most cheerful, but it can be realistic and humanistic.

About five years ago, Mark, aged 71, became severely depressed after his wife Debra's death. He thought about and attempted suicide, completely convinced that life was over for him and that all chances for happiness were past. "No one wants me" he later said had been his key conclusion before deciding to overdose on anti-depressants. Once out of the hospital, he saw a case manager who consulted with me (Emmett Velten). She convinced Mark to do some of the activities he had once enjoyed. At first he argued against her, "feeling" quite sure he wouldn't enjoy those activities at all, ever again. She kept after him to experiment and to see, despite the fact that he didn't want to do those activities and was sure he'd never feel better. She pushed him to do small, formerly enjoyable activities, even though he didn't feel like doing them. For several weeks it was slow going, but Mark, like many other depressed people, noticed that he did enjoy the activities a little more than he predicted. Progress continued. The last I heard, Mark had recovered from his depression, though he still mourned Debra's death.

Overcoming Fear of Death

Obsessing about death, dreading it, and refusing to do anything to consider its eventuality can be self-defeating and a waste of time. Worrying about death detracts considerably from living and enjoying life.

What may you tell yourself at B, your Belief system, to generate not only concern about death, but dread? And how do you counteract some of those Irrational Beliefs? Let's look at some of the points that I (Albert Ellis) made nearly 30 years ago in an essay, "Overcoming the Fear of Death," from a book, *How To Master Your Fear of Flying*. I showed how a sensible and rational fear of dying can lead to rational concern and caution. You normally want to live as long and as well as possible. If you are properly sane and cautious, you will do your best to avoid sickness, accidents, rash risk-taking, and other truly dangerous activities that will get you closer to being dead than, when you are alive, you would like to be. By all means be rationally cautious, vigilant, and concerned about possible dangers, and thereby try to live as long as you can live. Based on sensible concern, take sensible action, like making a will, purchasing a good life insurance policy, and adopting a healthful lifestyle. At the same time, resolve to live and enjoy life as much and as long as possible. Waste no time dreading the inevitable.

Concern, however, is not overconcern, which is obsessive worry or anxiety. Obsessive worry about death and about dying is likely to be much more harmful than helpful, for a number of reasons:

1. Excessive anxiety about death includes various Irrational Beliefs: "I MUST NOT die," "I MUST live forever," "It's *terrible and awful* to die," and "I *can't stand* dying." These IBs are unrealistic, illogical, and definitional, and they will most likely do you little good and probably distinct harm. They can all, as we show below in a section dealing with the Three Key Questions for your Beliefs, be actively and clearly disputed, and thus surrendered.

2. Terrifying anxiety about dying may easily facilitate your quicker demise. Great worrying often can make you act foolishly— get in a car accident, for example, because you feel so nervous about getting into an accident. Anxiety also disrupts your bodily functions and may cause or exacerbate high blood pressure, gastrointestinal problems, immune system deficiency, and a host of other psychosomatic disorders.

3. The more you worry about dying, and keep yourself preoccupied with its "horror," the less pleasure you will have in living. You presumably want to live for enjoyment. You will be a very odd person if you really *enjoy* worrying and being miserable over possible injuries, accidents, and dying itself.

4. Worrying does not magically ward off the dreaded events you think may occur. Caution and vigilance may help you prevent bad happenings. Intense worry not only will not prevent their happening, but may even increase their chances of happening. However, when you sit in a plane and worry, worry, worry that it will crash, you will hardly affect the pilot, the safety devices that the plane includes, the weather, or the objects that may possibly hit the plane. All of these people and things simply do not care about your worrying. Not a bit!

5. Worry often sidetracks you from preventive action. If you are taking a long automobile trip, for instance, you are wise to have your car checked before you start. It will be sensible for you to

drive at reasonable speeds, keep your eyes on the road instead of your companions, and stop for periodic rests. Bringing on a state of panic about the trip will hardly help you focus on and do these important things.

6. Obsessive worry is usually a demand for certainty—that you be absolutely, 100 percent certain that no dire events occur. Although there is a high degree of probability that no accident will seriously injure or kill you, there just is no certainty. It doesn't exist. Obsessing about it means you are demanding the impossible. Minimize your risks, if you will—but you still have to take certain chances if you are to get what you want and avoid what you don't want. Take reasonable chances—and don't ask for the absolute certainty that grim things won't happen. You can't get it.

7. If you incessantly worry about dying, you will have to forgo taking virtually any risks, trying any novelty, or experiencing any adventure. Your life, if you call it a life, will be exceptionally safe—and dull—even *deadly* dull.

8. Let's face it, no matter how much (or how little) you panic yourself about death and dying, you will inevitably die. Someday medical science may give you a new heart, new lungs, new toenails, and may keep you alive forever. But that day has definitely not come yet, and therefore you will die. So, instead of worrying, especially obsessively, about death, take care of the things that need to be taken care of to prepare for the inevitable.

    Perhaps science will discover how to stop or even reverse the aging process, and you would then be potentially immortal (though you could still die through some accident). If you think the world has overpopulation and other problems now, wait till then! Among the first million people to get the gift of immortality or even extremely extended life, you quite likely will not find yourself. You *will* probably find the dictators and other scalawags of the world. At any event, the universe, and certainly the earth, appear to have finite life spans. When they end, then so will you, "immortal" or not.

9. As far as we know, death itself is completely painless and worry-free. It is possible that you will have some kind of afterlife—but

don't count on it. No real knowledge of it exists, though some people are utterly certain that they communicate with the dead. Assume what is most likely, that a *painful* afterlife does not exist. Your woes and disabilities will end with your death—including your worries about your loved ones, who are still alive. If you accept that hypothesis, and not the fantasy that when you are dead you will simultaneously be alive and kicking, you can think of "being" dead with real calmness and equanimity. You may have loads of pains and troubles now—but not then!

10. Although you will most probably be free of any pain once you are dead, it's possible that you will suffer somewhat, or even greatly, during the process of dying. Yes, you may. Fortunately, however, few people experience very painful deaths. In addition, there are various safeguards you can take while living—such as making a living will—that may take care of some of the worst possibilities of dying. The chance that you will die a very painful death and be unable to take pain killers or lighten the process are slim. Even if the chances were rather large, worrying about these chances will not ward them off, and may well ruin your life while you are living.

All the things we have said about the futility of obsessively worrying about death and dying also relate to worrying about dying painfully. Most likely you won't. But the NEED for certainty that you won't, and your consequent obsessive worrying about whether you will, won't magically prevent painful death from occurring. Not at all. This brings us to our Nineteenth Rule for Optimal Living:

Rule #19: Accept Uncertainty

Healthy people tend to acknowledge and accept the idea that we live in a world of probability and chance where absolute certainties do not, and probably cannot, exist. They realize that it is often fascinating and exciting, but not *awful*, to live in such a world. They enjoy a good degree of order, but they do not demand to know exactly what the future will bring or what will happen to them.

The Three Key Questions and the NEED for Certainty

Let's now look at the Three Key Questions for examining Beliefs and see how they apply to the demands for certainty that underlie most fears about death and dying.

- Practical Disputing: *Does my demand for certainty help me or hinder me over the long run?* Start with the prospective Adversities (A) of death and dying. Show yourself in detail that NEEDING certainty (B) about death and dying can detract from your happiness and successful living and make you miserable (C). Then show yourself how the alternative Rational Beliefs promote your happiness and successful living. Show yourself how acceptance of uncertainty helps you if you vow to do what you can to minimize dangers without minimizing your life.

- Factual Disputing: *Is my Belief, I MUST have certainty, consistent with reality and the facts?* Of course it isn't. If you HAD TO have certainty, you would. There would be a law of the universe to that effect. If something MUST be, it is so. If something truly is certain, then you don't even have to think about it, much less worry about it. It simply is. If it MUST be. Think about and list all the facts you can think of that contradict your Belief that *not* having certainty is *horrible*. Gayle, for example, thought being dead was *awful*. She happened not to believe in life after death, but still feared "being" dead. I (Emmett Velten) asked her once what some of her feared experiences might be during the eons she would "be" dead. After a pause, she laughed, realizing that—from her point of view—when you're dead, you're dead, and you won't be having "being" type experiences.

- Logical Disputing: *Just because certainty about some things might be desirable and you'd like to have it, does it logically follow that you MUST have certainty?* Show yourself repeatedly that the Belief that you MUST be certain that you won't die before your time, that you absolutely MUST not die inconveniently, and that you *couldn't stand* joining the ranks of the dead that way, does not logically follow from your preferences. Namely, your preferences for a long, healthy life capped off by dying peacefully in your sleep. You can also show yourself that since *some* things about aging are adverse, it does not follow that *all* things about aging—including being dead—are adverse. Similarly, since it may be *harder* to contend with difficulties in some ways as you get older, it's quite an illogical overgeneralization to tell oneself that *everything* will be *awful* and *unbearable* about older age.

There is something most people fear more than death. No, we don't mean public speaking, which does indeed rank as worse than death in most surveys of people's fears. It's NURSING HOMES. To be more exact, it's *going* to a nursing home yourself.

How To Keep Your Home From Being a Nursing Home and What To Do If You're Stuck There

What about going to a nursing home? Is that the one thing that really is *awful*? True, it's something very few people jump with joy when contemplating. How can you face this unappetizing prospect without undue horror? Better, how can you avoid it? How can you minimize your suffering if you DO end up there?

How to select a nursing home for yourself or someone you love is a topic beyond the scope of this book. However, if you face that unfortunate prospect, this book will help you do the research and make the decision with less anxiety. It will also help galvanize your determination to work out an arrangement, such as shared living, that could be a much better alternative to living in a nursing home. Nevertheless, if you might ever live in a nursing home, or already are stuck there, you'd better develop the attitude now that it is—or might be—*home*. It would be a group living situation where you are the *employer* of the people who work there. Yes, of course, they have a job to do and rules and routines can make it easier. But you have a life to live, and after all, it's your home and you are the employer. Adopt, as far as is practicable, an activist attitude. Exercise as much control over your environment and your life as you can.

Might you go to a nursing home someday? If you are like most people, just reading those words may produce a little shiver of fear. It may give you a sinking feeling of dread. From some things you've read or seen first hand, strong feelings of concern are justified. We only wish we could deny it. In fact, however, only one out of 20 Americans over 65 lives in a nursing home or has Alzheimer's. As many as 20 percent of the people who reach 65 may get stuck in a nursing home somewhere along the line. It can happen involuntarily and you may have no other option. You may be bedridden, partly paralyzed, or otherwise infirm. Getting out of the nursing home, and even rational suicide may not be options. You always have your first and best option, philosophical acceptance.

Research by Morton Lieberman and others suggests that institutions can be the death of you. Old people living in a variety of institutional settings are psychologically worse off and more likely to die sooner than are comparable people living in the community. If you are stuck in a nursing home, and if you view yourself as "old," a number of undesirable effects become more likely. These include depression, lack of energy, unhappiness, rigidity, intellectual ineffectiveness, negative self-image, feelings of personal insignificance and impotency, a low range of interests, withdrawal, unresponsiveness to others, and a tendency to live in the past rather than in the future. And death. Whether or not you have any disease at the time you get "placed" in a nursing home, there's a fair chance you will die within six months. Yes, unpleasant words! What happens? Not only do you face loss of cherished surroundings, isolation, lack of challenge and incentives, which would be bad enough. You may also buy into the idea that life is already over for you, that you have no remaining potential for any growth, activity, or fun.

There are several ways you can use REBT methods to (1) de-horrify yourself about the possibility of ending up in a nursing home; (2) reduce or avoid the possibility; and (3) figure out alternatives. If you are to make emotional and practical progress on this subject, you'd better face and work through the unpleasant prospects rather than avoid them.

One sensible way to reduce dread of nursing homes is to determine to make them better places to live. If you live in a nursing home and the conditions are bad, make waves if you can. You and your relatives are missing a bet if you don't form tenants' organizations, write letters to the authorities and the press, conduct rent strikes, and otherwise militantly push for better conditions. You can raise legal issues. Does it take informed consent to "place" someone in a nursing home? We say it does. Who really decides about "placement"? What about conflicts of interest? Is the decision to "place" really based on the older person's best interests? Or based on someone else's convenience?

Life Extension

Ellen Langer and Judith Rodin conducted a simple experiment that revealed the latest solid information about life extension. They found that nursing home residents who were allowed to own and water plants and to arrange their furniture lived significantly longer than people in a matched control group subjected to the usual nursing home routine. If you allow people to make choices, if you treat them as individuals, if they get to live with shared responsibility, choice, and dignity, they live longer. They are healthier and feel happier—even if their home is a nursing home.

If you may need to go into a nursing home someday and have options, be proactive. Do comparison shopping, contact the relevant monitoring agencies, and narrow down the choices. Maybe you can make your selection before it's required. You could consider one of the set-ups with "levels of care." Get up the courage to schedule yourself to go look at some of the places. The more you feel in charge of yourself and can exercise options, the better you may feel and do.

If you are stuck, or might get stuck in a nursing home, you can still devote yourself to remaining as active, stimulated, and involved as possible. You can focus on obtaining the enjoyments possible to you and can refrain from awfulizing about the many crummy aspects of your "home." At the same time, wherever possible, do what you can to improve your surroundings and your life.

A much smaller percentage of older people lives in nursing homes than is commonly supposed. If you are 80 or older, there's still only one chance out of six that you live in a nursing home. Still, many would rather take their chances playing Russian roulette! If not a nursing home, then what? There are several real-life communities that are unconventional and well-working alternatives to nursing homes. One source we recommend is Betty Friedan's *The Fountain of Age*. It provides some information about such communities and is an inspiring delineation of the mystique of age. There are in-depth studies about ways and means to select and develop such communities.

Shared Housing

If you think a nursing home could be in your future and you don't like that idea, one excellent option is to arrange ahead of time—way ahead of time—for *shared housing*. Charlotte Muller found that people who moved into shared housing survived longer and were less likely to enter nursing homes or be hospitalized. Moreover, they were healthier, felt better, and had fewer limitations in activity even if they were in poor health when they applied. Of these findings, Betty Friedan pointed out in *The Fountain of Age*:

> The worsening of health and the deterioration assumed by the mystique of age *was not found* in these people who moved into shared housing in their seventies or eighties. In fact, they became less worried about their health, but also seemed more realistic about their disabilities. Another study found that those who moved to shared housing participated more in activities, had more good friends and social involvement. They were more likely to "get out" and "dress up" than before. They participated and were more integrated within the outside community than residents of "care" facilities. (p. 408)

In a study conducted in Philadelphia, older people who moved to a shared living arrangement did much better at six-month follow-up than a control group of people of comparable status. The people who shared housing showed much better health, were happier, had more friends, and experienced fewer limitations of activity. At a follow-up three years later, two-thirds of those who had not moved had died. Only 11 percent of those who had moved to shared housing had died.

Let me (Albert Ellis) tell you the story of my mother, Hettie. She was quite an independent individual and after she divorced my father, Henry, when she was 43, she lived with my sister, brother, and me for a number of years. Finally, at the age of 65 she moved to sunny California and spent over 20 years living alone by the beach in Venice, a section of Los Angeles. She got along very well by herself, saw my sister (who lived in Los Angeles) every week, had occasional boyfriends, and led a good life. At the age of 87, however, she was stricken with what was then called arteriosclerosis of the brain, but today would probably be called Alzheimer's disease, and couldn't consistently take care of herself. So, my sister, brother, and I urged her to go to a nursing home.

Well, she would have none of it. She loved her independence and loathed the idea of being taken care of, even though at times she would forget to shop and eat and neglect other necessities of living. My sister was getting desperate, for mother obviously was deteriorating and wasn't taking care of herself, and took her to check out several nursing homes. No sale. Finally, it was either a nursing home or the hospital, and she tentatively chose the former, while saying she probably wouldn't stay very long. Surprise, surprise! Within two weeks, she loved it. She had three good meals a day, plus snacks; her room had a large television set, and best of all, she had many other residents to socialize with. She still independently did many things for herself, but she also was cared for and had companions. Some companions were not exactly the greatest, like one of her roommates who never stopped talking to herself. Nevertheless, she became real friends with others, as well as with members of their families, genuinely mourned their deaths, and in some cases, kept up contacts with their family members. On the whole, she lived happily until age 93, when she had a stroke and then survived only a few weeks. She regretted going to the hospital, at the end, because she felt so strongly attached to her nursing home.

You, too, may delight in independent living, and may shy away from nursing homes. But if you really cannot fully take care of yourself, visit several of them, tentatively try the one you think will be the best for you, and relax and enjoy it. Your declining years may be, as happened with my mother, among your best.

If you figure out your plan to avoid a nursing home, or to find one for yourself that will be relatively tolerable, you are ahead of the game. Let's hope you succeed in that effort, and that you live as long and as lustily, and as happily, as you can. We cannot promise you success in that effort—or in your efforts to get what you want out of life and avoid what you do not want. We cannot promise you heaven on earth. We predict, however, that if you follow this book's rules for optimal aging, you will give yourself the best chance possible. And this brings us to the Final Rule for Optimal Living:

Rule #20: Don't Expect Heaven On Earth

Healthy people accept the fact that heaven on earth is probably not achievable and that they are never likely to get everything they want or to avoid everything they don't want. They refuse to strive unrealistically for total joy, complete happiness, perfection, or total lack of anxiety.

To strengthen your knowledge about successfully helping yourself, we will conclude with a brief review of the Rules for Optimal Living we've advocated in this book. Let's fit them all together. And then put them to work in our lives!

Conclusions:
Twenty Rules for Optimal Living in the 21st Century

The goal of all life is death.

Sigmund Freud

The goal of all life is to have a ball.

Albert Ellis

By this point you have a firm foundation for enjoying the rest of your life with a minimum of unnecessary disturbance about your age and the implications of your being "too old." Don't forget to look at the advantages of older age, just in case you—as do most people—tend to forget that there are any. Then acknowledge some of the negatives that do tend to accompany older age. Find your root attitudes that create psychological disturbances, including dread about the prospect of growing old. Keep in mind that our culture has many ageist attitudes that you'd better oppose in it and in yourself.

Once you have detected the Irrational Beliefs that could give you trouble as you age, apply the simple but profound methods of **REBT**. Dispute those negative attitudes that can add to your irreducible woes and that can prevent your enjoyment of life. Then construct, and practice, more helpful Beliefs in their place. Once you feel undisturbed about hassles, then you will be able to deal more effectively with those you can change. You will also be more able to accept more gracefully those hassles you cannot change. After that, concentrate on the many positive ways to create enjoyment in the last half of your life.

Let's now recap this book's Rules for Optimal Living, 20 rules for the 21st Century:

Rule #1: Face Reality

Accept the fact that reality has bad aspects. Then change them if you can. If you cannot do much about some aspect of reality, live with it and make the best of it. Then look for and focus on reality's pluses.

Rule #2: Take Action

Build your life actively and you will usually get more of what you want and less of what you do not want. Passivity will not work.

Rule #3: Create Yourself

You create yourself—your Beliefs (B's), your actions and your feelings (C's). You can change your Beliefs about life's circumstances, including aging itself.

Rule #4: Accept Responsibility

Life deals you a hand of cards, but YOU play that hand. That is your responsibility and you'd best accept it. If you do accept responsibility for your thoughts, feelings, and actions, including your emotional disturbances, you will save much time and energy by not defensively blaming others and social conditions.

Rule #5: Do It Now

If you're going to change, there's no time BUT the present.

Rule #6 : You Can't Change the Past

Your childhood is irrelevant to handling your present problems. The past is gone forever. Your present Beliefs about the past really *can* affect you. If they make you unduly upset, you can fortunately always change them now.

Rule #7: Act Like a Scientist

You will get better results from your efforts by trying to think more objectively and scientifically about yourself, others, and the world.

Rule #8: Work, Work, Work, and Practice, Practice, Practice

It takes work and practice to change how you think, feel, and act. This is probably the most important "insight" you can ever have.

Rule #9: Push Yourself

Change is uncomfortable. It's usually better to push yourself, uncomfortably, rather than wait to feel comfortable, before doing what you know would likely be best for you to do. High frustration tolerance is basic to optimal living.

Rule #10: Do and Feel

No matter how you voice Rational Beliefs, without acting on them, without consistently and strongly feeling them, they will remain unconvincing.

Rule #11: There's No Gain Without Pain

There is no *easy* way to solve your emotional problems and deal with practical problems more effectively. No pain, no gain.

Rule #12: Accept and Forgive Yourself Unconditionally

You can choose to accept yourself unconditionally. You can refuse to measure your intrinsic worth by your achievements or by your popularity. Try to completely avoid rating your worth—your totality or your being—and try to refrain from labeling yourself. Enjoy life rather than trying to prove yourself.

Rule #13: Live for Now *and* for the Future

Try to balance both of these old ideas: Live as if this is to be the last day of your life; live today as if you are going to live forever.

Rule #14: Commit Yourself

Most people tend to be healthier and happier when they are vitally absorbed in something outside themselves and preferably have at least one strong creative interest, as well as some major human involvement.

Rule #15: Take Risks

Emotionally healthy people tend to take a fair amount of risk and try to do what they want to do, even when there is a good chance that they may fail. They tend to be adventurous, but not foolhardy.

Rule #16: Be Interested in Yourself *and* in Others

To remain emotionally healthy, have interest not just in your own welfare but in that of others too. However, sensible and emotionally healthy people tend to put their own interests at least a little above the interests of others. If you do not act morally, protect the rights of others, and promote social survival, it is unlikely that you will create the kind of world in which you yourself can live comfortably and happily.

Rule #17: Remain Flexible

Healthy and mature people tend to be flexible in their thinking, open to change, and unbigoted in their view of other people. They do not make rigid rules for themselves and others.

Rule #18: Use It Or Lose It

Use your mind, your body, your talents, your human potential, or you will lose opportunity for optimal living and optimal aging.

Rule #19: Accept Uncertainty

Healthy people tend to acknowledge and accept the idea that we seem to live in a world of probability and chance where absolute certainties do not and probably never can exist. They realize that it is often fascinating and exciting, but not *awful*, to live in such a world. They enjoy a good degree of order, but they do not demand to know exactly what the future will bring or what will happen to them.

Rule #20: Don't Expect Heaven on Earth

Why not? Because your expectations will be dashed. Nevertheless, strive for optimal living and optimal aging. The rest of the trip is up to you. Have a good journey!

About the Authors

Albert Ellis, born in Pittsburgh and raised in New York City, holds a bachelor's degree from the City College of New York and M.A. and Ph.D. from Columbia University. He has been Adjunct Professor of Psychology at Rutgers University, Pittsburg State College, and other universities, and has served as Chief Psychologist of the New Jersey Department of Institutions and Agencies. He is the founder of Rational Emotive Behavior Therapy and the grandfather of cognitive-behavior therapy. Currently President of the Albert Ellis Institute for Rational Emotive Behavior Therapy in New York City, he has practiced psychotherapy, marriage and family therapy, as well as sex therapy, for over 55 years and continues this practice at the Psychological Clinic of the Institute in New York.

Dr. Ellis has published over 800 articles in psychological, psychiatric, and sociological journals and anthologies and has authored or edited 70 books, including *How To Live With a "Neurotic," Reason and Emotion in Psychotherapy, A Guide To Rational Living, A Guide to Personal Happiness, The Practice of Rational Emotive Behavior Therapy,* and *How To Stubbornly Refuse to Make Yourself Miserable About Anything—Yes, Anything!*

Emmett Velten was born and raised in Memphis, Tennessee, and holds a bachelor's degree from the University of Chicago and a Ph.D. in psychology from the University of Southern California. His doctoral dissertation produced the Velten Mood Induction Procedure, widely used in research on mood states. Dr. Velten has been a clinical school psychologist with the Memphis City Schools, staff psychologist in the Division of Gastroenterology of the University of Alabama School of Medicine, and Chief Psychologist at Yuma County Behavioral Health Services in Arizona. For fifteen years he was Clinical Development Director of Bay Area Addiction Research and Treatment in San Francisco, and remains an Assistant Clinical Professor at the University of California, San Francisco. A recent immigrant to Tucson, Arizona, he maintains a private practice there. Drs. Velten and Ellis have previously co-authored *When AA Doesn't Work For You: Rational Steps for Quitting Alcohol* (1992).

Rational Emotive Behavior Therapy, launched by Albert Ellis in the 1950s, has spearheaded the cognitive-behavioral revolution in psychotherapy. For more information about REBT, contact the Albert Ellis Institute for Rational Emotive Behavior Therapy, 45 East 65th Street, New York, NY 10021 (212-535-0822; http://www.rebt.org).

Recommended Reading and Listening

This list includes all the works mentioned in this book, plus a number of others we believe you may find helpful. Many of these materials are available from the Albert Ellis Institute for Rational Emotive Behavior Therapy (Phone: 212–535–0822).

Adler, Alfred. 1927. *Understanding Human Nature*. Garden City, NY: Greenberg.

Alberti, Robert, and Michael Emmons. 1995 [1970]. *Your Perfect Right*. 7th edn. San Luis Obispo: Impact.

Baldon, A., and Albert Ellis. 1993. *RET Problem Solving Workbook*. New York: Albert Ellis Institute.

Benson, Herbert. 1975. *The Relaxation Response*. New York: Morrow.

Berne, Eric. 1972. *What Do You Say after You Say Hello?* New York: Grove.

Birren, James. 1985. Age, Competence, Creativity, and Wisdom. In James Birren and K. Werner Schaie (eds.), *Handbook of the Psychology of Aging*. New York: Van Nostrand.

Broder, Michael. 1994. *The Art of Staying Together*. New York: Avon.

———. (Speaker) 1995. *Overcoming Your Anxiety in the Shortest Period of Time*. Cassette Recording. New York: Albert Ellis Institute.

Burns, David. 1980. *Feeling Good: The New Mood Therapy*. New York: Morrow.

———. 1993. *Ten Days to Self-Esteem*. New York: Morrow.

Clark, Lynn. 1998. *SOS: Help for Emotions*. Bowling Green, KY: Parents Press.

Csikszentmihalyi, Mihaly. 1997. *Finding Flow: The Psychology of Engagement with Everyday Life*. New York: Basic Books.

Dryden, Windy. 1998. *Developing Self-Acceptance*. Chichester, England: Wiley.

Dychtwald, Ken, and John Flower. 1989. *Age Wave: The Challenges and Opportunities of an Aging America*. Los Angeles: Jeremy P. Tarcher.

Edelstein, Michael, and David Ramsay Steele. 1997. *Three Minute Therapy: Change Your Thinking, Change Your Life*. Lakewood, Co: Glenbridge.

278   *Recommended Reading and Listening*

Ellis, Albert. 1963. *The Intelligent Woman's Guide to Man-Hunting*. New York: Lyle Stuart.

_____. 1972. *How to Master Your Fear of Flying*. New York: Albert Ellis Institute.

_____. (Speaker) 1973. *How to Stubbornly Refuse to Be Ashamed of Anything*. Cassette. New York: Albert Ellis Institute.

_____. (Speaker) 1973. *Twenty-One Ways to Stop Worrying*. Cassette. New York: Albert Ellis Institute.

_____. (Speaker) 1975. *RET and Assertiveness Training*. Cassette. New York: Albert Ellis Institute.

_____. 1976. *Sex and the Liberated Man*. Secaucus, NJ: Lyle Stuart.

_____. 1976 [1958]. *Sex Without Guilt*. North Hollywood: Wilshire.

_____. (Speaker) 1976. *Conquering Low Frustration Tolerance*. Cassette. New York: Albert Ellis Institute.

_____. (Speaker) 1977. *A Garland of Rational Humorous Songs*. Cassette and Songbook. New York: Albert Ellis Institute.

_____. (Speaker) 1977. *Conquering the Dire Need for Love*. Cassette. New York: Albert Ellis Institute.

_____. 1985 [1957]. *How to Live With a Neurotic*. North Hollywood: Wilshire.

_____. 1985. *Intellectual Fascism*. New York: Albert Ellis Institute. Revised edn. 1991.

_____. 1988. *How to Stubbornly Refuse to Make Yourself Miserable about Anything—Yes, Anything!* Secaucus, NJ: Lyle Stuart.

_____. 1991. Achieving Self-Actualization. *Journal of Social Behavior and Personality*, 6(5), 1–18. Reprinted: New York: Albert Ellis Institute.

_____. 1994. *Rational Emotive Imagery*. Revised edn. New York: Albert Ellis Institute.

_____. 1996. *How to Maintain and Enhance Your Rational Emotive Behavior Therapy Gains*. Revised edn. New York: Albert Ellis Institute.

_____. 1998. *How to Control Your Anxiety Before It Controls You*. Secaucus, NJ: Carol.

Ellis, Albert, and Irving Becker. 1982. *A Guide to Personal Happiness*. North Hollywood: Wilshire.

Ellis, Albert, and Robert A. Harper. 1998. *A New Guide to Rational Living*. 3rd revised edn. North Hollywood: Melvin Powers.

Ellis, Albert, and William Knaus. 1977. *Overcoming Procrastination*. New York: New American Library.

Ellis, Albert, and Arthur Lange. 1994. *How to Keep People from Pushing Your Buttons.* New York: Carol.

Ellis, Albert, and Chip Tafrate. 1997. *How to Control Your Anger—Before It Controls You.* Secaucus, NJ: Birch Lane Press.

———. 1997. *How to Control Your Anger Before It Controls You.* Two audio cassettes. Read by Stephen O'Hara. San Bruno: Audio Literature.

Ellis, Albert, and Emmett Velten. 1992. *When AA Doesn't Work for You: Rational Steps to Quitting Alcohol.* New York: Barricade.

Emery, Gary. 1982. *Own Your Own Life.* New York: New American Library.

Epictetus. 1983. *The Handbook of Epictetus.* Indianapolis: Hackett.

FitzMaurice, Kevin. 1997. *Attitude Is All You Need.* Omaha: Palm Tree.

Frankl, Victor. 1959. *Man's Search for Meaning.* New York: Pocket Books.

Freeman, Art, and Rose DeWolf. 1989. *Woulda, Coulda, Shoulda.* New York: Morrow.

———. 1993. *The Ten Dumbest Mistakes Smart People Make and How to Avoid Them.* New York: Harper Perennial.

Friedan, Betty. 1993. *The Fountain of Age.* New York: Simon and Schuster.

Glasser, William. 1965. *Reality Therapy.* New York: Harper and Row.

Goleman, Daniel. 1991. Missing in Talk of Right to Die: Depression's Grip on a Patient. *New York Times* (4 December).

Grieger, Russell, and Paul Woods. 1993. *The Rational-Emotive Therapy Companion.* Roanoke: Scholars Press.

Hauck, Paul A. 1991. *Overcoming the Rating Game: Beyond Self-Love—Beyond Self-Esteem.* Louisville: Westminster/John Knox.

Heubusch, Kevin. 1997. *The Rating Guide to Life in America's Small Cities.* Buffalo: Prometheus.

Jacobson, Edmund. 1938. *You Must Relax.* New York: McGraw-Hill.

Johnson, Warren. 1981. *So Desperate the Fight.* New York: Albert Ellis Institute.

Korzybski, Alfred. 1933. *Science and Sanity.* San Francisco: International Society of General Semantics.

Langer, Ellen, and Judith Rodin. 1976. The Effects of Choice and Enhanced Personal Responsibility for the Aged: A Field Experiment in an Institutional Setting. *Journal of Personality and Social Psychology,* Vol. 34, No. 2.

Lazarus, Arnold, Cliff Lazarus, and Allen Fay. 1993. *Don't Believe It for a Minute: Forty Toxic Ideas That Are Driving You Crazy*. San Luis Obispo: Impact.

Lieberman, Morton. 1969. Institutionalization of the Aged: Effects on Behavior. *Journal of Gerontology*, Vol. 24, No. 3.

Low, Abraham A. 1952. *Mental Health through Will Training*. Boston: Christopher.

Marcus Aurelius. 1984. *Meditations*. Indianapolis: Hackett.

Masters, William, Virginia Johnson, and R. C. Kolodny. 1982. *Human Sexuality*. Boston: Houghton Mifflin.

Moore, Pat, with Charles Paul Conn. 1985. *Disguised: A True Story*. Waco: Word Books.

Muller, Charlotte. 1989. Shared Housing for the Elderly. In Marilyn Petersen and Diana L. White (eds.), *Health Care of the Elderly*. Newbury Park, Ca: Sage.

Ogilvie, Daniel. 1986. Meaningful Activities and Temperament Key in Satisfaction with Life. *New York Times* (23 December).

Oliver, Rose, and Frances Bock. 1987. *Coping with Alzheimer's: A Caregiver's Emotional and Survival Guide*. New York: Dodd, Mead.

Palmore, Erdman. 1981. *Social Patterns in Normal Aging: Findings from the Duke Longitudinal Study*. Durham, NC: Duke University Press.

Russell, Bertrand. 1950. *The Conquest of Happiness*. New York: New American Library.

Seligman, Martin. 1991. *Learned Optimism*. New York: Knopf.

Simon, Julian. 1993. *Good Mood: The New Psychology of Overcoming Depression*. Chicago: Open Court.

Svanborg, Alvar. 1985. Biomedical and Environmental Influences on Aging. In Robert N. Butler and Herbert P. Gleason (eds.), *Productive Aging*. New York: Springer.

Tillich, Paul. 1953. *The Courage to Be*. New York: Oxford University Press.

Velten, Emmett. (Speaker) 1987. *How to Be Unhappy at Work*. Cassette. New York: Albert Ellis Institute.

Wiener, Daniel. 1988. *Albert Ellis: Passionate Skeptic*. New York: Praeger.

Wolfe, Janet L. 1977. *Assertiveness Training for Women*. Cassette. New York: BMA Audio Cassettes.

Wolfe, Janet L. 1992. *What to Do When He Has a Headache*. New York: Hyperion.

————. (Speaker) 1993. *Overcoming Low Frustration Tolerance*. Video-cassette. New York: Albert Ellis Institute.

Young, Howard S. 1974. *A Rational Counseling Primer*. New York: Albert Ellis Institute.

Zilbergeld, Bernie. 1992. *The New Male Sexuality*. New York: Bantam.

Index